MW00629939

THE

F·R·I·E·N·D·S
THE TELEVISION SERIES

BOOK OF LISTS

THE FRIENDS BOOK OF LISTS

THE OFFICIAL GUIDE

TO ALL THE CHARACTERS, QUOTES,
AND MEMORABLE MOMENTS

MICHELLE MORGAN

Running Press

PHILADELPHIA

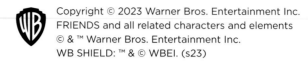
Running Press
Hachette Book Group
1290 Avenue of the Americas, New York, NY 10104
www.runningpress.com
@Running_Press

Printed in China

First Edition: March 2023

Published by Running Press, an imprint of Perseus Books, LLC, a subsidiary of Hachette Book Group, Inc. The Running Press name and logo are trademarks of the Hachette Book Group.

The Hachette Speakers Bureau provides a wide range of authors for speaking events. To find out more, go to www.hachettespeakersbureau.com or call (866) 376-6591.

The publisher is not responsible for websites (or their content) that are not owned by the publisher.

Print book cover and interior design by Glen Nakasako

Names: Morgan, Michelle, author.
Title: Friends book of lists : the official guide to all the characters, quotes, and memorable moments / Michelle Morgan.
Description: First edition. | New York, NY : Running Press, an imprint of Perseus Books, LLC, a subsidiary of Hachette Book Group, Inc., 2022.
Identifiers: LCCN 2021059546 | ISBN 9780762480593 (hardcover) | ISBN 9780762480609 (ebook)
Subjects: LCSH: Friends (Television program)--Miscellanea.
Classification: LCC PN1992.77.F76 M67 2022 | DDC 791.45/72--dc23/eng/20220318
LC record available at https://lccn.loc.gov/2021059546

ISBNs: 978-0-7624-8059-3 (hardcover), 978-0-7624-8060-9 (ebook)

APS

10 9 8 7 6 5 4 3 2

CONTENTS

INTRODUCTION

When *Friends* premiered in 1994, nobody could have imagined that the new hit show would be just as popular, if not more so, almost thirty years later. Whether it's Ross's luminous white teeth, Phoebe's questionable homemade crafts (Gladys, anyone?), or Rachel's nightgown worn as a dress, *Friends* has always kept us laughing.

So, what is it that keeps us coming back for more? Of course, the laughs are a huge part of our attraction, but more than that is the feeling of connection with the characters. Monica, Rachel, Phoebe, Ross, Chandler, and Joey are not just visions on the screen. For many of us, they are just as genuine as any person we see in real life. They all have flaws, they all have quirks, but they all persevere, grow, and have dreams like anyone of us does. Not to mention, we feel like they really are our friends.

Included on the following pages are more than one hundred lists that recall the fun, happiness, heartbreak, and friendships from our favorite show. Perhaps you want to relive all the times Joey said, "How you doin'?" or revisit all the times our favorite character Janice (Oh. My. Gawd.) appeared throughout the series. Ultimately, in the pages of this book, we hope that you are reminded of how much you loved *Friends* then and now and why—after almost three decades—it remains one of the most beloved shows on television. As Chandler said of apartment 20 in the finale: "It was a happy place. Filled with love and laughter." We hope you find this book to be the same way.

CHAPTER ONE:
The One about
their Families,

the Friends, and the People They Know

THE FRIENDS

→ SIBLINGS ←

MONICA GELLER

Monica is Ross's younger sister. She works as a chef and is known for her obsessive need to clean, which she sees as just good sense. She is bossy and competitive, loves to organize teams and committees, and wants everybody to like her. Monica has a secret love of karaoke and once made up a dance routine with her brother. She has always dreamed of getting married and having children, and she eventually marries Chandler and adopts twins.

HIGH SCHOOL FRIENDS

INTRODUCED
THROUGH
ROSS

RACHEL GREEN

Rachel has two sisters and was spoiled as a child but is now living an independent life in the city. She works first as a waitress and then finds her way into the fashion industry. Rachel is a terrible driver and has been known to flirt her way out of awkward situations, but she is also a strong and confident woman. She is the on-off girlfriend (and one-time wife) of Ross and mother to Emma.

INTRODUCED
THROUGH ROSS AND
REACQUAINTED
THROUGH MONICA

PHOEBE BUFFAY

Phoebe is a twin who does not get along with her sister. She works as a masseuse but has also acted and worked in an office to earn extra money. She is a hippy at heart, though she has an edge due to her hard childhood and time spent living on the street. She is incredibly quirky and is very proud of the song she wrote and likes to perform, "Smelly Cat." Phoebe finds long-term relationships elusive, though she does eventually marry Mike.

MONICA'S ROOMMATE
BEFORE MOVING INTO HER
GRANDMOTHER'S APARTMENT

The six main characters on *Friends* are each unforgettable in their own way, and each has unique traits, hobbies, and habits we know and love them for.

ROSS GELLER

Ross is Monica's older brother. He works as a paleontologist and professor and loves to talk about dinosaurs. Known (to himself) as Ross, the Divorce Force, he has been married three times and is father to Ben and Emma. He enjoys kicking back with a puzzle and ordering Pottery Barn items. He once slept with someone while he was in a relationship with Rachel but insists that they were on a break.

COLLEGE ROOMMATES

CHANDLER BING

Chandler is an only child and endures a strained relationship with his parents. Emotionally scarred from his parents' divorce, he often uses humor as a defense and is known to be both funny and sarcastic. Chandler works in an office, though his friends seem quite confused about what it is he actually does. He has a fear of commitment but eventually marries Monica. He is a reformed smoker, though he still likes a cigarette whenever the opportunity arises.

BECAME ROOMMATES AFTER JOEY ANSWERED AN ADVERTISEMENT

JOEY TRIBBIANI

Joey is the only boy in a large family of girls. He is an actor, though arguably not a very good one, and is the flirt of the group, with many one-night stands and short-term girlfriends. He once loved Rachel, but they decided to just be friends. Known to be a little childish at times, Joey adores his friends and is protective and loyal, but will never share his food.

FAMILY TREES

Here is the family tree of each friend.
Just don't get lost in Phoebe's complicated
lineage or Ross's divorce history.

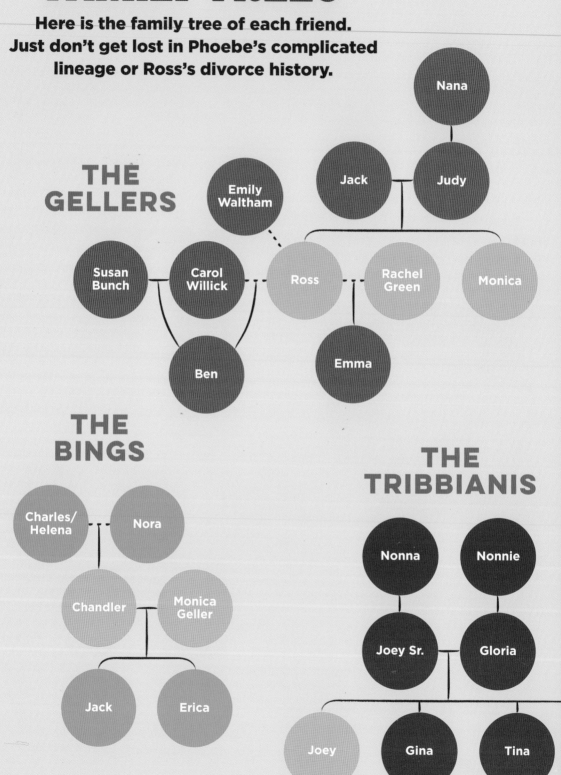

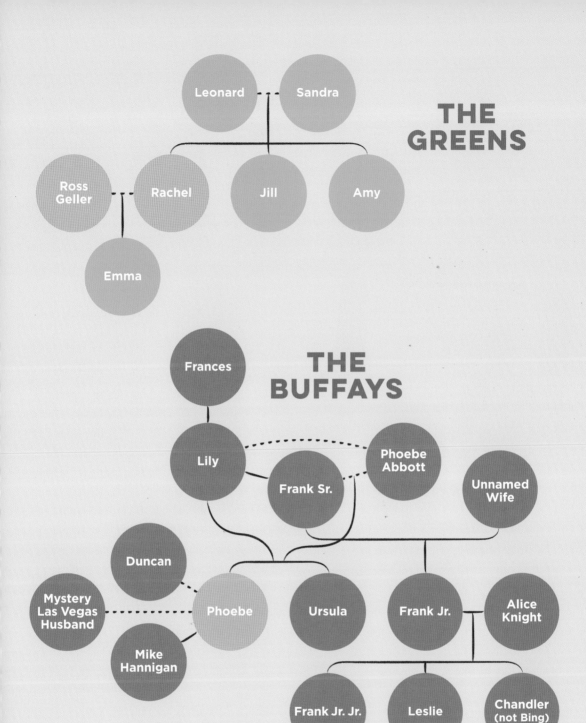

THE GREENS

THE BUFFAYS

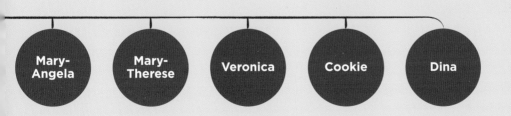

JOBS

Throughout the series, the friends make their way through dozens of different jobs. Can you remember who became obsessed with the ANUS and who was sent on sabbatical for shouting at their boss? Here is our rundown of all the jobs featured in the series, including all of Joey's questionable acting roles and auditions.

CHANDLER

- Chandler is a data processor at an unnamed company, dealing with statistical analysis and data reconfiguration, though nobody seems to know what that means. In *THE ONE WITH THE STONED GUY*, he quits after being offered the position of processing supervisor, but when his boss offers him more money, Chandler becomes "Boss Man Bing." He then worries about such things as the WENUS (Weekly Estimated Net Usage Statistics) and the ANUS (Annual Net Usage Statistics).

- Chandler goes to an interview for a job that is exactly the same as the one he currently does, but they're offering more money. Phoebe coaches him on interview techniques, and the real interview goes well—until Chandler mentions poo (because of the way the interviewer says *duties*), and his potential new boss is not impressed. *(THE ONE WITH THE COOKING CLASS)*

- Chandler receives a transfer to Tulsa when he accidentally falls asleep during a meeting. *(THE ONE WHERE EMMA CRIES)* He quits in *THE ONE WITH CHRISTMAS IN TULSA*, when he needs to work over the holiday season and realizes he wants to do something different.

- Chandler takes a job as an unpaid intern for an advertising company. He is the oldest intern there, but he impresses his boss with his commercial idea for a sneaker/roller-skates combo. Because he's not earning any money, Chandler and Monica see their savings deplete, which leads to them both borrowing $2,000 from Joey. This causes a misunderstanding when Chandler—thanks to Joey—thinks that Monica has borrowed the money to pay for a boob job. *(THE ONE WITH THE MUGGING)*

- Chandler is anxious to hear if he got an assistant job at the ad agency, but when all of the positions are filled, he fears the worst. However, his boss calls and says that he was too good to be an assistant and offers him the job of junior copywriter instead. *(THE ONE WITH THE LOTTERY)*

ROSS

- Ross is a curator at the Museum of Prehistoric History, which is also the location of Ross and Rachel's first night together. When his marriage to Emily doesn't work out, Ross screams at his boss because he ate his sandwich. This altercation leads to the boss forcing Ross to take a sabbatical. (THE ONE WITH ROSS'S SANDWICH)

- After demonstrating his "sound" (the way he refers to his keyboard playing), Ross gets a gig playing the keyboards on the stage of Central Perk. Everyone hates the noise, but Phoebe thinks he's a musical genius and refuses to play after him. Eventually, Ross apparently loses his ability to play "well," which gives Phoebe the confidence to return to the stage. (THE ONE WHERE CHANDLER CROSSES THE LINE)

- Ross is asked to be a guest lecturer at NYU, which could lead to a full-time job. When Monica and Rachel visit him during a lecture, they're shocked to discover he's speaking to his students in a British accent. He tries to phase it out, but then that's all the students want to talk about. (THE ONE WHERE JOEY LOSES HIS INSURANCE)

- During Ross's time at NYU, he dates a student, two other students pretend they're in love with him to get higher grades, and he has to roller-skate to get to and from a faraway class, before he eventually achieves tenure. (THE ONE WITH PRINCESS CONSUELA)

- When Phoebe moves in with Ross for a couple of days, she takes over his living room with her massage business. When an attractive woman shows up for a massage, Ross tells her that he can do it, but it turns out the treatment is actually for her father. Unable to say no, Ross pokes at the man with wooden spoons, exfoliates him with a mop, does acupressure with chopsticks, and rolls a Tonka truck up and down his back. (THE ONE WITH RACHEL'S BOOK)

- Ross is invited to speak at a paleontology convention in Barbados, and all his friends go with him. While they are baffled by the "jokes" he tells during his speech, the other dinosaur nerds think he's hilarious and, much to Joey's confusion, famous. (THE ONE IN BARBADOS, PARTS 1 AND 2)

- Ross beats hundreds of applicants to become a finalist for a research grant. If he wins, he'll be awarded $25,000 so that he can complete his field research and will have an article published in the *Paleontology Review*. The problem is that Ross's girlfriend Charlie's ex-boyfriend, Benjamin Hobart, is the one who makes the final decision, and the only way he'll give the grant to Ross is if he'll break up with Charlie. During the interview, Benjamin asks Ross all kinds of bizarre questions that have nothing to do with paleontology and then gets back together with Charlie. (THE ONE WITH ROSS'S GRANT)

JOEY
(ACTING AND MODELING)

- Chandler mentions that Joey was once in a production of *Pinocchio*. (THE ONE WHERE MONICA GETS A ROOMMATE)

- Joey is in an unnamed production, where he plays a prisoner on death row who smokes. (THE ONE WITH THE THUMB)

- Joey plays the famous psychiatrist in a musical production called *Freud!* (THE ONE WITH THE BUTT)

- Joey apparently once played a troll in an unnamed play. (THE ONE WITH THE BUTT)

- Joey is the body double for Al Pacino's bottom, but he's fired after acting too hard. (THE ONE WITH THE BUTT)

- Joey takes a gig as an actor/model for a City Free Clinic poster and hopes it's for Lyme disease, but he's cast as Mario, a guy with VD. (THE ONE WHERE UNDERDOG GETS AWAY)

- Joey contemplates changing his name to one more suitable for the stage. Chandler suggests Joseph Stalin, and Joey goes for it—until he finds out who Stalin was. Phoebe suggests Flame Boy, but for his next audition, Joey goes for the unlikely choice of Holden McGroin. (THE ONE WITH THE FAKE MONICA)

- It's revealed that Joey was once in a porn film. He couldn't perform, so he acted as the copy repair guy, who watches the others have sex. (THE ONE WITH PHOEBE'S HUSBAND)

- Joey performs in an unnamed play, where he plays a king and accidentally flashes the audience while sitting on a throne. The friends rush out for the reviews in the middle of the night, but they all stink. (THE ONE WITH RUSS)

- When Joey goes for an audition as a taxi driver on *Days of Our Lives*, Lori the casting lady wants to sleep with him in exchange for the part. He can't do it, so she offers him the role of Dr. Drake Ramoray. (THE ONE WITH RUSS) Joey gets the part, but in THE ONE WHERE DR. RAMORAY DIES, after claiming that he writes a lot of his own lines, his character is killed off when he's pushed down an elevator shaft.

- Joey gets the role of a dying man when *Outbreak 2* is filming in Manhattan. He hams it up so much that they have to change the

role to that of a dead man. (THE ONE AFTER THE SUPERBOWL, PART 2)

- Joey goes for the part of Cab Driver Number 2 in *Another World* but can't control his ego after being Dr. Drake Ramoray. (THE ONE WHERE EDDIE WON'T GO)

- During an audition, Joey has to kiss a guy, but director Warren Beatty tells him he's a bad kisser. Joey tries to enroll his male friends to practice kissing them, but they're not keen on the idea. In the end, Ross kisses him, but then Joey reveals that the audition was earlier and he didn't get the part. (THE ONE WITH BARRY AND MINDY'S WEDDING)

- Joey plays Kevin for an *Amazing Discoveries* infomercial. The ad demonstrates Kevin spilling milk all over himself until he finds the Milk Master 2000. The commercial comes back to haunt Joey later when actress Kate Miller recognizes him as the guy who doesn't know how to pour milk and makes fun of him. (THE ONE WITH THE METAPHORICAL TUNNEL)

- Under Phoebe's representation, Joey goes for a number of acting jobs. He wins one, but the others are a disaster. Reasons given for Joey not getting the parts include: Never met an Italian actor with a worse Italian accent; Not believable as a human being; Pretty dumb. (THE ONE WITH THE METAPHORICAL TUNNEL)

- One of Joey's acting students is going for the role of Nick the boxer in *All My Children*. Joey is up for the part as well, so he gives the student some advice designed to sabotage him. It backfires, and the guy gets the part. (THE ONE WITH THE RACE CAR BED)

- Joey has an audition for a musical version of *A Tale of Two Cities*. He's invited to the dance audition, but there's just one problem—even though Joey's résumé says he can dance, it's actually a lie. He's left in charge of teaching his fellow auditionees "the combination," which leads to a routine that looks like zombies with jazz hands. When asked to show how it's really done, Joey runs away. (THE ONE WITH ALL THE JEALOUSY)

- Joey plays Victor in *Boxing Day*, a crazy play that looks like a family drama. (THE ONE WITH THE TINY T-SHIRT) It is revealed to be a science fiction piece, where Victor is beamed up into his spaceship. It's in this play that Joey meets love interests Kate Miller and Lauren. (THE ONE WITH THE SCREAMER)

- Before Joey films a movie with Charlton Heston, he goes on a three-day fishing trip with his dad. On his return, Joey stinks but forfeits a shower so that he can learn his lines. The next morning, he oversleeps and has to head to the set still smelling like fish. He takes a shower in Charlton Heston's dressing room and is caught by the man himself. He gives Joey some advice but warns him never to use his shower again. (THE ONE WITH JOEY'S DIRTY DAY)

- Joey appears on a PBS telethon. He thinks that he's going to be a host and is offended when he's just answering the telephone. When he realizes that his desk isn't in view of the camera, he asks another volunteer to switch with him, and they end up in a fight. (THE ONE WHERE PHOEBE HATES PBS)

- Joey auditions for the part of a twenty-nine-year-old Italian actor from Queens but loses out to a woman. Ross suggests that Joey create a part for himself by writing his own script. Ross takes control of Joey's writing schedule, which leads to an argument between Ross and Chandler. Joey writes a makeup scene for his two friends—and then a would-be porno, which he tries to get Rachel and Monica to star in. (THE ONE WITH THE INAPPROPRIATE SISTER)

- Joey is auditioning to play the role of a sophisticated man, so he plans on wearing a top hat to the audition. Rachel invites him to Bloomingdale's, where she dresses him up and gives him a man bag. At first Joey thinks bags are only for women, but he gets so obsessed with the bag that he carries it

everywhere and then gives the director a sales pitch for it during the audition. The director sends Joey away immediately. (THE ONE WITH JOEY'S BAG)

- When Ben gets an audition for a soup commercial, Joey tries out for the role to play his dad. They both get callbacks but go up against each other in the next interview. Joey is furious that Ross won't pull Ben out of the audition and tries to put him off acting when they're alone together. In the end, neither gets the part. (THE ONE WHERE RACHEL SMOKES)

- Joey lands a part in *Law & Order* and invites his grandmother to watch it on Monica's TV. Unfortunately for Joey, his part has been cut out, so he films his own makeshift role to try and fool her. (THE ONE WHERE ROSS CAN'T FLIRT)

- Joey wins a role in *Shutter Speed*, a movie being shot just outside Las Vegas, but he

won't be paid until the movie makes money. When Chandler refuses to believe that this will be Joey's big break, Joey throws him out of the cab and heads to Vegas on his own. There, he discovers that the movie has gone bust and he's out of a job. (THE ONE WITH JOEY'S BIG BREAK)

- When his movie goes bust, Joey passes the time by working as a gladiator at Caesars Palace, having his photo taken with tourists. (THE ONE IN VEGAS, PART 1)

- While hanging out in the casino, Joey is convinced that he's found his hand twin. He tries to persuade the "twin" to team up with him so that they can earn big money but is thrown out of the casino. (THE ONE IN VEGAS, PARTS 1 AND 2)

- While suffering from a hernia, Joey goes on an audition for an unnamed show, but he comes across as weird and creepy—especially when he sticks his hand down his pants to relieve his pain. He then has an audition for a pet food commercial but is in too much agony to lift the bag. Finally, he lands a winning role—the part of a dying man on a TV show. (THE ONE WHERE JOEY LOSES HIS INSURANCE)

- While working at Central Perk, Joey is offered an audition with one line: "I'm sorry, that seat's saved." Gunther has a hair appointment, so he tells Joey he can't go. Joey closes the coffee shop and goes anyway, doesn't get the part, and almost loses his job at Central Perk. (THE ONE WITH THE JOKE)

- Joey mentions that a couple of years ago, he went for an audition for a Minute Maid commercial. He didn't get it because a guy called Carl acted as his brother and messed it up. (THE ONE WITH UNAGI)

- When Chandler knows the director of an Al Pacino movie, Joey begs Chandler to give her a call. Chandler takes her out for coffee and dinner in the hope that he can persuade her, but she ends up thinking he has a crush on her. Playing along, Chandler tells her that he'll accept her rejection if she'll give Joey an audition. She does, but Joey forgets to go. (THE ONE WHERE ROSS DATES A STUDENT)

- Joey gets the male lead in *Mac and C.H.E.E.S.E.*, a TV show about a detective who solves crimes with his robot partner. (THE ONE WITH MAC AND C.H.E.E.S.E.) On the first day of shooting in THE ONE WHERE ROSS MEETS ELIZABETH'S DAD, Joey makes fun of the robot, which prompts controller Wayne to try to have him fired. When Joey tries to get back in Wayne's good graces by helping him speak to women, Joey gets his job back but not for long. Chandler describes the show as one of the worst things ever, and in THE ONE WITH RACHEL'S ASSISTANT, the show is canceled.

- Joey has an audition to play a nineteen-year-old, so he practices by wearing "young" clothes and saying "'Sup, dude" and "whack" a lot. (THE ONE WITH MONICA'S THUNDER)

- Joey thinks he's been offered the role of Dr. Drake Ramoray's twin brother, Stryker, and is appalled when he has to audition. He walks out, but when *Mac and C.H.E.E.S.E.* is canceled, he begs for another chance. The role of Stryker goes to another actor, and Joey is asked to revive his old role of Drake. (THE ONE WITH RACHEL'S ASSISTANT) In THE ONE WITH JOEY'S NEW BRAIN, Drake gets a new brain and wakes from his coma.

- Joey is nominated for a Soapie Award and is furious when he doesn't win. (THE ONE WITH JOEY'S AWARD)

- Joey auditions for a movie about three Italian brothers who arrive in America at the turn of the century. Trouble is, the part calls for an uncircumcised man, so Monica fashions him a little something out of Silly Putty, but it falls off during the audition. (THE ONE WITH ROSS AND MONICA'S COUSIN)

- Joey wins a roll in a WWI movie, but his drunk costar keeps spitting as he talks and then holds up production so much that Joey is late for Monica and Chandler's wedding. In the end, Joey picks him up and escorts him from the building just so that he can get away. (THE ONE WITH MONICA AND CHANDLER'S WEDDING, PARTS 1 AND 2)

- In THE ONE WHERE RACHEL IS LATE, Joey invites Chandler to his movie premiere but is furious when he falls asleep.

- Joey is up for the role of a game show host on a crazy new show called *Bamboozled*, and Chandler and Ross help him prepare. At first, they're thoroughly confused, but they soon get competitive and excited about the game. However, when Joey gets to the audition, the producer has changed the format to simple questions and answers because they thought the original was too complicated. Joey is sorely disappointed until he is told that there will be bikini-wearing women holding up the scores. (THE ONE WITH THE BABY SHOWER)

- Joey remembers getting a "good" review for a production of *Our Town*. The review said that everything in the play was terrible, but Joey was abysmal. Joey apparently has no idea what *abysmal* means and takes it as a huge compliment. (THE ONE WITH THE COOKING CLASS)

- Joey gets an audition for a Broadway play with legendary Leonard Hayes as the director. Joey is in awe, but Hayes thinks Joey can't act. However, Hayes agrees that Joey can come back as long as he realizes

that the role needs urgency. During the second audition, Joey is desperate to use the bathroom, which creates exactly the kind of urgency that Leonard is looking for. He uses the same technique when he comes for the final callback and gets the part. However, he's so desperate for the toilet that he ends up peeing all over the director. (THE ONE WITH THE MUGGING)

- When Chandler's agency wins a huge advertising campaign, Joey asks if he can be in it. Chandler doesn't think the part of Stuffy Professor is Joey's thing, but Joey thinks otherwise and gives him a video to watch. Chandler doesn't want to look like an idiot to his bosses, so he tells Joey that he liked the reel, but his boss did not. Joey knows he's lying, so he pops the video into the machine and reveals a Japanese commercial he once made for Ichiban, a blue lipstick for men. He then makes Chandler wear some to show how sorry he is for lying to Joey. (THE ONE WITH ROSS'S GRANT)

- Joey reveals that he recently had an unsuccessful audition for *Family Honor 2: This Time It's Personal*. (THE ONE WITH PHOEBE'S WEDDING)

- Joey has an audition for a play, which requires him to speak French. According to his résumé, he can speak it fluently, but of course that's a lie. Phoebe agrees to teach him, but Joey can't pick it up, which leads to an awkward—and failed—audition. (THE ONE WHERE JOEY SPEAKS FRENCH)

- Joey thinks that his agent, Estelle, is not putting him up for auditions so he fires her, but as it turns out, Estelle died and Joey's one of the last people to find out. (THE ONE WHERE ESTELLE DIES)

- When the new chick and duck get stuck in the Foosball table, Joey recites a speech that he gave during a recent audition for a sci-fi movie. He does not get the part. *(THE LAST ONE, PARTS 1 AND 2)*

JOEY
(NON-ACTING)

- Joey once worked at Macy's as the Aramis guy. *(THE ONE WHERE UNDERDOG GETS AWAY)*

- Joey is Santa's helper in a department store. He was up for the role of Santa, which he had last year, but lost out to a guy who was sleeping with the manager. *(THE ONE WITH THE MONKEY)*

- Joey takes part in a fertility study at NYU Med School. The research lasts for two weeks, and he earns $700. *(THE ONE WHERE RACHEL FINDS OUT)*

- Joey works in a department store spritzing customers with Bijan for Men but is then moved to selling Hombre. This leads to competition between Joey and the original Hombre Man, who ends up spritzing a customer in the eye. *(THE ONE WITH THE BREAST MILK)*

- Chandler gets Joey a job at his company as an entry-level processor, except Joey decides to be Joseph, a whole new character to fit the role. He ends up driving Chandler crazy with his lies and sucking up to the company bosses. *(THE ONE WITH THE CHICKEN POX)*

- Joey takes on a part-time job of teaching acting for soap operas at a local college. The nuggets of information he shares with the class include:

- Reacting does not mean acting again.
- Some of the students will have to become much more attractive.
- If you have to cry during a scene, cut a hole in your pocket, take a pair of tweezers, and just start pulling.
- If you want to convey that you've done something evil, pretend you have a fishhook in your eyebrow and you like it.
- If your character receives bad news, try to divide 232 by 13.
(THE ONE WITH THE RACE CAR BED)

- Joey sells Christmas trees when he's between acting gigs. However, Phoebe is against innocent trees being cut down in their prime and is mortified that the older trees go into a chipper. She tries to persuade customers to buy the dead trees, which interferes with Joey's commission. In the end, the friends gather the old trees in Monica's apartment so that the trees can fulfill their Christmas destiny. *(THE ONE WHERE RACHEL QUITS)*

- It is revealed that Joey gave up a job of declawing cats to be in the terrible play *Boxing Day*. *(THE ONE WITH THE SCREAMER)*

- Monica employs Joey at Alessandro's so that she can fire him, thereby appearing authoritative and in control to her colleagues. Only trouble is, Joey loves the holiday tips, so it takes several attempts before he finally plays along and leaves. *(THE ONE WITH THE GIRL FROM POUGHKEEPSIE)*

- Joey is employed as a guide in the museum where Ross works but is disappointed when Ross won't sit with him in the cafeteria. It's the unwritten rule that the scientists and tour guides can't sit together. In the end, Ross decides that this rule should change and gives a dramatic speech about having less division in the museum and how they should share more about themselves. (THE ONE WITH PHOEBE'S UTERUS)

- Joey takes a job as a waiter at Central Perk but is fired for leaving work to go to an audition. Rachel gets his job back (THE ONE WITH THE JOKE), and in THE ONE WITH RACHEL'S SISTER, Joey keeps giving free food and drinks to attractive women. Gunther makes him pay for the treats and tells Joey that only those celebrating a birthday can have free stuff—suddenly twenty pretty ladies have their birthdays in one day. He eventually quits, but Gunther doesn't notice.

- Determined to make some spare money, Joey takes part in an identical twin study. Only problem is, Joey doesn't have an identical twin. Joey hires a "look-alike" to pretend that they're related, but since they look nothing like each other, it all fails. (THE ONE WITH UNAGI)

MONICA

- When we first meet Monica, she is one of several chefs at Iridium. (THE ONE WHERE MONICA GETS A ROOMMATE) In THE ONE WITH FIVE STEAKS AND AN EGGPLANT, she's promoted to head lunch chef and head of purchasing but is fired when she accepts some steaks from the meat vendor.

- Monica hosts a dinner for Phoebe's friend Steve, who is looking for a head chef for his new restaurant. The evening ends up being a disaster because Steve turns up stoned, eats the entire first course in one bite, and then tries to raid Monica's pantry. (THE ONE WITH THE STONED GUY)

- Monica goes for a job interview with Leon Rastatter, who works for a firm promoting Mockolate, a synthetic—and revolting—form of chocolate. Rastatter wants to turn Thanksgiving into the Mockolate holiday and asks Monica to create recipes. She does, using just tiny bits of the food, but the FDA approval doesn't come through, citing something about laboratory rats. (THE ONE WITH THE LIST)

- Monica gets the job as Carol and Susan's wedding caterer. When the wedding is almost called off, Monica's biggest concern is whether or not she'll still get paid. (THE ONE WITH THE LESBIAN WEDDING)

- Monica goes for a job as a chef, with Chandler listed as her reference. The boss wants her to make a salad, but he has a weird sexual fetish for vegetables and starts to make Monica uncomfortable, so she leaves. (THE ONE WITH THE PROM VIDEO)

- Judy Geller gets Monica a job as a caterer for an old friend, Dr. Richard Burke. Phoebe acts as a waitress at the party, where she notices a definite spark between Monica and Richard. (THE ONE WHERE ROSS AND RACHEL . . . YOU KNOW)

- Monica goes to an interview at the fifties-style Moondance Diner but hates the thought of working there. Instead, she plays the stock market and does well for a while but when she goes broke, she takes the waitress job. This involves her wearing fake boobs, a blonde wig, and fifties clothes. When she's not jumping on the counter to dance, she can be seen gliding around the place on roller skates. *(THE ONE WITH THE BULLIES)*

- Pete buys a restaurant and wants Monica to be the head chef. This is Monica's dream job, and when Pete assures her that he no longer has a crush on her, she agrees to work there. While visiting the restaurant, Monica and Pete kiss, and she realizes she has feelings for him. *(THE ONE WITH A CHICK AND A DUCK)*

- After her breakup with Pete, Monica is without a job, so she accepts her mother's offer of a catering gig for a party she's hosting. *(THE ONE WITH THE CUFFS)*

- Monica caters a funeral party using money that Phoebe loaned to her. The next day, they team up and cater another funeral, where the widow tries to get out of paying them. Phoebe does such a good job of getting the money that she and Monica decide to go into business together. It doesn't last. *(THE ONE WITH THE DIRTY GIRL)*

- When Monica fills in as a food critic for a local newspaper, she writes an article attacking Alessandro's restaurant. The owner demands an explanation and then offers Monica a job. She gives up her catering business and takes the position, only to find that the staff hates her because some of them are the sacked chef's children. *(THE ONE WHERE THEY'RE GOING TO PARTY!)*

- When Chandler has to move to Tulsa, Monica agrees to go with him, but then she's offered a job at the posh restaurant Javu and quickly changes her mind. *(THE ONE WITH THE PEDIATRICIAN)*

RACHEL

- After leaving Barry at the altar and moving in with Monica, Rachel gets her first job as a waitress at Central Perk. She's a terrible employee and frequently serves the wrong drinks, as well as sneeze muffins to rude customers. *(THE ONE WHERE MONICA GETS A ROOMMATE UNTIL THE ONE WHERE RACHEL QUITS)*

- Rachel acts as a waitress when Monica is trying to impress Phoebe's stoner friend, Steve. *(THE ONE WITH THE STONED GUY)*

- Rachel applies for dozens of jobs but receives rejection letters from most of them. She goes on an interview at Saks Fifth Avenue but receives a rejection call while in the middle of a poker game. *(THE ONE WITH ALL THE POKER)*

- When Gunther tells Rachel that she needs to retrain at Central Perk, she's shocked. She's not interested in where the "tray spot" is or why she shouldn't trap spiders under cups and leave them there. Joey and Chandler tell Rachel to "feel the fear" and go after something she wants instead. She follows their advice and finally quits. *(THE ONE WHERE RACHEL QUITS)*

- When she can't find a job, Rachel wants to retract her notice at Central Perk. However, Joey saves the day when he reveals that his dad has been doing a plumbing job at Fortunata Fashions and they have an opening. Rachel gets the job, serves her last cup of coffee at Central Perk, and then is asked to make coffee for the bosses at Fortunata. (THE ONE WHERE RACHEL QUITS)

- Rachel gets a job as an assistant at Bloomingdale's after meeting fellow assistant Mark in the Moondance Diner. (THE ONE WHERE CHANDLER CAN'T REMEMBER WHICH SISTER)

- Rachel goes for an internal job as assistant buyer in the Junior Miss department at Bloomingdale's. Once at the interview, however, her existing boss, Joanna, does not want to lose Rachel, so she downplays Rachel's new filing system and responsibilities, claims she gets too friendly with designers, and says she's an alcoholic. (THE ONE WHERE THEY'RE GOING TO PARTY!)

- When Bloomingdale's eliminates her department, Rachel ends up working in personal shopping, which she thinks is a huge step down. She's proved right when she has to help an eighty-one-year-old woman into a thong and the woman doesn't even buy it. However, her days become brighter when Joshua, a newly divorced customer, walks in and Rachel falls head over heels. (THE ONE WITH RACHEL'S CRUSH)

- When Rachel goes for the position of coordinator of the women's collection at Ralph Lauren, she thinks that it will be the ideal job for her. However, first she has to get through the interview, which proves rather difficult when her would-be boss leans over to open the door and she misunderstands and kisses him. Despite that (and subsequent faux pas), Rachel gets the job. (THE ONE WITH RACHEL'S INADVERTENT KISS)

- Ralph Lauren promotes Rachel to merchandising manager for Polo Retail, a job that comes with her own assistant. During interviews, Rachel has the opportunity to hire middle-aged Hilda or young, good-looking Tag. She chooses Tag, who is so pretty she could cry. (THE ONE WITH RACHEL'S ASSISTANT)

- A headhunter from Gucci contacts Rachel and asks her to go for an interview. Unfortunately, it takes place in a restaurant at the table right next to her current boss, Mr. Zelner. When Rachel tries to disguise the interview, she embarrasses herself and ends up losing the Gucci job and her Ralph Lauren one. (THE ONE WITH PRINCESS CONSUELA)

- Old colleague Mark offers Rachel a job at Louis Vuitton. The only problem is it's in Paris, which means leaving her old life behind. (THE ONE WITH PRINCESS CONSUELA)

- Ross begs Mr. Zelner to give Rachel her job back and a pay raise. Rachel accepts the offer to come back but then admits to Ross that she's desperate to go to Paris. He tells her she should go. (THE ONE WHERE ESTELLE DIES)

PHOEBE
(MASSAGE THERAPIST)

- Client (and Rachel's boyfriend) Paolo makes a pass at Phoebe while lying on the massage table. (THE ONE WITH THE DOZEN LASAGNAS)

- Mrs. Adelman, an eighty-two-year-old massage client, dies on the table. Her spirit goes into Phoebe and refuses to leave until she finally sees everything. (THE ONE WITH THE LESBIAN WEDDING)

- Frank Jr. thinks Phoebe is a prostitute because she works in a massage parlor. When Phoebe tells him that a colleague will give him a massage, he thinks her colleague must

be one, too, and tries to sleep with her. (THE ONE WITH FRANK JR.)

• Phoebe has a crush on one of her massage clients, and when she makes a move on him, she ends up being fired for "being a whore." Undeterred, Phoebe walks the streets, asking random people if they want massages, and then a cop thinks she's a prostitute, too. (THE ONE WITH THE BALLROOM DANCING)

• When Phoebe finds out that Monica has been going to another massage therapist for the past three years, she's furious. She persuades Monica into a massage, but when Monica starts making inappropriate noises, Phoebe wishes she'd never asked. (THE ONE WITH THE SECRET CLOSET)

• Phoebe reveals that her massage license has been revoked again. She's vague about the reason, although she does admit that when there's a lot of oil involved, sometimes her hand just slips. (THE ONE WITH RACHEL'S DREAM)

• Rachel has a gift certificate for a massage at Lavender Day Spa in Soho, but Phoebe lectures her about corporate greed destroying hearts and leaving behind hollow shells. Phoebe then tears up the voucher, but Rachel goes anyway. When she arrives, she's surprised to meet her Swedish therapist Ikea, who is none other than Phoebe. (THE ONE WITH THE FERTILITY TEST)

PHOEBE
(OTHER JOBS)

• Phoebe says her first job was in a Dairy Queen. Her first paycheck happened to coincide with a mine caving in, and eight people were killed. (THE ONE WITH GEORGE STEPHANOPOULOS)

• After teaching a massage-yourself-at-home course, Phoebe loses some clients. To earn more money, she goes to work as Chandler's temporary secretary. She discovers that nobody likes Chandler now that he's Boss Man Bing, and some even do impressions of him behind his back. (THE ONE WITH THE ICK FACTOR)

- Phoebe has always been the resident (and voluntary) Central Perk singer, but she's fired when Terry hires a professional entertainer. Rachel persuades the boss to have her back, but Phoebe will no longer work for free. Instead, she sings libelous songs outside Central Perk, until she eventually returns to the inside stage. (THE ONE WITH THE BABY ON THE BUS)

- Phoebe gets a job as a singer in a children's library. Unfortunately, her inappropriate songs lead her to be fired, but the kids love her anyway and christen her the Singing Lady Who Tells the Truth. (THE ONE AFTER THE SUPERBOWL, PART 1)

- Phoebe acts as a waitress for Monica during Dr. Richard Burke's party. (THE ONE WHERE ROSS AND RACHEL . . . YOU KNOW)

- Phoebe forgot to give Joey a message about an audition, which he ends up missing. To apologize, she calls the casting director and arranges a new appointment for Joey. Phoebe then becomes his temporary agent, but she can't stand the terrible things people say about him, so she has to give it up. (THE ONE WITH THE METAPHORICAL TUNNEL)

- Phoebe teams up with Monica to cater a funeral, and then they decide to go into business together. (THE ONE WITH THE DIRTY GIRL) The plan is that Monica will cook while Phoebe deals with the money. She even buys a van for their supplies, but in the end, the business doesn't take off when Monica accepts a chef job in THE ONE WHERE THEY'RE GOING TO PARTY!

- After finding out that she's carrying triplets, Phoebe wants to raise money to help Frank and Alice. She ponders insider trading, selling knives, and working at a Saturn dealership. She then comes up with the idea of maybe opening her own massage/cab business in the back of her van. She and Rachel come up with two possible names—Relaxitaxi or Relaxicab. (THE ONE WITH THE FREE PORN)

- Phoebe takes on a charity job collecting donations outside Macy's department store. Unfortunately, her happy holiday mood disappears when she catches a shopper using the bucket for change. When a woman donates trash and then the bucket catches fire as a result of a discarded cigarette and a cup of liquor, Phoebe returns as Street Phoebe, with a variety of homemade signs. When she is spotted shouting at shoppers, Phoebe is removed from her corner. (THE ONE WITH THE INAPPROPRIATE SISTER)

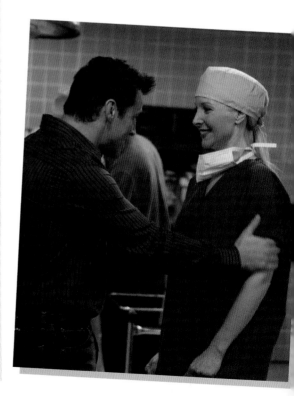

Scott Alexander: A processor at the company. He is introduced when Joey temporarily joins the company as an entry-level processor. Joey thinks he's a dork. (*THE ONE WITH THE CHICKEN POX*)

Fleischman: Chandler and Scott Alexander mention Fleischman when they're talking about Joey joining the company. Scott advises Joey to never touch Fleischman's sandwiches. (*THE ONE WITH THE CHICKEN POX*)

Jeannie: Head of East Coast Operations. Her husband is Milton. Joey says he had a lovely chat with her while he's working as an entry-level processor. He invites her and her husband to his imaginary boat and then calls her a phony behind her back. (*THE ONE WITH THE CHICKEN POX*)

Doug: Doug is a new boss who loves to slap Chandler on the backside in *THE ONE WITH THE ULTIMATE FIGHTING CHAMPION*. Chandler asks his boss not to do it but then feels deprived when other colleagues get slapped and he doesn't. Doug returns in *THE ONE WITH CHANDLER'S WORK LAUGH*, when Chandler reveals his work laugh to Monica, and then Doug and his wife, Kara, go up against the couple during a game of tennis. When Doug divorces his wife in *THE ONE WITH ROSS'S STEP FORWARD*, he wants to have dinner with Monica and Chandler. Monica refuses because she finds Chandler's boss annoying, so to explain her absence, Chandler tells his boss that they've separated. Doug then takes him to a strip club, and when Chandler won't give him his wedding ring, his boss throws a soda can at a bird.

Phil, Stephen, and Goldberg: The colleagues that Doug slaps while Chandler gets jealous. (*THE ONE WITH THE ULTIMATE FIGHTING CHAMPION*)

Drew and Patrick: When Chandler offers to find a date for Rachel, he ends up attracting the attentions of various workmates. They all want to take her out, so they try to bribe Chandler with whiskey, sports tickets, and much more. (THE ONE WITH THE GIRL FROM POUGHKEEPSIE)

Eldad: Another colleague who Chandler tries to set up with Rachel, but she's not interested since Monica and Chandler put too much pressure on her. (THE ONE WITH JOEY'S FRIDGE)

Bob and Mr. Franklin: Bob works on the sixth floor. He has mistakenly called Chandler Toby for the past five years, and now it's too late to correct him. When Mr. Franklin says that Bob might come to work on the eleventh floor, Chandler puts him off because of the name situation. Bob finds out that someone called Chandler has thwarted his promotion and smashes up Chandler's office—with the help of "Toby." (THE ONE WITH RACHEL'S DATE)

Walter and Elaine McKenna: When Chandler falls asleep during a staff meeting, he wakes up just before he snuggles into colleague Walter's shoulder. When he falls asleep again, Walter wakes Chandler just in time to be told by Elaine that he'll be moving to Tulsa. (THE ONE WHERE EMMA CRIES)

Ken and Claudia: During a staff meeting, Ken asks if it's true that Chandler had to move to Tulsa after falling asleep in a meeting. Chandler tells him not to believe everything he hears but admits it's true. Claudia then lights up a cigarette, which inspires Chandler and the rest of the office to do the same. (THE ONE WITH PHOEBE'S BIRTHDAY DINNER)

Jo Lynn: Jo Lynn is Chandler's assistant in the Tulsa office. She is single, loves cats, and insists on showing Chandler photographs of

them. Joey knows her as the crazy assistant. (THE ONE WITH RACHEL'S PHONE NUMBER)

Wendy: When Chandler has to work in Tulsa over Christmas, Wendy, the regional vice president and runner-up Miss Oklahoma, chooses to stay in the office after the other colleagues have left. Wendy tries to seduce Chandler, which prompts him to quit his job and return to New York. (THE ONE WITH CHRISTMAS IN TULSA)

Steve: Chandler's new boss at the advertising company. Steve is two years younger than Chandler, but Chandler still calls him "sir." (THE ONE WITH THE MUGGING)

Jordan: An intern at the advertising company, who thinks of Chandler as an old man. (THE ONE WITH THE MUGGING)

Nate, Susan, and Charlie: Interns who become full-time assistants at the ad agency. (THE ONE WITH THE LOTTERY)

Zack: After discovering that it will be almost impossible for him and Monica to get pregnant, Chandler brings home his colleague Zack in the hopes that he can be their sperm donor. After an evening of inappropriate questions, Zack thinks that they're weirdos, and Monica doesn't want his sperm anyway. If Chandler can't get Monica pregnant, then she doesn't want to get pregnant at all, so the couple decides they'll adopt instead. (THE ONE WITH THE DONOR)

Jeanette: Pregnant colleague, who walks in just as Chandler is talking to Zack. Chandler asks Zack if Jeanette is planning on keeping her baby. (THE ONE WITH THE DONOR)

ROSS

Marsha: While working at the museum, Marsha arranges the cave people to look angry. She decides that the woman is furious because she is at home while her husband is out hitting other women over the head. *(THE ONE WITH THE SONOGRAM AT THE END)*

Celia the Bug Lady: Celia is the curator of insects, and Ross dates her for a short time. Also see page 153. *(THE ONE WITH THE STONED GUY)*

Joey: A temporary tour guide in the museum. He, Rhonda, Peter, Dr. Andrew Phillips, Ted, and Scott are in the cafeteria during Ross and Joey's who-should-sit-where debacle. Also see page 13. *(THE ONE WITH PHOEBE'S UTERUS)*

Donald: Donald is one of the bosses at the museum. He has to speak to Ross after hearing reports that he's refusing to meet deadlines and is "mental." Ross explains that it's because of a note he left after someone ate his sandwich, but when Donald admits that he ate Ross's sandwich, Ross freaks out and is sent on sabbatical. *(THE ONE WITH ROSS'S SANDWICH)* Donald visits him in *THE ONE WHERE EVERYBODY FINDS OUT* and invites him back to the museum—just before Ross freaks out after seeing Chandler and Monica making out and taking off each other's clothes through his window.

Professor Kurt Rathman: One of Ross's fellow lecturers at NYU. He asks if he can speak to Ross about his first lecture, and Ross replies in a British accent, prompting visiting Rachel and Monica to talk with accents of their own. *(THE ONE WHERE JOEY LOSES HIS INSURANCE)*

Burt, Lydia, and Mel: Professors at NYU. When Ross dates a student, they tell him that it's against the rules, and if anyone finds out, he'll be fired. *(THE ONE WHERE ROSS DATES A STUDENT)*

Professor Newman: Professor Newman is the head of the paleontology department, but he's retiring. Ross gets to teach one of his advanced classes but wonders why he didn't get the head of department job instead. *(THE ONE WHERE JOEY DATES RACHEL)*

Professor Charlie Wheeler and Professor Spafford: The two professors are new to the university, and Ross is in charge of showing them around. Ross loves Professor Charlie, but the same can't be said for Professor Spafford. He's a boring guy who insists on telling a story about when he and his wife went on a cruise. According to the professor, there was a magnificent seafood buffet with clams, mussels, oysters, cracked crab, snow crab, and king crab, but he couldn't eat any of it because he is allergic to seafood—and peanuts, cashews, almonds, and filberts. When he goes to the bathroom, Ross and Charlie ditch him. *(THE ONE WITH THE SOAP OPERA PARTY)*

Professor Sherman: When Ross is up for keynote speaker at the National Paleontology Conference, he must first impress Professor Sherman. However, Ross bores the guy so much that he falls asleep. Ross is afraid to wake him up, so he tries to get out, but with the professor sitting right next to the door, it's impossible. As he scrambles past, Ross accidentally falls onto Sherman's knee, and when he wakes up, Ross pretends that he's just been offered the job. *(THE ONE WITH THE DONOR)*

JOEY
(ACTING)

Estelle Leonard: Estelle offered Joey representation after seeing him in the musical *Freud!* She isn't particularly good at her job and at one time even bad-mouths him around town when she thinks he's left the agency. However, she did get Joey an audition for *Days of Our Lives*, which was his biggest role. Estelle passes away in THE ONE WHERE ESTELLE DIES, but Joey doesn't realize it; he thinks she's not getting him auditions and fires her. (Actually, he fires Phoebe, who is impersonating her at the time). (THE ONE WITH THE BUTT ONWARD)

Lori: The casting lady on *Days of Our Lives*. Joey has to sleep with her to get the part. (THE ONE WITH RUSS)

Jean-Claude Van Damme: The main star of *Outbreak 2*. Joey has a small role as the dying/dead man. (THE ONE AFTER THE SUPERBOWL, PART 2)

Kate Miller and Lauren: Kate is Joey's costar and Lauren is the stand-in for his family drama/sci-fi play, *Boxing Day*. (THE ONE WITH THE TINY T-SHIRT) He sleeps with both of them but falls in love with Kate. However, she leaves before they can become a couple. (THE ONE WITH THE SCREAMER)

Charlton Heston: Joey has a small part in a Heston movie but is caught using the main star's shower. (THE ONE WITH JOEY'S DIRTY DAY)

Wayne: The controller of the robot in Joey's short-lived TV show, *Mac and C.H.E.E.S.E.* (THE ONE WHERE ROSS MEETS ELIZABETH'S DAD)

Cecilia Monroe: Actress on *Days of Our Lives* and short-term love interest of Joey. Her character donates her brain to Dr. Drake Ramoray. (THE ONE WITH JOEY'S NEW BRAIN)

Jessica Ashley: Actress on *Days of Our Lives*. She doesn't care that she won a Soapie Award, so Joey keeps it. (THE ONE WITH JOEY'S AWARD)

Richard Crosby: Joey's drunk, spitting costar in a WWI movie. (THE ONE WITH MONICA AND CHANDLER'S WEDDING, PARTS 1 AND 2)

Cash: Actor on *Days of Our Lives*. He goes on a date with Rachel but leaves when she tells him she's pregnant. (THE ONE WITH RACHEL'S DATE)

Phoebe: See Phoebe's colleagues: Joey, page 29.

Leonard Hayes: A Broadway director who casts Joey in a play. However, after Joey pees on him, he never makes it to the stage. (THE ONE WITH THE MUGGING)

Jan Rogers: Colleague on *Days of Our Lives*. She leaves a message on Joey's phone, which leads to Rachel finding out about Joey's secret party. (THE ONE WITH THE SOAP OPERA PARTY)

JOEY
(NON-ACTING)

Annabel and Todd: While working as a cologne spritzer, Joey's colleagues are assistant Annabel and fellow spritzer Todd, aka the Hombre Man. (THE ONE WITH THE BREAST MILK)

Chandler: See Chandler's colleagues: Joey, page 20.

Monica: Monica hires Joey so that she can fire him in front of her bullying staff. During the

gig, he adopts the name Dragon and earns $565 in tips. (*THE ONE WITH THE GIRL FROM POUGHKEEPSIE*)

Ross: See Ross's colleagues: Joey, page 23.

Gunther: Gunther is Joey's boss at Central Perk. He reprimands Joey for taking time off to go to an audition and giving free muffins to female customers. (*THE ONE WITH THE JOKE / THE ONE WITH RACHEL'S SISTER*)

MONICA

Franny: Chef at Iridium who tells Monica that she cured Paul the Wine Guy of his impotence. (*THE ONE WHERE MONICA GETS A ROOMMATE*)

Paula: Gives Monica advice about her friends' reactions to her boyfriends. (*THE ONE WITH THE THUMB*)

Wendy: A waitress Monica asks to assist during the evening with Steve the Stoner, but Wendy cancels at the last minute. (*THE ONE WITH THE STONED GUY*)

Leon: Manager of Iridium and Monica's boss. He promotes her after firing the head lunch chef and then fires her when she takes a steak gift from the meat vendor. (*THE ONE WITH FIVE STEAKS AND AN EGGPLANT*)

Julio: A waiter at the Moondance Diner who loves reading and writing pretentious poetry, which appeals to Monica. That is, until they date, and he writes an insulting poem about American women. (*THE ONE WITH ALL THE JEALOUSY*)

Jeannine: A waitress at the Moondance Diner who leaves early so that Monica can speak to Julio, but once Monica ditches him, he comes on to Jeannine. (*THE ONE WITH ALL THE JEALOUSY*)

Phoebe: For a short time, Monica and Phoebe work together as caterers. *(THE ONE WITH THE DIRTY GIRL)*

Tony, Carlos, and Marie: They are the children of Emilio, the chef who was fired from Alessandro's to make way for Monica. They (and the rest of their colleagues) hate her. *(THE ONE WHERE THEY'RE GOING TO PARTY!)*

Joey: See Joey's colleagues: Monica, page 24.

Stu: Stu makes Monica's life miserable when she first starts at Alessandro's. *(THE ONE WITH THE GIRL FROM POUGHKEEPSIE)* They later become friendly, and when Monica is organizing a stripper for Chandler's late bachelor celebration, he gives her a phone number. The woman is really a hooker, but Monica doesn't find out until she's already naked in the apartment. *(THE ONE WITH THE STRIPPER)*

Hillary: An assistant chef at Alessandro's. Ross thinks she's into him and asks Monica to set them up, but their date ends in disaster when his bright white teeth glow in the dark. *(THE ONE WITH ROSS'S TEETH)*

Tim: The new sous-chef at Alessandro's. Monica thinks he's terrible, but Phoebe (who is dating him) begs her to give him another chance. Later, Monica wants to fire him again, but Phoebe now wants to dump him, so they argue over who'll go first. In the end, they do it together, but then Monica takes pity and rehires him. *(THE ONE WITH RACHEL'S DATE)*

Jeffrey: The maître d'hôtel at Javu. Monica tells Chandler that Jeffrey's the funniest guy she's ever met, which sends him into a joke-telling obsession. When Joey tells Monica that Chandler is paranoid about Jeffrey, she tries to make it better by laughing at everything Chandler says. There is so much laughter that Chandler realizes Joey must have told Monica about the paranoia, so she tells him that Jeffrey isn't so funny after all. She's fibbing of course—the night before, he told a joke that was so funny, a little bit of pee came out. *(THE ONE WITH THE MALE NANNY)*

RACHEL

Gunther: The manager of Central Perk. With hair "brighter than the sun," Gunther is madly in love with Rachel, though he doesn't admit this to her until the very end of the series. *(THE ONE WITH THE SONOGRAM AT THE END ONWARD)*

Terry: The owner of Central Perk. First appears in *THE ONE WHERE UNDERDOG GETS AWAY*. He thinks that Rachel is a terrible waitress, and he can't stand Phoebe's singing. In *THE ONE WITH THE BABY ON THE BUS*, he tells Rachel that Phoebe is so bad that she makes him want to stick his finger through his eye, into his brain, and swirl it around. In *THE ONE WHERE RACHEL QUITS*, he insists that Gunther retrain Rachel, which prompts her to quit.

Mr. Kaplan: One of the old bosses at Fortunata Fashions. *(THE ONE WHERE RACHEL QUITS)* In *THE ONE WHERE CHANDLER CAN'T REMEMBER WHICH SISTER*, Mr. Kaplan admits to Rachel that coffee makes him gassy, but she already knows. He then gives her the "fabulous" job of sorting out a store cupboard full of tangled coat hangers.

Myra: The arthritic seamstress at Fortunata Fashions. Rachel has to walk her to the bathroom. *(THE ONE WHERE CHANDLER CAN'T REMEMBER WHICH SISTER)*

Mark: Rachel meets Mark at the Moondance Diner. He works at Bloomingdale's, which leads to Rachel being hired as an assistant in his department. (THE ONE WHERE CHANDLER CAN'T REMEMBER WHICH SISTER) Mark leaves Bloomingdale's in THE ONE WITH PHOEBE'S EX-PARTNER, but returns to Rachel's life in THE ONE WITH PRINCESS CONSUELA when he offers her a job in Paris.

Nancy: A colleague of Rachel's at Bloomingdale's. When she kisses Mark in the office, Ross overhears and thinks that it's Rachel and Mark making out. (THE ONE WITH ALL THE JEALOUSY)

Joanna: Rachel's boss at Bloomingdale's. Rachel and Mark are her assistants until Mark leaves and Sophie takes his place. Joanna has a fling with Chandler in THE ONE WITH THE DOLLHOUSE and THE ONE WITH THE CUFFS. She then sabotages an interview for Rachel and then promises her a better job. Unfortunately, she gets hit by a cab before she can put anything in writing. (THE ONE WHERE THEY'RE GOING TO PARTY!)

Sophie: Rachel's colleague at Bloomingdale's. First seen in THE ONE WHERE ROSS AND RACHEL TAKE A BREAK. Joanna hates Sophie and insults her at every opportunity. When Joanna dies in THE ONE WHERE THEY'RE GOING TO PARTY!, Sophie is ecstatic that her bullying boss is dead.

Mrs. Lynch: She's part of the interview committee when Rachel goes for another position at Bloomingdale's and then later breaks the news of Joanna's death. (THE ONE WHERE THEY'RE GOING TO PARTY!)

Mr. Waltham: Rachel's boss when she gets moved to the personal shopping department at Bloomingdale's. Very proper and quite snooty, he is the uncle of Emily, which is how Rachel (and Ross) come to be introduced to her. (THE ONE WITH RACHEL'S CRUSH)

Mr. Zelner: Rachel's browbeaten boss at Ralph Lauren. He puts up with many of Rachel's dramas from the moment she arrives until she finally leaves at the end of season 10. (THE ONE WITH RACHEL'S INADVERTENT KISS ONWARD)

Kim and Nancy: Kim is one of Rachel's bosses at Ralph Lauren, and Nancy is one of Kim's favorite employees. They make lots of decisions in the smokers' area, which leads Rachel to try smoking just so that she can be included. She still can't infiltrate their clique, however, and is gutted when Kim asks Nancy to go with her on a trip to Paris. (THE ONE WHERE RACHEL SMOKES) In an attempt to be more popular with the boss in THE ONE WITH ROSS'S TEETH, Rachel tells Kim that someone fooled around with Ralph Lauren in the copy room. Kim thinks it must be Rachel and that she's doing it to steal her job, so Rachel pretends that Ralph has dumped her.

Ralph Lauren: The owner of Ralph Lauren and the person Phoebe thinks she made out with in the company copy room. (THE ONE WITH ROSS'S TEETH) In THE ONE WITH RACHEL'S ASSISTANT, Ralph promotes Rachel to merchandising manager for Polo Retail.

Tag: Rachel knows she should hire the best person for the job of her assistant, but instead she chooses Tag primarily because she has a crush on him. (THE ONE WITH RACHEL'S ASSISTANT) They start dating in THE ONE WHERE CHANDLER DOESN'T LIKE DOGS—even though it's against company rules—and are almost caught when a naughty performance evaluation is accidentally sent to Mr. Zelner. *(THE ONE WITH ALL THE CANDY)*

Melissa: She walks in on Rachel as she's sniffing and hugging Tag's T-shirt. Melissa wants to ask Tag out, so Rachel tells her he's busy and then threatens to call her supervisor. *(THE ONE WITH THE ENGAGEMENT PICTURE)*

Betty: Betty is Mr. Zelner's secretary who has breakfast at her desk. Rachel plans to lure her away from the office with chocolates while Tag retrieves the sexy performance evaluation. *(THE ONE WITH ALL THE CANDY)*

Lee: Lee works in Human Resources. Mr. Zelner asks him to be in on the meeting with Rachel during a discussion about the "misunderstanding" regarding buying her baby. *(THE ONE WITH THE TEA LEAVES)*

Gavin Mitchell: An overly confident colleague who says he took over Rachel's job while she was on her "baby vacation." Mr. Zelner describes him as Super Gavin, and Rachel is so scared that he'll take over permanently that she cuts her maternity leave short and returns two weeks early. *(THE ONE WHERE RACHEL GOES BACK TO WORK)*

Heather: A colleague at Ralph Lauren. Gavin stares at her when she delivers a file to Rachel's office. He assures Rachel that he was staring at her skirt . . . or maybe it was her pants . . . *(THE ONE WITH PHOEBE'S RATS)*

PHOEBE

Jasmine: A colleague at the massage parlor who first appears in *THE ONE WITH THE DOZEN LASAGNAS*. In *THE ONE WITH FRANK JR.*, Frank Jr. propositions her, thinking that she's a prostitute. Jasmine is also Gunther's

roommate and plays a part in the Chloe to Rachel trail that leads to Rachel and Ross's big breakup. See page 54 and Ross's Love Interests: Chloe, pages 153–154.

Chandler: See Chandler's Colleagues: Phoebe, page 20.

Leslie: A childhood friend of Phoebe's and her former singing partner. The partnership split up when Leslie left to write jingles. When she's fired from her jingle job, Leslie and Phoebe reunite, but then Leslie sells "Smelly Cat" for use in a cat litter ad, and the friendship is fractured for good. *(THE ONE WITH PHOEBE'S EX-PARTNER)*

Monica: See Monica's Colleagues: Phoebe, page 26.

Joey: Phoebe works as an extra on Joey's show, *Days of Our Lives*. *(THE ONE WHERE RACHEL GOES BACK TO WORK)*

Tara: Tara is the receptionist at Lavender Day Spa. Phoebe is annoyed by the way she speaks and is confused that Tara seems to like working there so much. *(THE ONE WITH THE FERTILITY TEST)*

MEMORABLE AND EMBARRASSING SECRETS

The friends have more than a few embarrassing secrets in their closets, and many are revealed at the most inappropriate times. Here are some of the most memorable.

- Monica's underwear is on the telephone pole after having sex on the terrace with Fun Bobby. (THE ONE WITH PHOEBE'S HUSBAND)

- Chandler has a third nipple. (THE ONE WITH PHOEBE'S HUSBAND)

- Joey was in a porn movie. (THE ONE WITH PHOEBE'S HUSBAND)

- Ross smoked pot in college. (THE ONE WHERE ROSS GOT HIGH)

- The fired mailman didn't steal Jack's *Playboy* magazine—Ross did. (THE ONE WHERE ROSS GOT HIGH)

- Hurricane Gloria didn't break the porch swing—Monica did. (THE ONE WHERE ROSS GOT HIGH)

- Ross hasn't worked at the museum for a year. (THE ONE WHERE ROSS GOT HIGH)

- Monica and Chandler are living together before marriage. (THE ONE WHERE ROSS GOT HIGH)

- Ross married Rachel in Vegas and got divorced again. (THE ONE WHERE ROSS GOT HIGH)

- Phoebe loves Jacques Cousteau. (THE ONE WHERE ROSS GOT HIGH)

- Ross pooped himself on Space Mountain. (THE ONE WITH RACHEL'S ASSISTANT)

- Chandler accidentally kissed a man in a bar. (THE ONE WITH RACHEL'S ASSISTANT)

- In college, Ross used to wear leg warmers. (THE ONE WITH RACHEL'S ASSISTANT)

- Chandler entered a Vanilla Ice look-alike contest and won. Ross came in fourth and cried. (THE ONE WITH RACHEL'S ASSISTANT)

- Monica was once sent to her room without dinner, so she ate the macaroni off a jewelry box she'd made. (THE ONE WITH RACHEL'S ASSISTANT)

- Ross used to stay home every Saturday night to watch *The Golden Girls*. (THE ONE WITH RACHEL'S ASSISTANT)

- Monica couldn't tell time until she was thirteen. (THE ONE WITH RACHEL'S ASSISTANT)

- Chandler once wore Monica's underwear to work. (THE ONE WITH RACHEL'S ASSISTANT)

- In college, Ross got drunk and slept with the lady who cleaned their dorm. Ross claimed that it was Chandler who slept with the cleaning lady. (THE ONE WITH RACHEL'S ASSISTANT)

- Chandler hates dogs. (THE ONE WHERE CHANDLER DOESN'T LIKE DOGS)

- Ross doesn't like ice cream because it's too cold and hurts his teeth. (THE ONE WHERE CHANDLER DOESN'T LIKE DOGS)

- In high school, Ross and Will Colbert founded an I Hate Rachel Club. The club created a rumor that Rachel had both male and female reproductive parts. (THE ONE WITH THE RUMOR)

- Ross made out with his fifty-year-old high school librarian. (THE ONE WITH THE RUMOR)

- When Monica and Ross were kids, Monica couldn't get braces because their dog Chi-Chi needed knee surgery. (THE ONE IN MASSAPEQUA)

- Ross still sees his pediatrician. (THE ONE WITH THE PEDIATRICIAN)

- Chandler took his security blanket to college even though he insists it was a wall hanging. (THE ONE WITH THE PEDIATRICIAN)

- Chandler gets pedicures. (THE ONE WITH ROSS'S TAN)

- Chandler kissed Rachel at college. (THE ONE WHERE THE STRIPPER CRIES)

- Ross thinks he kissed Rachel at college. Actually, he kissed Monica, who was lying on the bed in the dark. So technically, Monica was Ross's first kiss with Rachel. (THE ONE WHERE THE STRIPPER CRIES)

- Ross was Monica's midnight mystery kisser and her first kiss ever. (THE ONE WHERE THE STRIPPER CRIES)

- One summer as a teenager, Ross lived with his grandmother while trying to make it as a dancer. (THE LAST ONE, PARTS 1 AND 2)

I HATE RACHEL CLUB

QUOTABLE QUOTES

They say there is a *Friends* quote for every occasion. Here are a few of the most loved, funniest, and most memorable.

"How you doin'?"

See page 36.

"Oh my God!"

Janice's favorite catchphrase, which she says at every opportunity. In fact, they are the first words she says when we meet her in *THE ONE WITH THE EAST GERMAN LAUNDRY DETERGENT*.

"I'm going to Yemen!"

Just to get rid of her, Chandler tells Janice that he's going to Yemen. When she won't leave the airport, he really is forced onto the plane for Yemen.
(*THE ONE WITH ALL THE RUGBY*)

"He's her lobster."

Phoebe says that all lobsters fall in love and mate for life, and she believes that Rachel is Ross's lobster. (*THE ONE WITH THE PROM VIDEO*)

"I know!!"

See page 67.

"Could that report *be* any later?"

Chandler has a habit of emphasizing words such as *be* and *more*, which his colleagues (and sometimes friends) do impressions of. (*THE ONE WITH THE ICK FACTOR*)

"We were on a break!"

See page 48.

"PIVOT!"

When Ross buys a new couch for his apartment, he refuses to pay the delivery charge. Instead, he and Rachel carry it home themselves, and then Chandler is recruited to help them get it up to the apartment. Unfortunately for Ross, the couch won't fit up the stairs despite his incessant cries of "Pivot!" as they try to round the corner. *(THE ONE WITH THE COP)*

"I don't even have a *pla*."

When it comes to life, Phoebe doesn't even have a *pla*, never mind a plan. *(THE ONE WITH GEORGE STEPHANOPOULOS)*

"You fell asleep?"

Rachel writes an eighteen-page letter (front and back!) to Ross, explaining all the ways he did her wrong. It's late and the letter is so long that he falls asleep and doesn't read the part where Rachel says he has to take responsibility for everything that went wrong if he wants to get back together with her. *(THE ONE WITH THE JELLYFISH)*

"They don't know that we know they know we know."

Phoebe and Rachel's plans for getting Monica and Chandler to confess to being in love look thwarted when the couple finds out. But then Phoebe decides that "they don't know that we know they know we know," and the plan is back on. *(THE ONE WHERE EVERYBODY FINDS OUT)*

"I wasn't supposed to put beef in the trifle!"

When Rachel makes an English trifle for Thanksgiving dessert, she makes one tiny mistake—one of the layers is made of meat! *(THE ONE WHERE ROSS GOT HIGH)*

"Could I *be* wearing any more clothes?"

When Chandler steals the chair cushions from apartment 20, Joey puts on all of Chandler's clothes and does an uncanny impression of him.

"I got off the plane."

Rachel has second thoughts about moving to Paris and turns up at Ross's apartment, just as he's hoping she would. (THE LAST ONE, PARTS 1 AND 2)

"I needed a plan. A plan to get over my man."

When Monica and Richard split up, she needs something to occupy her mind, so she makes jam. Apparently, jam is the opposite of man. (THE ONE WITH THE JAM)

"Get off my sister!"

Ross screams this when he sees Monica and Chandler making out (and possibly more) from across the street. (THE ONE WHERE EVERYBODY FINDS OUT)

"This is all a moo point."

According to Joey, a *moo* point is a cow's opinion. It doesn't matter. It's *moo*. (THE ONE WHERE CHANDLER DOESN'T LIKE DOGS)

"I'm the Holiday Armadillo!"

Ross wants to teach Ben about Hanukkah, but Ben is more interested in Santa. Ross tries to rent a Santa costume to appease Ben, but there aren't any left at the shop, so he's forced to rent an armadillo costume and retells the story of Hanukkah to Ben. (THE ONE WITH THE HOLIDAY ARMADILLO)

"Joey doesn't share food!"

Joey loves to eat and won't even consider sharing a grape with baby Emma. When his date takes food off his plate without asking, he makes it clear that "Joey doesn't share food," although that doesn't stop him from stealing her dessert because it looks nicer than his. (THE ONE WITH THE BIRTH MOTHER)

EVERY TIME JOEY SAYS, "HOW YOU DOIN'?"

Perhaps one of the most infamous one-liners to come out of *Friends*, Joey's "How you doin'?" pickup line was sometimes successful with the ladies, sometimes not, but always hilarious and unforgettable.

- Joey gives advice to Rachel about how to ask somebody out. He tells her that he normally looks a woman up and down and then says, "How you doin'?" Later, Rachel tries it out during an imaginary conversation between her driver's license and Joshua's driver's license. *(THE ONE WITH RACHEL'S CRUSH)*

- Despite being half-asleep during a visit to the sleep clinic, Joey still manages to say, "How you doin'?" to the whole room. *(THE ONE WITH ALL THE WEDDING DRESSES)*

- Bridesmaid Felicity loves Joey to "talk New York," which of course involves his famous catchphrase. *(THE ONE WITH ROSS'S WEDDING, PART 2)*

- While flirting with the hot girl across the street, Joey attempts to mime the words "How you doin'?" It works and she waves him over. *(THE ONE WITH RACHEL'S INADVERTENT KISS)*

- While looking for his hand twin in Vegas, Joey attempts to flirt with a dealer at the gambling table by using his catchphrase but gets nowhere. *(THE ONE IN VEGAS, PART 2)*

- Joey uses his catchphrase to flirt with two girls who think he has a Porsche underneath a car cover. Unfortunately for him, it's really a pile of cardboard boxes, which is destroyed when a young guy runs into it. *(THE ONE WITH JOEY'S PORSCHE)*

- To release some of his flirting energy (so that he doesn't use it up on Janine), Joey tries out his catchphrase on Chandler. Later that day he uses the line on Janine, but it doesn't work on her at all. *(THE ONE WHERE PHOEBE RUNS)*

- When Rachel's sister Jill comes to stay with her, Joey asks how she's doing, but it's Ross who ends up going on a date with her. *(THE ONE WITH RACHEL'S SISTER)*

- When the friends wonder what could have been if they had taken different directions in life, Joey meets Rachel for the first time and immediately uses his catchphrase. *(THE ONE THAT COULD HAVE BEEN, PART 1)*

- While trying to convince a research study that he is an identical twin, Joey hires Carl to be his brother. He tries to teach Carl his catchphrase, but Carl says it all wrong. *(THE ONE WITH UNAGI)*

- When Joey asks a colleague how she's doing on the set of *Mac and C.H.E.E.S.E.*, it prompts the robot developer to ask for lessons on how to talk to women. *(THE ONE WHERE ROSS MEETS ELIZABETH'S DAD)*

- When Rachel asks Joey to spend time with Tag, he teaches him to be "all Joey." When a woman walks into the office the next day, Tag asks, "How you doin'?" *(THE ONE WITH THE ENGAGEMENT PICTURE)*

- Rachel decides to move out of Joey's apartment because she doesn't want her baby's first words to be "How you doin'?" *(THE ONE WITH THE STAIN)*

- When Joey meets Molly, the hot nanny hired by Ross and Rachel, his first reaction is "How do you think she's doin'?" Ross pretends that he doesn't find her that attractive but then admits to the guys that she's so hot he cried himself to sleep. *(THE ONE WITH PHOEBE'S RATS)*

- After having his eyebrows plucked by Chandler, Joey practices his catchphrase while admiring himself in the mirror. *(THE ONE WHERE MONICA SINGS)*

- When a female producer takes a liking to Joey during an audition, he interrupts his pleas with the director to ask how she's doing. *(THE ONE WITH THE MUGGING)*

THINGS THAT HAPPEN DURING AND AFTER JOEY'S DIY HOBBY

Joey's DIY hobby causes chaos for Monica and Chandler.

DURING

- He wears snug pants.

- He cuts Chandler's bedroom door in half with a power saw.

- He drills a hole through Chandler's bedroom wall.

- He gouges a hole in Monica's bathroom floor tiles.

- He disguises the hole with the toilet brush.

- He leaves the varnish lid on the couch, and it sticks to Chandler's pants.

- He replaces Monica's tiles.

- He makes a TV unit that's so huge it takes up most of the wall and the bedroom doors.

- He forgets to tell Chandler that the side of the cabinet is still wet, and Chandler leans on it.

(THE ONE WITH FRANK JR.)

AFTER

- The humongous TV unit destroys one of Chandler's jacket sleeves, and he demands that it be sold.

- Joey places a $300 ad in the paper, asking $5,000 for the TV unit. Chandler changes this to $50 or best offer.

- Joey turns down several buyers because they are unsuitable.

- Joey voluntarily sits in the cupboard when a potential buyer bets that he won't fit in it. The guy then steals almost everything they own—except for Joey's white ceramic dog.

- Left with no furniture, the guys are forced to accept a canoe in exchange for the TV unit.

(THE ONE WITH THE CAT)

WACKY THINGS IN JOEY'S *BAMBOOZLED* GAME

When Joey auditions for a new game show, he tries out his script on Ross and Chandler. However, they weren't at all prepared to discover what the game actually involved.

- Wicked Wango Cards (they determine whether you go higher or lower).

- Spin the wheel of mayhem.

- Hold your breath until you hear the question.

- Use an angel pass for a free turn.

- Spin the wheel or pick a google card.

- If you pick a gimmie card, you get all your opponent's points.

- You can get a bonus for saying words backward.

- You can go up the ladder of chance to the golden mud hut.

- A monkey chant hails the hungry monkey section.

- There's a super speedy speed round with hopping bonus, but if you forget to switch legs between questions, there's no bonus.

- To win the game, you need to spin the wheel of mayhem to go up the ladder of chance. You go past the mud hut and through the rainbow ring to get to the golden monkey, then you yank his tail and—boom—you're in paradise pond.

(THE ONE WITH THE BABY SHOWER)

WICKED WANGO CARD

GIMME CARD

IMAGINARY THINGS ON JOEY'S RÉSUMÉ

Joey has a real problem with being truthful on his résumé. Here are the imaginary things that he claims to have experienced.

JOEY TRIBBIANI, NYC

- Three years of modern dance with Twyla Tharp.

- Five years with the American Ballet Theatre.

- One of the *ZOOM* kids.

- He can play the guitar (which is why he eventually takes lessons).

- He can speak fluent French.

- He can tap-dance.

- He does archery.

- He does horseback riding.

- He can drink a gallon of milk in ten seconds (he really believes he can do this).

(THE ONE WITH ALL THE JEALOUSY / THE ONE WHERE JOEY SPEAKS FRENCH)

parlez-vous français?

MILK

THINGS THAT HAPPEN IN THE LIFE OF JOSEPH THE PROCESSING GUY

When Joey starts working at Chandler's company, he creates a fictional character called Joseph. Joseph may be loved by some of his colleagues, but Chandler grows to hate him. Here are some of the things that happen to Joseph the Processing Guy.

- He has two daughters, Ashley and Britney. Ashley copies everything Britney does.

- His kids and the kids of the head of East Coast Operations go to the same school.

- He's married to Karen and thinking of having a third kid.

- Then they do have a third kid.

- The baby doesn't feel very well.

- He invites department head Jeannie and her husband to join him and Karen on their boat.

- He sides with Mr. Douglas when he's complaining about people taking time off for a holiday.

- He mixes things up and ruffles some feathers. Apparently, if you try to pull something sneaky, Joseph will always call you on it.

- He tells Mr. Douglas that it was Chandler who dropped the ball on the Lender project.

- He's upset when Chandler tells him that he just slept with Joseph's wife, Karen (under the guise of his own character, Chandy).

- He believes that Chandler has Karen's panties in his desk drawer.

(THE ONE WITH THE CHICKEN POX)

41

JOEY'S CAREER-RELATED ITEMS, PAID FOR BY CHANDLER

Before Joey became successful, Chandler paid for many of his career expenses. Here are some of the items that he covered over the years.

- First set of headshots

- Second set of headshots (showing a booger)

- Acting classes

- Stage combat classes

- Secret tap-dancing classes

- Dialogue coach, hired to teach Joey how to speak with a southern accent, but his accent turned out Jamaican.

(THE ONE WHERE RACHEL IS LATE)

EVENTS THAT JOEY SENDS (OR TRIES TO SEND) HIS FRIENDS TO SO THEY WON'T ATTEND HIS SOAP OPERA PARTIES

Joey can't stand the idea of his friends attending his annual soap opera party because he thinks they'll make a big deal out of being around famous stars, so he makes sure to send them to various questionable activities.

- A one-woman play called *Why Don't You Like Me: A Bitter Woman's Journey through Life*.

- A trip to a medieval times restaurant.

- A nighttime tour of a button factory.

(THE ONE WITH THE SOAP OPERA PARTY)

SUGGESTIONS FOR CHANDLER'S NEW NAME

When Chandler becomes paranoid that his name is stupid, he decides on a series of alternatives—with help from Joey and Phoebe.

No first name
No name
Clint
Gene
Mark Johnson
John Markson
Barney

(THE ONE WITH RACHEL'S NEW DRESS)

CHANDLER'S ADVERTISING SLOGANS

When Chandler decides that his future lies in advertising, he tries out some slogans for various household items.

- Cheese—it's milk that you chew.
- Crackers—because your cheese needs a buddy.
- A grape—because who can get a watermelon in their mouth?
- The phone—bringing you closer to people who have phones.
- Bagels and donuts—round food for every mood.
- Pants—like shorts but longer.

(THE ONE WHERE RACHEL GOES BACK TO WORK)

ALL THE TIMES CHANDLER SMOKES

The only smoker of the group, Chandler gave up the habit some time ago, but whenever the opportunity arises, he's tempted to give it another go.

- Chandler helps Joey prepare for an acting role playing a smoker, and Chandler ends up enjoying the cigarettes too much. He's forced to smoke on the balcony, sneaks cigarettes in his work cubicle, and enrages all of his friends. He quits when Phoebe offers him $7,000. *(THE ONE WITH THE THUMB)*

- When Ross and Rachel break up, Chandler finds it too similar to his own parents' breakup, so he starts smoking again. *(THE ONE WITHOUT THE SKI TRIP)*

- Rachel gives Chandler a hypnosis tape to help him quit smoking. Unknown to him, the tape is actually designed for women, and it accidentally brings out his feminine side. *(THE ONE WITH THE HYPNOSIS TAPE)*

- When Rachel is tormented by her smoking colleagues at Ralph Lauren, Chandler goes down to the office and takes a drag of the boss's cigarette. *(THE ONE WHERE RACHEL SMOKES)*

- While the residents of the building shout for more of Monica's candy, Chandler takes a drag from Smokes a Lot Lady's cigarette. *(THE ONE WITH ALL THE CANDY)*

- A nervous Chandler smokes in the hotel just before his wedding to Monica. *(THE ONE WITH MONICA AND CHANDLER'S WEDDING, PART 2)*

- Chandler starts smoking again after all his Tulsa colleagues light up during an office meeting. When he comes back to New York, Chandler sprays himself with (unscented) oven cleaner, and then Monica smells the smoke and freaks out. She forbids him to smoke again (so he lights up) and then tricks him into bed because she wants to have sex with him when she's ovulating. *(THE ONE WITH PHOEBE'S BIRTHDAY DINNER)*

- While waiting for the adoption social worker to arrive, Chandler admits to having a pack of cigarettes taped to the back of the toilet tank. *(THE ONE WITH THE HOME STUDY)*

- After looking at houses with Nancy the realtor, Chandler comes home smelling of perfume and cigarettes. The perfume is Nancy's, but the cigarettes are Chandler's. *(THE ONE WHERE CHANDLER GETS CAUGHT)*

ALL THE WAYS ROSS'S LEATHER PANTS WERE A DISASTER

When Ross tries out leather pants as part of his New Year's resolution, little does he know that they'll cause absolute chaos in a variety of ways.

- They are very tight.

- They cause him to burn up.

- They make weird gassy sounds against the couch.

- They won't go back up when he takes them down.

- After smearing his legs in powder and lotion, they still won't go up, which causes him to slap his face when his hands slip off the leather.

- They make him look like a weirdo in front of his date, Elizabeth.

- Because he can't get them back on, he's forced to travel back to Monica's without any pants on.

- They're stupid leather pants that don't even fit.

(THE ONE WITH ALL THE RESOLUTIONS)

EVERY TIME ROSS SAYS,

"WE WERE ON A BREAK!"

This is Ross's never-ending excuse as to why he "cheated" on Rachel with the girl from the copy shop. While it becomes Ross's catchphrase, it was actually Rachel who suggested a break in *THE ONE WHERE ROSS AND RACHEL TAKE A BREAK.*

- While Ross is visiting ex-wife Carol, she sympathizes with him that Rachel "fell in love with that Mark guy." However, Phoebe overhears the conversation while on the phone to Carol and explains what really happened. Ross responds with his trademark saying, "We were on a break!" *(THE ONE WITHOUT THE SKI TRIP)*

- After helping when Phoebe's cab breaks down on the way to a ski trip, Rachel makes a dig at Ross for sleeping with somebody else. He tells her that they were on a break, and Rachel replies that he should put the phrase on his answering machine. *(THE ONE WITHOUT THE SKI TRIP)*

- After Ross reads Rachel's super-long letter asking him to take responsibility for everything that went wrong in their relationship, he screams, "We were on a break!" in the middle of Central Perk. Chandler tells Ross that if he says that one more time, *he'll* break up with him. *(THE ONE WITH THE JELLYFISH)*

- Rachel is happy that Ross has taken full responsibility for what went wrong in their relationship. While in bed, she lectures him on how much he's grown and how her mother thought it would never work out because "once a cheater, always a cheater." Ross finally loses his patience and screams, "We were on a break!" The relationship is then off again. *(THE ONE WITH THE JELLYFISH)*

- When Chandler tells his friends that Kathy has cheated on him, Ross replies that perhaps she thought they were on a break. *(THE ONE WITH RACHEL'S CRUSH)*

- Ross may not have said it himself but would have agreed with the passenger on Rachel's flight from New York to London. After listening to her Ross and Rachel story, the passenger tells Rachel that it's perfectly clear that when Ross cheated, the two were on a break. *(THE ONE WITH ROSS'S WEDDING, PART 2)*

- The friends think it's hilarious when Chandler apologizes to Monica by proposing. Afterward, they make fun of him by proposing to each other as a way of saying sorry for slight misdemeanors. Ross takes it too far, however, when he asks Rachel if she remembers "that whole we were on a break thing" and then asks her to marry him. Nobody thinks it's funny. *(THE ONE WITH THE GIRL WHO HITS JOEY)*

- When Rachel discovers that Ross didn't annul their Vegas marriage, she tells him she has never been so angry. He replies by reminding her of the time he said they were on a break. *(THE ONE WITH JOEY'S PORSCHE)*

- Ross tells baby Emma that no matter what Mommy says, they really were on a break. *(THE ONE WITH ROSS'S INAPPROPRIATE SONG)*

- When Ross and Rachel get together for the last time, Ross makes a joke that they're back together for good, unless they're on a break. *(THE LAST ONE, PARTS 1 AND 2)*

ROSS'S SPRAY TAN DISASTER

When our favorite paleontologist decides to get a spray tan, what could possibly go wrong?

He gets a number 2 (meaning the strength of the dye) on his front.

He counts "Mississippily" before turning around, and ends up with a second number 2 on his front.

He returns to the booth to do his back.

He turns around and accidentally gets another number 2 on his front.

And then another number 2 on his front.

He goes back to the spray tan place.

He requests four 2s, all of them on his back.

He gets confused by the two sets of nozzles.

He gets another 2 on his front.

He turns around and receives another 2 on his front.

He hides in his apartment until Chandler tricks him into opening the door.

Chandler takes a photo.

(THE ONE WITH ROSS'S TAN)

PERSONAL DETAILS REVEALED WHEN ROSS ENCOURAGES LESS DIVISION IN THE MUSEUM

Joey is surprised at the division in the dinosaur museum, so Ross steps in to fix it. He may have wished he hadn't, however, when he hears what his colleagues have to say.

- Ross is divorced and has a kid.

- Joey is an actor and knows squat about dinosaurs.

- Ted moved to New York a month ago, and it really scares him.

- Andrew did not pay for his pear.

- Rhonda's breasts are not real.

- Scott needs to turn the light switch on and off seventeen times before he leaves the room, or his family will die.

(THE ONE WITH PHOEBE'S UTERUS)

TYPES OF COOKIES SOLD BY ROSS WHEN HE'S AN HONORARY BROWN BIRD

When Ross accidentally breaks a Brown Bird's leg, he steps in to sell her holiday cookies. Here's what cookies Ross has to offer.

Santa

Rudolph

Cream-Filled Baby Jesus

Hanukkah Menoreses

Mint Treasures

(THE ONE WHERE RACHEL QUITS)

PRACTICAL JOKES THAT RACHEL TEACHES BEN

Rachel's idea of being a cool babysitter is to teach Ben some practical jokes. Here are a few things he learns from her.

- Repeat everything the other person says.

- Jump out of closets to scare people.

- Switch the sugar for the salt.

- Take a quarter, blacken the edge, and then bet a person that they can't roll the coin from their forehead to their chin without it leaving their face.

- Put Saran wrap on the toilet seat so the pee goes everywhere.

(THE ONE WITH THE TRUTH ABOUT LONDON)

RACHEL DRAMAS THAT MR. ZELNER PUTS UP WITH

Rachel may be terrific at her job, but she sure does bring a lot of drama. Here are some of the events that her boss, Mr. Zelner, has to deal with over the years.

- She accidentally kisses him during the interview. (*THE ONE WITH RACHEL'S INADVERTENT KISS*)

- She accuses him of hiring her for sex. (*THE ONE WITH RACHEL'S INADVERTENT KISS*)

- She accidentally touches his groin. (*THE ONE WITH RACHEL'S INADVERTENT KISS*)

- She dates her assistant, Tag, and then writes a sexy evaluation for him, which causes stress for Mr. Zelner when he has to investigate whether or not Rachel and Tag are dating. (*THE ONE WITH ALL THE CANDY*)

- She tells Joey the fictitious story that Mr. Zelner wants to buy her baby, which leads to Joey storming into his office. (*THE ONE WITH THE TEA LEAVES*)

- He has to apologize if he implied that he wanted to buy her baby. (*THE ONE WITH THE TEA LEAVES*)

- He has to give her one extra month's paid maternity leave to say sorry for the baby-buying incident. (*THE ONE WITH THE TEA LEAVES*)

- He overhears Rachel on an interview with Gucci, just feet from where he is having lunch. (*THE ONE WITH PRINCESS CONSUELA*)

- He has to listen to Ross begging for Rachel's job back. (*THE ONE WHERE ESTELLE DIES*)

- He has to listen to Ross asking if he'll offer Rachel a raise. (*THE ONE WHERE ESTELLE DIES*)

THE TRAIL FROM CHLOE TO RACHEL

When Ross and Rachel have a fight and Ross thinks they're on a break, he sleeps with Chloe. Joey and Chandler tell him that he needs to think about the trail from Chloe to Rachel.

Chloe works with Isaac at the copy shop.

Isaac's sister is Jasmine.

Jasmine works at the massage place with Phoebe.

Jasmine does not tell Phoebe, but she does tell her roommate, Gunther.

Gunther tells Rachel.

ITEMS THE GUYS KNOW WILL BE IN RACHEL'S SHOPPING BAG

Joey and Chandler think they know exactly what is in Rachel's shopping bag.

A half-eaten box of cookies
Apples
Tortilla chips
Yogurt
Diet soda
Scotch tape

(THE ONE WITH THE EMBRYOS)

PHOEBE'S FUNKY BICYCLE

**When Phoebe reveals that she's never owned a bike,
Ross gifts her one that has some very funky accessories.**

Pink helmet

Pink mirrors

Pink, blue, and purple bell

Purple, blue, green,
and pink tassels

Pink saddle

White basket with yellow,
red, blue, purple,
and pink flowers on it

Pink frame

Pink and white
reflectors in the spokes

Gray wheels

Stabilizers

(THE ONE WITH ALL THE CANDY)

PHOEBE'S HOMEMADE MACY'S SIGNS

When Phoebe works as a charity collector outside Macy's, she's not prepared for the lack of respect for the bucket. She comes back the next day with the following signs.

RESPECT THE BELL, NO LOUD MUSIC!

HAPPY HOLIDAYS!

I HAVE NO MACYS INFO

WE ARE NOT A BANK!

WE ARE NOT A URINAL!

HAPPY HOLIDAYS!

PLEASE DON'T INVADE MY PERSONAL SPACE!

(THE ONE WITH THE INAPPROPRIATE SISTER)

PHOEBE'S ALIASES

We all like to play pretend sometimes, but Phoebe takes her false persona and fake names to a whole other level.

- After Ross says the wrong name at the altar, Phoebe calls Emily's stepmother as Dr. Phalange, Ross's personal physician. She tells Mrs. Waltham that Ross forgot his brain medicine, so women's names become interchangeable. (THE ONE AFTER ROSS SAYS RACHEL)

- Phoebe plays Regina Phalange—"a business woman in town on business"—when she tries to persuade the Las Vegas croupier that he is Joey's hand twin. (THE ONE IN VEGAS, PART 2)

- When Rachel's old sorority sister asks if Phoebe has ever been in a sorority, she tells her that it had to be shut down when Regina Phalange died of alcohol poisoning. (THE ONE WITH RACHEL'S BIG KISS)

- Monica refuses to believe that a couple they met on their honeymoon gave her and Chandler false names. Joey reveals that his fake name is Ken Adams, while Phoebe's is Regina Phalange. (THE ONE WITH THE VIDEOTAPE)

- Phoebe introduces herself as Regina Phalange while helping Chandler prepare for a job interview. (THE ONE WITH THE COOKING CLASS)

- When Joey tries (and fails) to speak French to a producer, Phoebe steps in to help. She tries to persuade the man that she's a French woman called Régine Philange and that Joey is really speaking a French dialect. (THE ONE WHERE JOEY SPEAKS FRENCH)

- When Phoebe hears that she can change her name to absolutely anything, she chooses Princess Consuela Banana Hammock (Valerie to her friends). However, she forgets the idea when Mike tells her he's changing his name to Crap Bag. (THE ONE WITH PRINCESS CONSUELA)

- When Phoebe wants Rachel to get off the plane to Paris, she tells her that there is something wrong with the left phalange. There is no such thing, but that doesn't stop fellow passengers from panicking and running from the plane. (THE LAST ONE, PARTS 1 AND 2)

HELLO my name is REGINA PHALANGE

PHOEBE'S SONGS

Phoebe might not be the best singer in the world, but she certainly puts her heart into her songwriting.

- Phoebe has written a song about that moment when you realize what life is really about. Unfortunately, a blackout prevents the performance. *(THE ONE WITH THE BLACKOUT)*

- Phoebe writes "New York City Has No Power" during the blackout. *(THE ONE WITH THE BLACKOUT)*

- Phoebe sings "The Snowman," a song about her mother's suicide. *(THE ONE WITH THE MONKEY)*

- Phoebe sings "My Mother's Ashes," another song about her mother, this time focusing on what happened after her death. *(THE ONE WITH THE MONKEY)*

- Phoebe starts to sing "You Don't Have to Be Awake to Be My Man," a song about the guy in a coma, but it's interrupted when Phoebe sees Monica heading to the hospital without her. *(THE ONE WITH MRS. BING)*

- Phoebe sings a song about naughty children while in the waiting room of the hospital. Ross pays her to shut up. *(THE ONE WITH THE BIRTH)*

- While locked in a broom cupboard, Phoebe traumatizes Ross and Susan by singing a song about bodies being found. *(THE ONE WITH THE BIRTH)*

- Phoebe wrote a song in the shower, and the lyrics involve pretty much everything she saw while in there. *(THE ONE WITH THE BABY ON THE BUS)*

- After Terry hires a professional singer for Central Perk, Phoebe sings a series of furious songs outside. When she returns, she teaches the professional how to sing "Smelly Cat." *(THE ONE WITH THE BABY ON THE BUS)*

- When Ross kisses Rachel and then struggles to decide between Rachel and Julie, Phoebe sings a song called "Two of Them Kissed Last Night." It is—according to her—a totally fictitious story of a love triangle between Neil, Betty, and Lulie. *(THE ONE WITH THE LIST)*

- Phoebe sings a series of songs for kids at a library all about dying grandparents, how they make hamburgers, and things you don't want to do. *(THE ONE AFTER THE SUPERBOWL, PART 1)*

- Phoebe teaches "Smelly Cat" to love interest Rob Donan. *(THE ONE AFTER THE SUPERBOWL, PART 1)*

- A record producer wants to do a demo and video for "Smelly Cat." However, Phoebe may have the look, but she doesn't have the voice, so they use her for the video and dub

it with another woman's track. She later sings the song in Central Perk with her friends. *(THE ONE WHERE EDDIE MOVES IN)*

• Phoebe sings a song about a crusty old man and maraca-playing rats, performed during her gig at Central Perk. *(THE ONE WHERE DR. RAMORAY DIES)*

• Joey asks if Phoebe's song "Salt Water Taffy Man" is written for Phoebe's love interest, Ryan, but she denies it. *(THE ONE WITH THE CHICKEN POX)*

• Phoebe sings "Sticky Shoes" in Central Perk with her ex-songwriting partner. *(THE ONE WITH PHOEBE'S EX-PARTNER)*

• Phoebe shares "Smelly Cat" and "Magician Box Mix-Up" with Leslie, her ex–songwriting partner. *(THE ONE WITH PHOEBE'S EX-PARTNER)*

• Phoebe writes "Jingle Bitch Screwed Me Over" when Leslie sells "Smelly Cat" for use in a cat litter commercial. *(THE ONE WITH PHOEBE'S EX-PARTNER)*

• Phoebe sings "Crazy Underwear" in Central Perk just moments before she's dumped by her two boyfriends, Jason and Vince. *(THE ONE WITH ROSS'S THING)*

• Phoebe is singing "66 Colors of My Bedroom" when her birth mother walks into Central Perk. *(THE ONE WITH THE JELLYFISH)*

• Phoebe sings an angry song called "Drunken Bitch," but no one knows who Phoebe is singing about. *(THE ONE WITH THE CAT)*

• Phoebe has a stinking cold, which makes her renditions of "Smelly Cat" and "Sticky Shoes" seem sexy. She assures customers in Central Perk that if she sneezes, it's not on purpose, except for when she sings the last verse of a song called "Pepper People." When her cold clears up, Phoebe sings "Goats Are Parading" but is disappointed that she no longer has her sexy voice, so she adopts a French accent to sing "Papier-Mâché Man." (THE ONE WITH JOEY'S NEW GIRLFRIEND)

- Phoebe practices "Tiny Tarzan" in Monica's apartment. Ross gives her some songwriting advice, and then he introduces everyone to his keyboard—he's horrible at playing it. (THE ONE WHERE CHANDLER CROSSES THE LINE)

- Phoebe's holiday song is "Happy Hanukkah," which goes through various drafts before she performs it in Central Perk. (THE ONE WITH THE GIRL FROM POUGHKEEPSIE)

- Phoebe sings "Are You in There Little Fetus?" while lying upside down on Monica's armchair, waiting to hear if she's pregnant. (THE ONE WITH THE EMBRYOS)

- After being so pregnant that it's uncomfortable to use her guitar, Phoebe sings "Smelly Cat" while playing a drum. (THE ONE WITH RACHEL'S NEW DRESS)

- Phoebe's dad tells her that when she was a baby, he would sing a song for her called "Sleepy Girl." The song has the same tune as Phoebe's "Smelly Cat." (THE ONE WITH JOEY'S BAG)

- Phoebe sings "Little Black Curly Hair" during her gig at Central Perk and puts Ross off his cake. (THE ONE WITH ROSS'S DENIAL)

- When the friends imagine what their lives would be like if they'd taken other paths, Phoebe sings a song about how her heart attack set her free. (THE ONE THAT COULD HAVE BEEN, PART 2)

- Phoebe is determined to sing at Monica and Chandler's wedding. First, she composes a

song about how she thought Chandler was gay and then demands a deposit. When they refuse, Phoebe writes an angsty song about how she'll never ask either of them to sing at her wedding and then sits outside Monica and Chandler's bedroom, where she performs a song about staying there all night. She finally gets a deposit and is sent on her way. (THE ONE WITH MONICA'S THUNDER)

- While trying to impress Mike's parents, Phoebe sings "Smelly Cat" and then mentions two of her other songs—"Pervert Parade" and "Ode to a Pubic Hair." (THE ONE WITH ROSS'S INAPPROPRIATE SONG)

- While singing outside Javu, Phoebe sings a song about buying a human spleen in Argentina. When Monica questions what's going on, Phoebe tells her that the customers were requesting a lot of her songs, including "You Suck" and "Shut Up and Go Home." When she returns (dressed in evening gear), she sings "The Woman Smelled Like Garbage" and later plans a performance of "The Uncircumcised Man." When she and Monica fight, Phoebe returns to the restaurant with a new song—"The Food Here at Javu Will Kill You!" (THE ONE WITH RACHEL'S DREAM)

- On Emma's first birthday, Phoebe writes and performs a "Happy Birthday" song, but after Joey's dramatic reading of a children's book, it falls flat with the party audience. (THE ONE WITH THE CAKE)

- Phoebe feels as though she's in a musical and compiles several songs, including "When the Sun Comes Up—Bright and Beaming" and "Don't Take No for an Answer." (THE LAST ONE, PARTS 1 AND 2)

PHOEBE'S NAMES FOR HER GUITAR CHORDS

When Phoebe offers to teach Joey to play guitar,
she has some interesting names for the chords.

Bear Claw

Old Lady

Turkey Leg

Tiger   Dragon   Iceberg

(THE ONE WITH ALL THE RESOLUTIONS)

PHOEBE'S WEIRD PAST

Phoebe never ceases to shock her friends, particularly when she's sharing a wild fact from her past.

- Phoebe was fourteen when she moved to New York. She came to the city after her mother committed suicide, and she lived with an albino guy who cleaned windshields outside Port Authority. He killed himself and then she found aromatherapy. *(THE ONE WHERE MONICA GETS A ROOMMATE)*

- Debbie was Phoebe's best friend in junior high. She was struck by lightning on a miniature golf course, and now Phoebe gets a Debbie vibe whenever she uses little yellow pencils. *(THE ONE WHERE NANA DIES TWICE)*

- The following people have all died while Phoebe has been sitting in a dentist chair: Aunt Mary, John her mailman, and her cowboy friend Albino Bob. *(THE ONE WITH THE GIANT POKING DEVICE)*

- By the time Phoebe was eighteen, her mother had committed suicide, her father had run away, and she was living in a Gremlin with a guy named Sidney who talked to his hand. *(THE ONE WITH THE JELLYFISH)*

- While discussing Ross's love life in Central Perk, Phoebe says that she had a similar problem when she lived in Prague. Since nobody knew she ever lived there, it comes as quite a surprise. *(THE ONE WITH THE GIRL FROM POUGHKEEPSIE)*

- Phoebe's friend Sylvie's husband said somebody else's name in bed, so Sylvie cursed him and turned his thingy green. *(THE ONE WITH THE YETI)*

- Phoebe once stabbed a cop but only because he stabbed her first. *(THE ONE WITH ROSS'S SANDWICH)*

- Phoebe has a roommate named Denise, who nobody has ever seen (and rarely even heard of), who may or may not be imaginary. *(THE ONE WITH ROSS'S DENIAL)*

- Phoebe never borrows money from friends. That's apparently why she and Richard Dreyfuss don't speak anymore. *(THE ONE WHERE RACHEL GOES BACK TO WORK)*

- When she lived on the street, Phoebe was a teenage mugger. One of her victims was Ross, whom she mugged outside a comic store. During the incident, she stole his backpack, which had a "Geology Rocks" sticker on the outside and a handmade *Science Boy* comic on the inside. Years later, Phoebe realizes who her victim was and shows Ross her box of crap from the street. Inside is a jar of Vaseline, a cat skull, and *Science Boy*. Phoebe knew a fellow criminal called Lowell and another called Stabby Joe. *(THE ONE WITH THE MUGGING)*

- When Phoebe and Ursula were kids, on their birthday, their stepdad would sell his blood to buy them food. (THE ONE WITH THE CAKE)

- Phoebe spent her sweet sixteen being chased around a tire yard by an escaped mental patient who, in his own words, "wanted to kill her or whatever." Her friend later shot him. (THE ONE WITH THE HOME STUDY)

PLACES WHERE PHOEBE'S "PHOTO FRAME" DAD TURNS UP

It comes as quite a shock to Phoebe when she discovers that her "dad" is really just a guy in a generic picture in a store-bought picture frame. Here are some of the places she sees him.

Close-up in Ross's frame

In front of a blue screen with a collie

In a meadow

Helping a little boy fly a kite

A graduation

Another graduation

Another graduation

(THE ONE WITH PHOEBE'S DAD)

EVERY TIME MONICA SAYS,

"I KNOW!"

This is Monica's standard screechy reply when she agrees with someone. It is first said by Monica in *THE ONE WITH ROSS'S NEW GIRLFRIEND.*

- Phoebe accidentally gives Monica the same haircut as Dudley Moore instead of Demi Moore. When Phoebe realizes and says that Demi has gorgeous hair, Monica shouts, "I know!" for the first time. (*THE ONE WITH ROSS'S NEW GIRLFRIEND*)

- Monica screams her catchphrase when Phoebe excitedly admits that she wants to be a Waxine girl. (*THE ONE WITH THE MORNING AFTER*)

- When Phoebe tells Monica that her dollhouse is beautiful, Monica can't help but shout, "I know!" (*THE ONE WITH THE DOLLHOUSE*)

- Ross sarcastically tells Monica that she's lucky to be going out with Chip Matthews, the most popular boy in school, but Monica enthusiastically agrees. (*THE ONE WITH THE CAT*)

- When Joey points out that Monica has been in the plane bathroom for half an hour, she says "I know" through gritted teeth. She is furious because Chandler was supposed to meet her there but has been delayed by Joey. (*THE ONE AFTER ROSS SAYS RACHEL*)

- Chandler remarks that Monica is naked in the Polaroid she just gifted to him.

"I know," she says with a smile. (*THE ONE WITH ROSS'S SANDWICH*)

- Monica is so enthusiastic about answering her own question at night class that she can't stop shouting her catchphrase over and over again. (*THE ONE WITH ROSS'S SANDWICH*)

- Joey thinks that Monica and Chandler are so cute, and Monica can't help but agree. (*THE ONE WITH THE COP*)

- When Rachel mentions that her moving out is the end of an era, Monica declares, "I know!" (*THE ONE WHERE ROSS HUGS RACHEL*)

- Monica gets a bit too enthusiastic when Chandler exclaims that she's perfected speaking quietly. *(THE ONE WITH THE APOTHECARY TABLE)*

- Chandler is overcome that he and Monica have had sex, and she agrees. *(THE ONE THAT COULD HAVE BEEN, PART 2)*

- Rachel can't believe that her old room is so beautiful and says that it didn't look that way when she lived there. "I know!" says Monica. *(THE ONE WHERE ROSS DATES A STUDENT)*

- Ross thinks Monica looks beautiful in her wedding dress, and she agrees. *(THE ONE WITH MONICA AND CHANDLER'S WEDDING, PART 2)*

- Monica is proud when Chandler points out that she said she'd move to Tulsa without gagging. *(THE ONE WITH THE PEDIATRICIAN)*

- "I know!" shouts Monica, when Chandler says that her hyper-organized, pain-in-the-ass stuff will pay off, as she helps him to find a new job. *(THE ONE WHERE RACHEL GOES BACK TO WORK)*

- In a flashback, Rachel tells Monica that she can tell she's lost four pounds. Monica agrees. *(THE ONE WHERE THE STRIPPER CRIES)*

THINGS THAT THE ALESSANDRO'S STAFF DOES TO MONICA

When Monica gets the job of head chef at Alessandro's, the staff is not impressed. Here are some of the things they do to try and get her to quit.

- Write "Quit Bitch" on her chef's hat.

- Bake her chef's coat.

- Invent fake specials and make her cook them.

- Pretend they can't hear her talk.

- Pretend they don't speak English.

- Lock her in the refrigerator, where she spills sauce all over herself.

(THE ONE WITH THE GIRL FROM POUGHKEEPSIE)

THINGS MONICA DOES DURING HER LIGHT SWITCH OBSESSION

When Monica discovers a redundant light switch in Joey and Chandler's apartment, she's determined to find out what it really does. Here are some of the ways she investigates.

- Switches it off and checks every outlet.

- Plugs noisy equipment into each outlet to see if the switch controls any of them.

- Goes to city hall to buy electrical plans for the building.

- Knocks holes in the wall and floor to follow the wire.

- Asks Mr. Treeger to figure out what it does (he can't).

- Hires a $200-an-hour electrician to figure out what it does (he can't).

- Gives herself seven pretty serious shocks.

- Gives up.

- Never discovers that it actually controls the television in her old apartment.

(THE ONE WITH ALL THE RUGBY)

EVERYTHING IN MONICA'S AND PHOEBE'S DOLLHOUSES

When Monica inherits a dollhouse from her late aunt, she bans Phoebe from playing with it because of her questionable choice of accessories. Phoebe decides to make her own, of course. Here are some memorable items from each dollhouse.

MONICA

Faded wallpaper

Ghost for the attic

Gigantic dog

Green dinosaur

Hardwood floors

Little man riding a giraffe

Loose carpet

Victorian furniture, including a new china cabinet

(THE ONE WITH THE DOLLHOUSE)

PHOEBE

Aroma room

Beads

Blue flower on the wall

Bubbles

Cow

Curtains with cat faces and
  Frankenstein's monster

Drawers made from
  matchstick boxes

Flowery wallpaper

Foster puppets

Giraffe

Hanging ball

Licorice room (you can eat
  all the furniture)

Little yellow teddy

Oven drawn onto the wall

Pirate

Red monkey

Santa

Silver paper slide instead
  of stairs

Sparkly lights

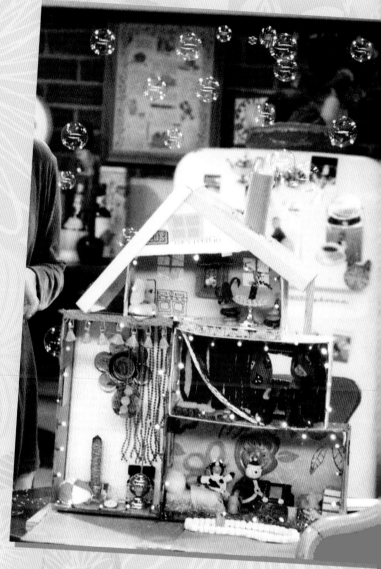

Table and chairs

Tassels

Teeny Etch A Sketch

Tootsie rollaway bed

Wand

Yellow duck in a pond

Yellow sofa

(THE ONE WITH THE DOLLHOUSE)

CHRISTMAS GIFTS FROM JOEY AND CHANDLER BOUGHT/STOLEN FROM THE SERVICE STATION

The friends seemed none too thrilled to receive the following Christmas presents from Joey and Chandler that were apparently stolen from a service station.

Wiper blades

Car smell spray

Toilet seat covers

Cola drink

Lemon lime drink

Ribbed condoms

(THE ONE WITH PHOEBE'S DAD)

INAPPROPRIATE QUESTIONS THAT MONICA AND CHANDLER ASK ZACK

When Monica and Chandler have trouble conceiving a child, Chandler decides that his colleague Zack might be the ideal sperm donor. Here are the questions the couple decides to ask when he visits their apartment— only he has no idea why they really asked him there.

- Do you have a history of mental illness in the family?

- Do you or any of your blood relatives have diabetes? Heart disease? Alzheimer's? Gout?

- You know what's not funny? Male-pattern baldness.

- Did you have braces as a child?

- Are you just tired now, or are you always tired? Because that can be a sign of clinical depression.

(THE ONE WITH THE DONOR)

PARENTS

Most of us deal with embarrassing parents at some point in our lives, but the friends seem to have more embarrassing parents than most. Here are all the memorable appearances from Jack and Judy Geller, Nora Tyler Bing and Charles Bing, Sandra and Dr. Leonard Green, and Joey Sr. and Gloria Tribbiani.

- Monica and Ross's parents, Jack and Judy, come over for dinner. Judy criticizes Monica, while her dad unintentionally insults her. In an effort to get the attention away from her, Monica persuades Ross to tell them about his divorce and Carol's pregnancy, but Monica gets into trouble for that, too. (THE ONE WITH THE SONOGRAM AT THE END)

- Chandler's mother, Nora Tyler Bing, is on a publicity tour for her new novel, and the friends go out to dinner with her. Ross kisses her in a drunken moment and then tells Chandler that it was Paolo. When Ross comes clean, Chandler is furious. This leads to a discussion with Nora about boundaries. (THE ONE WITH MRS. BING)

- Joey's dad, Joey Sr., comes to stay for a couple of nights, and it turns out that he's been having a six-year affair with Ronnie, a pet mortician. Joey insists he comes clean, but then his mother, Gloria, shows up and admits she knew (and approved) of the affair. (THE ONE WITH THE BOOBIES)

- Monica speaks to Gloria on the phone in THE ONE WITH RACHEL'S BIG KISS, when she's organizing her wedding guest list.

- Ross has lunch with his dad to discuss his feelings on fatherhood. (THE ONE WITH TWO PARTS, PART 2)

- Rachel's mother, Sandra, announces that she's considering leaving Rachel's father, Leonard. Sandra is keen to experience the life of a single woman, much to the embarrassment of Rachel. (THE ONE WITH THE LESBIAN WEDDING)

- Jack and Judy Geller drop by with boxes of Monica's possessions since they're changing her room into a gym. In one of the boxes is the prom video that finally gets Ross and Rachel together. While they're visiting, Monica tells her parents that she was fired from the restaurant, but they're not too worried because they assume she's always saved 10 percent of her paycheck. (THE ONE WITH THE PROM VIDEO)

- Monica and Ross head to their childhood home for their dad's birthday party. Their parents get more than they expected when Monica and Richard come clean about their relationship. (THE ONE WHERE JOEY MOVES OUT)

- It's Rachel's birthday party and her warring parents—Sandra and Leonard Green—both

• While Phoebe always believed that Frank and Lily were her parents, it's actually Phoebe Abbott—her mother's school friend—who's her birth mom. When Phoebe tracks her to a house at the beach, Phoebe Abbott tries to cancel their meeting, but Phoebe breaks in anyway. The truth about Phoebe's early life is revealed, and she storms out of Phoebe Sr.'s house. Later, her birth mother turns up at Central Perk, and the two realize they may have more in common than first thought. (THE ONE AT THE BEACH / THE ONE WITH THE JELLYFISH)

show up. Suddenly, one party becomes two in an effort to keep them away from each other. The parties are a success, but Rachel is upset when her parents complain about each other to her. (THE ONE WITH THE TWO PARTIES)

• The vision of Judy Geller comes into Ross's mind at an inappropriate moment—while acting out a Princess Leia fantasy with Rachel. (THE ONE WITH THE PRINCESS LEIA FANTASY)

• Monica's dad arrives for a little Monicuddle while she's watching Civil War documentaries to remind her of Richard. He has spoken to Richard and he's doing terribly—even worse than when he broke up with his wife. Monica falls asleep, so Jack watches the Civil War documentary and smokes a cigar. (THE ONE WITH THE PRINCESS LEIA FANTASY)

• Dr. Green takes Ross and Rachel to dinner, but it doesn't end well when Ross adds to the stingy tip that Dr. Green left. A brunch follows, but this time the two men manage to bond a little over Rachel's reliance on a terrible chiropractor called Bobby Bobby and her refusal to buy renters' insurance. (THE ONE WITH THE RACE CAR BED)

• Judy Geller is hosting a party and asks Monica to cater it. Determined that she will "pull a Monica" and do something wrong, Judy has already bought frozen lasagnas, which she hauls out when Monica loses a fake nail in the quiche. Undeterred, Monica makes a casserole, and nobody touches the lasagna. Even Judy has to admit that the job has been a success and she was wrong. (THE ONE WITH THE CUFFS)

• Phoebe visits her birth mom to talk about becoming a surrogate for Frank Jr. and Alice. Based on her own experience, Phoebe Sr. does not want Phoebe to go through with it, though she comes to understand her decision. (THE ONE WITH PHOEBE'S UTERUS)

• Jack and Judy are in London for Ross's wedding to Emily. They are late to the rehearsal dinner because Judy wanted to ride the tube (subway). They then argue with Mr. and Mrs. Waltham about the wedding expenses. When Jack declares that nobody takes advantage of the Gellers, Judy is giggly and tells him she had forgotten just how powerful he could be. (THE ONE WITH ROSS'S WEDDING, PART 2) The Gellers are also seen at the wedding reception in THE ONE AFTER ROSS SAYS RACHEL, when Jack declares that it was terrible timing for Ross to say the wrong name at the altar.

- During a flashback, Chandler reminisces about the Thanksgiving when his parents announced their divorce. In the memory, his mother tells him that the separation doesn't mean they don't love him—it just means that his father would rather sleep with the houseboy than her. (THE ONE WITH ALL THE THANKSGIVINGS)

- In a flashback to the 1980s, Jack and Judy Geller are seen hosting Monica, Ross, Rachel, and Chandler during two different Thanksgivings. In the first, Judy is seen wearing a gold pantsuit and perm, and Ross tries to look grown-up by calling his parents by their first names. In the second, Judy wears a silver suit, while Jack tells Rachel that he's had his mole cluster removed. (THE ONE WITH ALL THE THANKSGIVINGS)

- At her grandmother's memorial service, Phoebe bumps into her father, Frank, a strange, nervous little man with long hair and glasses. He runs out of the chapel but meets Phoebe at Central Perk after she pretends to be a will executor. She pretends that her grandmother willed him a used lipstick, but he has to answer a load of questions before he can take it. After an awkward conversation, Phoebe admits that she's Frank's daughter and has to break the news of her mother's death. (THE ONE WITH JOEY'S BAG)

- Jack and Judy arrive for Thanksgiving dinner, but they don't like Chandler, so Monica doesn't want them to know that she and

Chandler are living together. *(THE ONE WHERE ROSS GOT HIGH)*

• After Monica and Chandler get engaged, they go out for dinner with Jack and Judy. Monica is keen to know if they still have her wedding fund, but they spent it on a beach house. They started saving again when she was dating Richard but then used the money to redecorate the kitchen. *(THE ONE WITH RACHEL'S BOOK)*

• Chandler plays racquetball with Jack and afterward they go into the steam room. A combination of steam on Chandler's glasses and shortsightedness causes him to sit on Jack's knee and then accidentally head to the hot tub—naked. *(THE ONE WITH PHOEBE'S COOKIES)*

• On finding out that their childhood home is to be sold, Monica and Ross go over to look through their childhood possessions. They meet Jack in the garage, where it's revealed that he's been using Monica's boxes to protect his Porsche from floodwater. Ross puts some of his stuff in Monica's boxes to cover for his dad, but Monica finds out, so Jack then gifts her his Porsche. *(THE ONE WHERE ROSITA DIES)*

• During Monica's thirtieth birthday party, Jack reveals to Chandler that Ross was conceived close to the tux he's currently wearing. Then both parents are surprised to discover that Monica is drunk—for the first time ever that they know of. *(THE ONE WHERE THEY ALL TURN THIRTY)*

• When Monica and Chandler travel to Vegas before their wedding, they go to see Charles Bing in his drag show. Charles (as Helena Handbasket) comes into the audience and is

invited to Chandler and Monica's wedding. *(THE ONE WITH CHANDLER'S DAD)*

• When Monica and Chandler get married, their parents attend the rehearsal dinner and wedding. Jack and Judy show off their skills on the dance floor, while Nora and Charles bicker about each other's dresses. *(THE ONE WITH MONICA AND CHANDLER'S WEDDING, PARTS 1 AND 2 / THE ONE AFTER "I DO")*

• When Rachel wants to tell her father about her pregnancy, she takes Phoebe along for support. Dr. Green is horrified that Ross isn't marrying her and storms over to the apartment just as Ross is entertaining Mona. Dr. Green later calls Rachel, so she leaves the handset on the counter while she goes out. Joey then finds it, and Dr. Green shouts at him, too. *(THE ONE WITH THE STRIPPER)*

77

- Jack and Judy have a thirty-fifth anniversary party, where Monica gives a terrible speech. Jack had to shave his ears for the evening and wonders why they're serving food on a sharp stick. Judy thinks Monica's speech is "interesting" and then cries with joy when Ross gives a simple toast. (THE ONE IN MASSAPEQUA)

- Monica and Phoebe forget to invite Sandra Green to Rachel's baby shower. When Monica calls her, the woman gives her a hard time because she has actually known about the party for a month. When Sandra arrives, she's still furious with Monica (which drives Monica crazy) and then announces that she's going to move in with Rachel and Ross once the baby arrives. (THE ONE WITH THE BABY SHOWER)

- Judy comes to the hospital while Rachel is in labor and gives Ross his grandmother's engagement ring. She hopes that he'll give it to Rachel, but while Ross agrees to take it, he has no intention of proposing. (THE ONE WHERE RACHEL HAS A BABY, PART 1)

- After baby Emma arrives, Jack Geller comes to the hospital to see his granddaughter. While there, he practices his magic tricks and then hears a couple having sex. He takes a peek through the door and is mortified to discover that it's Monica and Chandler. When Jack finds out that they're trying for a baby, he horrifies them with his advice on technique and stamina. (THE ONE WHERE NO ONE PROPOSES)

- Ross and Rachel accidentally lock themselves out of their apartment with baby Emma still inside. Judy arrives with the spare key and lets them in, and then she tells a tale about how Ross once pretended to be a little girl so that he could go to the beauty parlor with

her. Judy then accompanies the couple to Phoebe's birthday dinner, where she sits at the bar with Emma, while Rachel shouts child-care instructions to her. (THE ONE WITH PHOEBE'S BIRTHDAY DINNER)

- Jack and Judy arrive to celebrate Emma's first birthday and tell a story about how Ross pulled on his testicles during Monica's first birthday because he was jealous of all the attention she was getting. During a video message for Emma's eighteenth birthday, they surmise that they may no longer be around and give a talk about heart disease. When they look at the birthday cake (mistakenly shaped like a penis), Jack and Judy can't get over how familiar it looks. They have to leave early because Jack can no longer drive in the dark—last winter he went up onto the curb and destroyed a manger scene, which people thought was a hate crime. (THE ONE WITH THE CAKE)

- Leonard Green is in the hospital after having a heart attack. Despite the fact that he's ill, he's still scary and seems to hate Ross just as much as ever. (THE ONE WHERE JOEY SPEAKS FRENCH)

REASONS RACHEL'S DAD HATES ROSS

Some people might find Ross to be an acquired taste, but Rachel's dad dislikes him for all the following reasons.

- Ross describes Dr. Green's surgical work as a game. *(THE ONE WITH THE TWO PARTIES)*

- Ross doesn't understand what "neat" means when making Dr. Green's whiskey. *(THE ONE WITH THE TWO PARTIES)*

- Ross is caught wearing Dr. Green's glasses and pretending to smoke his cigarettes. *(THE ONE WITH THE TWO PARTIES)*

- Ross holds the door closed so that Dr. Green can't leave the apartment. *(THE ONE WITH THE TWO PARTIES)*

- He wears too much gel in his hair. *(THE ONE WITH THE RACE CAR BED)*

- Ross corrects Dr. Green when he thinks Ross works in a library. *(THE ONE WITH THE RACE CAR BED)*

- Ross can't eat lobster, which means Dr. Green has to ask for a menu at a restaurant instead of just ordering seafood for everybody. *(THE ONE WITH THE RACE CAR BED)*

- Ross makes a joke about Dr. Green's boat being rusty. *(THE ONE WITH THE RACE CAR BED)*

- Ross leaves an additional tip in a restaurant, thereby making Dr. Green look cheap. *(THE ONE WITH THE RACE CAR BED)*

- Ross got Rachel "in trouble" and refused to marry her. *(THE ONE WITH THE STRIPPER)*

- Ross told Mona (in front of Dr. Green) that the evening he got Rachel pregnant meant nothing to him. *(THE ONE WITH THE STRIPPER)*

- Ross receives a phone call asking if he's hired a hooker, while Dr. Green is standing next to him. *(THE ONE WITH THE STRIPPER)*

- Ross puts his feet on Dr. Green's hospital bed and tugs on his catheter. *(THE ONE WHERE JOEY SPEAKS FRENCH)*

- Ross talks about sex with Rachel when Dr. Green is right behind him. *(THE ONE WHERE JOEY SPEAKS FRENCH)*

URSULA'S APPEARANCES

**Phoebe might not like her twin sister, Ursula,
but the two still have to see each other occasionally.**

- Ursula is mentioned as Phoebe's twin, a high-powered, career-driven waitress. *(THE ONE WITH THE SONOGRAM AT THE END)*

- Chandler and Joey meet Ursula in a restaurant and think she's Phoebe. When they discover the truth, Joey asks Phoebe if it's okay to ask Ursula out. She pretends not to be bothered but actually hates it, especially when Joey asks her to try on the sweater he bought for Ursula's birthday. *(THE ONE WITH TWO PARTS, PART 1)*

- Ursula is not interested in Joey anymore but doesn't bother to tell him. Phoebe confronts her and then feels obliged to break up with Joey on Ursula's behalf, but first she makes sure that Joey likes her better than her sister. *(THE ONE WITH TWO PARTS, PART 2)*

- Phoebe spots Ursula in a subway station while talking to Malcolm the stalker. *(THE ONE WITH THE JAM)*

- Phoebe visits Ursula to tell her the truth about their birth mother. Ursula says she already knows the truth—she read the news in Lily's suicide note. She then forges the letter so that Phoebe can read it herself. *(THE ONE WITH THE JELLYFISH)*

- Phoebe visits Ursula to tell her about their grandmother's death. Ursula refuses to invite Phoebe in and then says that she thought their grandma died five years ago. Ursula can't go to the memorial service because she's made her peace and is going to a concert. *(THE ONE WITH JOEY'S BAG)*

- When Phoebe discovers that Ursula is making porn movies under her name, she storms over to Ursula's apartment. Her sister is making a film at that very moment and even suggests that they team up to do a twin scene, for which Phoebe's payment would be $30. *(THE ONE WHERE CHANDLER CAN'T CRY)*

- Phoebe tries to make peace with Ursula on their thirtieth birthday, but Ursula informs her it's actually their thirty-first. When Ursula breaks the news, she reveals that she saw the information on her birth certificate but sold Phoebe's to a Swedish runaway. *(THE ONE WHERE THEY ALL TURN THIRTY)*

- Ursula is engaged to Eric after spinning him lies for the past two weeks about all the supposedly great things she's done in her life. She and Eric come to Monica's Halloween party, but when Ursula leaves, Phoebe tells Eric the truth about her sister. *(THE ONE WITH THE HALLOWEEN PARTY)*

JANICE'S APPEARANCES

Chandler's on-again, off-again girlfriend, Janice, has a way of turning up unexpectedly, often at inopportune times and in the most embarrassing of places. Here are all the times she appears.

- Chandler has been dating Janice but wants to break up with her. He drinks so much espresso that he's hyper, and Phoebe has to step in to break the news to Janice. *(THE ONE WITH THE EAST GERMAN LAUNDRY DETERGENT)*

- Chandler invites Janice to Monica's party so that he's not alone on New Year's Eve. Halfway through, he realizes he's made a terrible mistake and breaks up with her again. *(THE ONE WITH THE MONKEY)*

- Chandler agrees to go on a Valentine's double-date with Joey and his date, Lorraine, but the woman he's set up with turns out to be Janice. She torments Chandler for most of the evening, but they spend the night together. Janice presumes they're back together and presents Chandler with engraved candy hearts. He breaks up with her for the third time, but this time she accepts it because she knows he'll be back. *(THE ONE WITH THE CANDY HEARTS)*

- Chandler calls Janice when he's worried that he'll end up like Mr. Heckles. She arrives in Central Perk but is now married and heavily pregnant. *(THE ONE WHERE HECKLES DIES)*

- Chandler has been talking to a girl on the Internet. They visit virtual museums and talk about their lives. When she reveals that she's married to a guy who's sleeping with his secretary, Chandler wants to call it off, but they eventually agree to meet. When the mystery woman walks into Central Perk, it's Janice, but Chandler doesn't care. He's fallen in love with her online and wants to get back together with her. *(THE ONE WITH BARRY AND MINDY'S WEDDING)*

- Chandler is crazy about Janice, but Joey can't stand her. Every time she starts laughing, he wants to pull his arm off and throw it at her. Janice suggests they spend some quality time together during "Joey and Janice's Day of Fun." They go to a Mets game and get Chinese food, and Janice even comes home with a giant, fluffy toy and some flags, but at the end of it all, Joey still can't stand her. *(THE ONE WITH THE PRINCESS LEIA FANTASY)*

- Ross gives Chandler advice on how to move Janice in bed so that he can sleep better. Ross teaches a hug and roll technique, which ends with Chandler spinning Janice straight off the bed. *(THE ONE WITH THE JAM)*

- Chandler freaks out when he realizes that he and Janice are now a couple. Joey advises him to face his fear by committing to the relationship, but then Janice thinks things are moving too fast. (THE ONE WITH THE METAPHORICAL TUNNEL)

- Janice poses the question: Have any of you slept together or almost slept together? This leads to the friends thinking back to when some of them almost got together. (THE ONE WITH THE FLASHBACK) See Flashbacks, page 95.

- Joey catches Janice kissing her estranged husband even though she's currently dating Chandler. (THE ONE WITH THE RACE CAR BED)

- Janice admits to Chandler that she still loves her ex. Knowing that they have a baby together, Joey encourages Chandler to step aside. He does (reluctantly), and Janice gets back together with her husband. (THE ONE WITH THE GIANT POKING DEVICE)

- Janice is mentioned when Chandler sees her skating at Rockefeller Center with her husband. He's so upset, he throws a pretzel at them. (THE ONE WHERE CHANDLER CAN'T REMEMBER WHICH SISTER)

- Rachel takes Chandler to a nail salon and bumps into Janice. She is now divorced and is keen to get back together with Chandler. Even though he was crazy about her during their last encounter, Chandler now can't stand her and thinks she's picked up nine more annoying habits than she had before. He tries to break off the relationship, but Janice is adamant that he's not getting away this time. In an attempt to get rid of her, Chandler tells her that he's being transferred to Yemen and is then forced to board the plane when she insists on coming with him to the airport. (THE ONE WITH ALL THE RUGBY)

- When Ross disappears for the night, his friends are worried about him. However, the real reason is that he hooked up with Janice. She begs not to be judged, stating that she did it because Chandler is in Yemen. The two then hang out regularly until Janice eventually gets tired of his complaining, labels him whiny, and breaks up with him. (THE ONE WITH CHANDLER'S WORK LAUGH)

- After agreeing to make Valentine's Day gifts for each other, Monica ends up buying one of Phoebe's sock bunnies for Chandler, while Chandler gives Monica a mixtape that he found in his belongings. Unknown to him, the tape was actually given to him by Janice, whose voice pops up with a heartfelt message and a song of her own. (THE ONE WITH UNAGI)

- Janice is a customer in Monica's restaurant and complains that the chicken is too dry. During the conversation, Monica is forced to announce her engagement to Chandler. Janice then invites herself and her boyfriend, Clark, to the wedding and goes out for dinner with the happy couple. Later, Janice turns up at the apartment, and Monica untruthfully tells her that Chandler still has feelings for Janice, so she can't stay at their apartment or go to the wedding. (THE ONE WITH ROSS'S LIBRARY BOOK)

- Janice shares a room with Rachel while they're both in labor. While there, she manages to freak out everyone but especially ex-boyfriend Chandler, who is trying to make love to Monica in the room next door. When the babies arrive, Janice introduces Rachel to baby Aaron and lectures her on how Ross will eventually find a new family. (THE ONE WHERE RACHEL HAS A BABY, PARTS 1 AND 2)

- Monica and Chandler go to the fertility clinic, and just as Chandler's about to go into the room, Janice arrives. She thinks it's fabulous that she's there at the same time and tells Chandler to let her know if he needs a hand. (THE ONE WITH THE FERTILITY TEST)

- Monica and Chandler visit the house next door to the one they're buying. They want to see if it's a better home than theirs but are shocked to discover that Janice is currently viewing it. She sees them and puts in an offer, which leads Chandler to pretend that he wants them to have a fling so that she'll pull out. It works, and Janice gives him one last kiss and then says goodbye. (THE ONE WHERE ESTELLE DIES)

Ahh the "old Hug & Roll"!

F·R·I·E·N·D·S

FRANK JR. AND ALICE'S APPEARANCES

Phoebe's half-brother, Frank Jr., enjoys burning stuff and is in love with his much older home economics teacher, Alice. Here are all the times the couple appears on the series.

- Frank (as an anonymous teenager) accidentally drops a condom into Phoebe's guitar case while she's busking outside Central Perk. *(THE ONE WITH THE BABY ON THE BUS)*

- When Phoebe tries to meet her dad at his house, she discovers that he left four years ago. She does meet her half-brother, Frank Jr., who tells her that their dad used to love walking on stilts. They talk about being siblings and agree to keep in touch. *(THE ONE WITH THE BULLIES)*

- Frank comes into the city for a visit with Phoebe, but the two don't have much in common. His only hobby is melting stuff and inventing crazy karate moves. He also thinks that Phoebe's colleague is a hooker. *(THE ONE WITH FRANK JR.)*

- Frank and Alice get engaged. See Weddings: Frank Jr. and Alice, page 184. *(THE ONE WITH THE HYPNOSIS TAPE)*

- Frank and Alice arrive at Central Perk to share the news of their wedding. When Phoebe asks if they have anything in mind as a wedding gift, the couple says they'd love it if Phoebe could be the surrogate for their child. While she has some reservations, she

ultimately decides to go through with it. *(THE ONE WITH PHOEBE'S UTERUS)*

- Phoebe goes to the hospital to have the embryos transferred, accompanied by Frank and Alice. Frank recommends putting in hundreds of embryos to increase their chances of getting pregnant, but Alice reminds him that Phoebe is a woman, not a gumball machine. Later, they arrive at Monica's apartment with a pregnancy test, which confirms that Phoebe is carrying Alice and Frank's child. *(THE ONE WITH THE EMBRYOS)*

- Frank and Alice are excited to hear that Phoebe is having triplets, until she mentions the added expense. The couple thinks of different ways they can possibly afford to raise them, including Frank dropping out of refrigerator college. *(THE ONE WITH THE FREE PORN)*

- Alice comes to Central Perk to ask Phoebe for a favor. She wants to call one of the girl babies Leslie, and Frank wants to call the boy Frank Jr. Jr. Alice wonders if Phoebe would like to name the other baby but is not impressed by her first answer—Cougar. The quest for a name leads to a competition between Joey and Chandler when they both

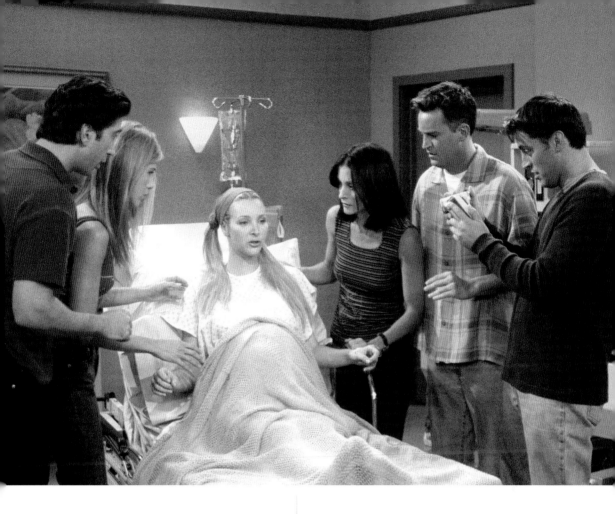

want Phoebe to choose their name—she chooses Chandler. *(THE ONE WITH RACHEL'S NEW DRESS)*

- Frank rushes to the hospital to see his babies being born, while Alice is delayed. When Phoebe decides that she wants to keep one of the babies, Rachel is in charge of asking Frank to give one up, but she chickens out. Alice arrives, and she and Frank celebrate the birth of their children by making out in the waiting room. *(THE ONE HUNDREDTH)*

- Frank brings the triplets to Central Perk and tells Phoebe that he hasn't slept in four years. For a moment, he wonders if Phoebe might want to take one of the children for herself, but which one? Certainly not Frank Jr. Jr., because he is funny and tells jokes. Not

Leslie because she can burp the alphabet, and not Chandler because she is a little genius who might be a doctor or a realtor when she grows up. *(THE ONE WHERE ROSS IS FINE)*

MEMORABLE GUNTHER MOMENTS

Central Perk would not be the same without Gunther. The waiter/manager might be a background character, but he frequently makes his presence, preferences, and feelings known.

- Gunther tells Joey that he once played Bryce on *All My Children*. His character was buried in an avalanche. (*THE ONE WHERE EDDIE WON'T GO*)

- Gunther first declares his love for Rachel (in his head) while also wondering what she sees in Ross. (*THE ONE WITH THE RACE CAR BED*)

- Gunther is devastated when Rachel quits Central Perk. As she gives her exit speech, he runs crying into the backroom. (*THE ONE WHERE RACHEL QUITS*)

- Keen to break up their relationship, Gunther tells Rachel that Ross had sex with Chloe, the girl from the copy shop. (*THE ONE WITH THE MORNING AFTER*)

- Gunther practices telling Rachel that he loves her in his head. Unfortunately for him, Mark comes into Central Perk and asks Rachel out. Gunther storms into the backroom and smashes what sounds like a pile of crockery, but he insists he just dropped a cup. (*THE ONE WITH THE TINY T-SHIRT*)

- After Phoebe kisses Gunther in an attempt to catch his cold, he apologizes to Rachel. This makes perfect sense to him since he's madly in love with her, but Rachel is completely confused. (*THE ONE WITH JOEY'S NEW GIRLFRIEND*)

- When Ross is trying to persuade Emily to move to New York, he agrees to sell all his belongings that may have been touched by Rachel. On overhearing the conversation in Central Perk, Gunther says that he will buy the whole lot. When Emily doesn't move after all, Ross goes in search of Gunther to get his stuff back. (*THE ONE WITH THE YETI*)

- Gunther is impressed that Ross is learning Dutch and tries to have a conversation with him. When Ross doesn't understand and tells him they're done, Gunther calls him *Ezel*, which means *donkey* or *ass*. (*THE ONE WITH THE STAIN*)

- On overhearing Joey admitting his love for Rachel, Gunther screams at him in the middle of Central Perk. (THE ONE WHERE JOEY TELLS RACHEL)

- Gunther tells Ross that he can't believe Rachel had his baby. In fact, he can't believe Rachel slept with Ross in the first place. He then watches in wonder as Ross goes to hit Joey and accidentally punches a post instead. (THE ONE WHERE EMMA CRIES)

- On Rachel's last day in New York, Ross decides to tell her exactly how he feels. The only trouble is, Gunther gets to her first and says he loves her in the middle of Central Perk. Rachel tells him that every time she sees a man with hair brighter than the sun, she'll think of him. (THE LAST ONE, PARTS 1 AND 2)

ALL THE BRITISH PEOPLE, REAL AND FAKE

There are a great many British people who turn up in the show, some more genuine than others.

Chandler: Chandler worries that he scared Janice away with his intensity and neediness. The girls recommend that he should "accidentally" run into her and then act aloof. He does, but his version of being aloof involves sporting a fake British accent, which Janice calls him out on immediately. (THE ONE WITH THE METAPHORICAL TUNNEL)

Mr. Waltham: He is Rachel's boss at Bloomingdale's after she is moved to the personal shopping department. He is also the uncle of Emily Waltham, who later marries Ross. (THE ONE WITH RACHEL'S CRUSH)

Emily Waltham: She is the niece of Mr. Waltham and Ross's second wife. Emily is from Shropshire and is introduced to Ross's friends when her uncle asks Rachel to take her to the opera and Ross goes in her place. (THE ONE WITH JOEY'S DIRTY DAY ONWARD)

Liam and Devon: Emily's British friends who invite Ross to play rugby with them in Riverside Park. (THE ONE WITH ALL THE RUGBY)

A Souvenir Seller and Sarah Ferguson, Duchess of York: While on a sightseeing trip of London, Joey buys a huge Union Jack hat from a gift seller, which embarrasses Chandler. After he storms off, Joey bumps into Sarah Ferguson, who records a little

message on his video camera. (THE ONE WITH ROSS'S WEDDING, PART 1)

The Waltham Housekeeper: While Phoebe is trying to tell Ross that Rachel is on her way to London to stop his wedding to Emily, she calls the Waltham home. The phone is answered by the snooty housekeeper, who tells off Phoebe for not introducing herself properly. (THE ONE WITH ROSS'S WEDDING, PART 2)

Stephen and Andrea Waltham: Emily's father and stepmother want the Gellers to pay for items completely unrelated to the wedding. Mrs. Waltham talks to Phoebe on the phone and thinks she's on a radio prank show and then flirts with a jilted Ross. (THE ONE WITH ROSS'S WEDDING, PART 2 / THE ONE AFTER ROSS SAYS RACHEL)

Plane Passenger: While Rachel is on the plane from New York to London, she irritates the Englishman sitting next to her by telling him about Ross. He responds by putting on his headphones, but he can still hear her talking to the guy on the other side of the aisle. The Englishman loses his temper and tells Rachel that she's a terrible person, that her plan to declare her love to Ross is awful, and that it is perfectly clear that they were on a break. *(THE ONE WITH ROSS'S WEDDING, PART 2)*

Drunk Guy: During Emily and Ross's rehearsal dinner, a drunk British man thanks Chandler for his moving performance in *Titanic* and then thinks that Monica is Ross's mother. *(THE ONE WITH ROSS'S WEDDING, PART 2)*

The Vicar: When Ross says Rachel's name at the altar, the vicar is forced to ask if the ceremony should go on and then reminds Ross which name he should actually say. *(THE ONE WITH ROSS'S WEDDING, PART 2)*

Jeweler: A posh man who works at the jeweler where Chandler is shopping for Monica's engagement ring. Phoebe is so busy trying on jewelry with the store owner that somebody buys the ring that Chandler wanted. He and Phoebe then have to go searching for it. *(THE ONE WITH THE RING)*

Dennis: Nora Bing brings Dennis as her date to Chandler and Monica's wedding. He is a director on Broadway, which impresses Joey so much that he takes to the stage and performs a dramatic audition piece. *(THE ONE AFTER "I DO")*

Don: Phoebe dates Don, who works with food and is centered, mature, and confident, but she actually thinks that he's Monica's soul mate (even though Monica is married to Chandler). While in Central Perk, Don and Monica bond over a hatred for sun-dried tomatoes, a love of food, and an interest in living in a house of cheese. But while Chandler is worried about their attraction, Monica assures him that there's nothing to worry about—she doesn't believe in soul mates and has gone off the cheese house idea because it would be hard to clean. *(THE ONE WHERE JOEY TELLS RACHEL)*

Amanda: Amanda once lived in the building but then moved to England and picked up a fake British accent. When she comes back to New York, Phoebe and Monica decide to cut her out and ignore her calls until she gets the message. This would work if only Chandler didn't pick up the phone and Monica didn't have an uncontrollable need to please people. They eventually meet up with Amanda in Central Perk, where she gets the girls to touch her abs and smell her neck, and then causes a fallout when she reveals that Phoebe once tried to cut out Monica. Back at the apartment, Amanda reveals that her flat is twice the size of theirs, tells Chandler that he looks ghastly, and then gives him an impromptu dance—even though she's had no "professional dance training." *(THE ONE WITH ROSS'S TAN)*

THINGS PARKER IS ENTHUSIASTIC ABOUT

Phoebe's new boyfriend is happy, excited, and positive but perhaps a little too enthusiastic. Here are some of the things Parker finds fantastic.

- Phoebe's friends
- Ross telling him it's time to go to the party
- Rachel's baby bump
- A photo of Chi-Chi the dog
- The idea of Massapequa
- Driving to Massapequa
- Event Room C
- Taking mental pictures of everyone
- Chandler's jokes
- The Long Island Expressway (a concrete miracle)
- Being alive
- The plate bouncy thing
- Feeding oysters to Phoebe, even though he's never had one
- The bunny hop dance
- Phoebe's well-lit hallway
- Phoebe's haven of an apartment
- Phoebe's comfortable couch
- Games (especially Jenga)
- Brake lights
- Fighting with Phoebe

(THE ONE IN MASSAPEQUA)

EVERYONE'S FREEBIE LISTS

**Most of the friends enjoy wondering
what celebrities they'd like to sleep with,
but perhaps Ross takes it a bit too seriously.**

RACHEL
- Chris O'Donnell
- John F. Kennedy Jr.
- Daniel Day Lewis
- Sting
- Parker Stevenson

CHANDLER
- Kim Basinger
- Cindy Crawford
- Halle Berry
- Yasmine Bleeth
- Jessica Rabbit

ROSS
(first draft)
- Elizabeth Hurley
- Susan Sarandon
- Isabella Rossellini

MONICA

First, she needs a
boyfriend, then she
can have a list.

**List of 5 Famous People
Ross Can Sleep With**

Uma Thurman
Winona Ryder
Elizabeth Hurley
Michelle Pfeiffer
Dorothy Hamill

ROSS
(laminated final draft)

(Isabella Rossellini has been bumped
for being too international, which is
unfortunate because she walks into
the coffee shop shortly after Ross
has laminated his final list.)
(THE ONE WITH FRANK JR.)

RESOLUTIONS FOR 1999

We all know that New Year's resolutions rarely work, but that doesn't mean we don't try. Here are the friends' resolutions for the year 1999.

Ross: Every day, Ross is going to do one thing he has never done before.

Phoebe: Phoebe is going to pilot a commercial jet.

Chandler: Chandler vows not to make fun of his friends after Ross bets him $50 that he won't last a week.

Joey: He wants to learn how to play guitar.

Rachel: She wants to gossip less.

Monica: She wants to take more photos of her friends.

(THE ONE WITH ALL THE RESOLUTIONS)

PEOPLE IN UNIFORM

There are many people in uniform throughout the series, some friendlier than others. (Find doctors in Medical Scenes and Illnesses on page 132.)

- Firefighters are called to Monica's apartment after Rachel pours alcohol on the girls' cleansing ritual fire and it gets out of control. Monica, Rachel, and Phoebe have been cleansing themselves of horrible men, but these guys are just as bad after they arrange a date with all three women, knowing they already have wives and girlfriends. *(THE ONE WITH THE CANDY HEARTS)*

- Louisa, the animal control officer, arrives when Marcel escapes from Monica and Rachel's apartment. She knew Monica and Rachel in high school and thought Rachel was a bitch. She accidentally shoots Phoebe in the back-side with a tranquilizer and then threatens to take Marcel away; that is, until Rachel says she'll call Louisa's boss about the dart incident, and suddenly Marcel is allowed to stay. *(THE ONE WHERE THE MONKEY GETS AWAY)*

- Ryan is a military man who works on a submarine. He always comes to visit Phoebe when he's in New York. *(THE ONE WITH THE CHICKEN POX)*

- While looking for change in Central Perk, Phoebe comes across a police badge. Instead of handing it in, she pretends that she's a cop and gives all kinds of warnings, including telling off a woman who stubs her cigarette out on a tree. In the end, the owner of the badge tracks her down. His name is Gary, he's an NYPD police officer, and he's rather keen on going out with Phoebe. *(THE ONE WITH THE COP)*

- When Gary wants to move in with Phoebe, Chandler is employed to talk him out of it. He goes to see him at the precinct but just ends up agreeing with Gary's reasons for wanting to move in with Phoebe. Later, Phoebe visits the station and is interrogated by Gary as to whether she really wants to move in with him. *(THE ONE WITH THE BALL)*

- When there is a fire at Phoebe and Rachel's apartment, the girls have to find somewhere else to stay. Phoebe moves in with Joey, while Rachel moves into her old room in Monica and Chandler's apartment, but they swap shortly after. *(THE ONE WHERE ROSS DATES A STUDENT)* When the apartment is repaired, Phoebe worries that Rachel will not want to live with her anymore since she's having so much fun with Joey. When the girls go to see the refurbished apartment, they find just one huge bedroom, sconces, and a new skylight, and suddenly Phoebe is quite happy to live alone again. *(THE ONE WITH THE HOLIDAY ARMADILLO)*

- When Phoebe smashes and disposes of her annoying, beeping fire alarm, it's retrieved and returned by a fireman. He informs her that it's against the law to disable the alarm and she should just press the reset button. Unfortunately, that fell off when she was smashing it up. *(THE ONE WHERE THEY'RE UP ALL NIGHT)*

- When Rachel and Ross take out Monica's Porsche, they both get stopped by the police: Rachel for driving too fast and Ross for driving too slowly. *(THE ONE WITH CHANDLER'S DAD)*

FLASHBACKS

Flashbacks become a recurring feature on the show, as the friends reminisce about past events and holidays.

an arm while working as a war nurse in 1862 and again in 1915; and Joey remembers having a turkey stuck on his head. The biggest flashback, however, is a 1980s Thanksgiving at the Geller house, when Monica overhears Chandler calling her fat. The next year, she has lost her weight and tries to make him fall for her, only it all goes wrong and he ends up with the tip of his toe sliced off when a knife falls on his foot. *(THE ONE WITH ALL THE THANKSGIVINGS)*

• While Joey is writing his speech for Monica and Chandler's wedding, it is revealed that when Monica and Chandler slept together in London, it was actually Joey she'd originally been looking for. *(THE ONE WITH THE TRUTH ABOUT LONDON)*

• Chandler and Ross are at college in 1987, publicizing their band, Way No Way. They both have a crush on a student named Missy Goldberg, so they make a pact that neither of them will go out with her (although it's later revealed that Chandler broke the pact). Just before graduation, there is a college party, and Rachel and Monica are there. The last time Monica saw Chandler, he called her fat, so she is in no mood to talk to him. He then sees Ross kissing Adrienne Turner, a student Chandler has a crush on. *(THE ONE WHERE THE STRIPPER CRIES)*

• When Janice asks if the friends have ever slept with each other, they think back to three years earlier: Phoebe secretly moves out of Monica's apartment; Chandler looks for a new roommate; Joey strips, thinking that Monica wants to have sex with him; Chandler hugs Monica and calls her beautiful; Phoebe and Ross kiss on a pool table after Ross finds out that his wife is a lesbian; and Rachel is engaged to Barry but fantasizes about Chandler—a random guy she met in the bar. *(THE ONE WITH THE FLASHBACK)*

• At Thanksgiving, the friends reminisce about Thanksgivings gone by. Chandler remembers when his parents announced their divorce; Phoebe thinks back to a past life when she lost

WHAT IF?

The friends wonder what would have happened had they gone in different directions in their lives.

- If Ross had still been married to Carol, he would have been sexually frustrated and ignored during a threesome with his wife and Susan. Afterward, a conversation with Rachel would confirm that his wife is gay. If Rachel had married Barry, she would have been a *Days of Our Lives* fan and contemplating an affair with Joey. In the end, she would discover that Barry is having an affair. If Monica was still overweight, she would be dating a boring doctor and wondering when she'd lose her virginity—until she got together with Chandler. If Chandler had left his job to become a writer, he'd have been poor and working as Joey's lowly assistant. The experience would inspire a comic book story. If Joey was still on *Days of Our Lives*, he would have been rich, successful, and bossing Chandler around. If Phoebe worked at Merrill Lynch, she would have been addicted to cigarettes, lost $13 million at work, had a heart attack, and been fired. She would later get a gig at Central Perk and sing a song about her heart attack and getting revenge on her old colleagues. *(THE ONE THAT COULD HAVE BEEN, PARTS 1 AND 2)*

- Phoebe wonders what would have happened if Monica and Joey had gotten together. The scenario involves an overweight Joey eating a feast made by Monica. *(THE ONE WITH THE TRUTH ABOUT LONDON)*

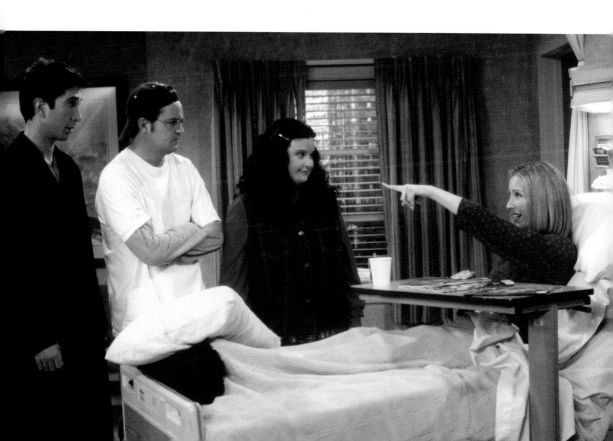

GUEST STAR APPEARANCES

From Robin Williams to Jill Goodacre and beyond, here are some of the most memorable actors who played recurring roles on *Friends*, and still others who made brief but no less memorable appearances.

James Michael Tyler: Gunther, the manager of Central Perk who's in love with Rachel. *(MULTIPLE EPISODES)*

Christina Pickles: Judy Geller, mother of Ross and Monica. *(MULTIPLE EPISODES)*

Elliott Gould: Jack Geller, father of Monica and Ross. *(MULTIPLE EPISODES)*

Maggie Wheeler: Janice, Chandler's on-again, off-again girlfriend. *(MULTIPLE EPISODES)*

Jill Goodacre: Plays herself. Chandler gets stuck in an ATM vestibule with her during a blackout. *(THE ONE WITH THE BLACKOUT)*

Larry Hankin: Mr. Heckles, Monica and Rachel's downstairs neighbor. *(MULTIPLE EPISODES)*

Dick Clark: Seen on the TV as host of *Dick Clark's New Year's Rockin' Eve*. *(THE ONE WITH THE MONKEY)*

Hank Azaria: Phoebe's scientist boyfriend, David. *(MULTIPLE EPISODES)*

Jay Leno: He plays himself and interviews Chandler's mother on his talk show. *(THE ONE WITH MRS. BING)*

Morgan Fairchild: Chandler's mother and best-selling author. *(MULTIPLE EPISODES)*

Robert Costanzo: Joseph Tribbiani Sr., Joey's father. *(THE ONE WITH THE BOOBIES)*

Brenda Vaccaro: Gloria Tribbiani, Joey's mother. *(THE ONE WITH THE BOOBIES)*

Jon Lovitz: Steve, the guy who ruins Monica's cooking interview and goes on a blind date with Rachel. *(THE ONE WITH THE STONED GUY / THE ONE WITH THE BLIND DATES)*

Helen Hunt: She thinks that Phoebe is Ursula in Central Perk. *(THE ONE WITH TWO PARTS, PART 1)*

George Clooney and Noah Wyle: Doctors who have a date with Monica and Rachel. *(THE ONE WITH TWO PARTS, PART 2)*

Jennifer Grey: Mindy, Rachel's former best friend who marries Barry. *(THE ONE WITH THE EVIL ORTHODONTIST)*

Harry Shearer: He wants Marcel for his animal-fighting attraction. *(THE ONE WITH THE FAKE MONICA)*

June Gable: First appeared as a nurse and then as Estelle Leonard, Joey's eccentric agent. *(MULTIPLE EPISODES)*

Leah Remini: Joey meets her in the hospital and becomes her birth partner. *(THE ONE WITH THE BIRTH)*

Jonathan Silverman: Dr. Franzblau, who flirts with Rachel while Carol gives birth. *(THE ONE WITH THE BIRTH)*

Steve Zahn: Phoebe's ice-skater husband, Duncan, who visits her to ask for a divorce. *(THE ONE WITH PHOEBE'S HUSBAND)*

Giovanni Ribisi: Phoebe's brother, Frank Jr. Phoebe is a surrogate for him and his wife. *(MULTIPLE EPISODES)*

Lea Thompson: Fawns over baby Ben when he's out with Chandler and Joey. *(THE ONE WITH THE BABY ON THE BUS)*

Chrissie Hynde: Stephanie, the professional singer at Central Perk. She knows all the chords. *(THE ONE WITH THE BABY ON THE BUS)*

Michael McKean: He hires Monica to create Mockolate recipes. *(THE ONE WITH THE LIST)*

Marlo Thomas: Sandra Green, mother of Rachel. *(MULTIPLE EPISODES)*

Brooke Shields: Erika, Joey's stalker girlfriend. *(THE ONE AFTER THE SUPERBOWL, PART 1)*

Adam Goldberg: Eddie, Chandler's crazy roommate. *(THE ONE WHERE EDDIE MOVES IN / THE ONE WHERE DR. RAMORAY DIES / THE ONE WHERE EDDIE WON'T GO)*

Chris Isaak: Rob, Phoebe's love interest. He hires Phoebe to play in a children's library. *(THE ONE AFTER THE SUPERBOWL, PART 1)*

Fred Willard: Works at the San Diego Zoo and lies to Ross about where Marcel has gone. *(THE ONE AFTER THE SUPERBOWL, PART 1)*

Jean-Claude Van Damme: He plays himself and dates Rachel and Monica. *(THE ONE AFTER THE SUPERBOWL, PART 2)*

Julia Roberts: Susie Moss, who takes revenge on Chandler for tormenting her in school. *(THE ONE AFTER THE SUPERBOWL, PART 2)*

Tom Selleck: Monica's boyfriend, Richard. *(MULTIPLE EPISODES)*

Ron Leibman: Leonard Green, Rachel's father. *(MULTIPLE EPISODES)*

Charlie Sheen: Ryan, Phoebe's submarine boyfriend. *(THE ONE WITH THE CHICKEN POX)*

David Arquette: Malcolm, Ursula's stalker ex-boyfriend and Phoebe's short-term boyfriend. *(THE ONE WITH THE JAM)*

Isabella Rossellini: She is on Ross's freebie list—until she's bumped for being too international. *(THE ONE WITH FRANK JR.)*

Jon Haugen: Ugly Naked Guy. Ross sublets his apartment. (THE ONE WITH THE GIANT POKING DEVICE / THE ONE WHERE EVERYBODY FINDS OUT)

Mae Whitman: Brown Bird Sarah. Ross sells her cookies when he accidentally causes her to break her leg. (THE ONE WHERE RACHEL QUITS)

Debra Jo Rupp: Frank Jr.'s wife and older teacher. (MULTIPLE EPISODES)

Jon Favreau: Monica's rich boyfriend, Pete. He wants to be the Ultimate Fighting Champion. (MULTIPLE EPISODES)

Dina Meyer: Joey's costar and love interest, Kate Miller. (THE ONE WITH THE TINY T-SHIRT / THE ONE WITH THE DOLLHOUSE / THE ONE WITH THE SCREAMER)

Ben Stiller: Tommy, Rachel's angry boyfriend. (THE ONE WITH THE SCREAMER)

Billy Crystal and Robin Williams: They sit next to the friends in Central Perk and argue about a woman. (THE ONE WITH THE ULTIMATE FIGHTING CHAMPION)

Sam McMurray: Chandler's boss, Doug. He likes to slap good employees on the backside. (MULTIPLE EPISODES)

Christine Taylor: Phoebe's (not so) bald friend, Bonnie, who goes out with Ross. (THE ONE WITH THE ULTIMATE FIGHTING CHAMPION / THE ONE AT THE BEACH)

Teri Garr: Phoebe's birth mother who lives in Montauk. (THE ONE AT THE BEACH / THE ONE WITH THE JELLYFISH / THE ONE WITH PHOEBE'S UTERUS)

Penn Jillette: Door-to-door encyclopedia salesman. He sells volume *V* to Joey. (THE ONE WITH THE CUFFS)

Paget Brewster: Joey's girlfriend, Kathy, who dumps Joey for Chandler. (MULTIPLE EPISODES)

Rebecca Romijn: Ross's dirty girlfriend, Cheryl. (THE ONE WITH THE DIRTY GIRL)

Michael Vartan: Richard Burke's son, Timothy. (THE ONE WITH CHANDLER IN A BOX)

Sherri Shepherd: Rhonda from the museum. She tells Joey that Ross won't sit with him, and she's right. (THE ONE WITH PHOEBE'S UTERUS)

Tate Donovan: Rachel's boyfriend, Joshua. She asks him to marry her after four dates. (MULTIPLE EPISODES)

Charlton Heston: Plays himself and catches Joey using his shower on a film set. (THE ONE WITH JOEY'S DIRTY DAY)

Helen Baxendale: Ross's ex-wife, Emily. (MULTIPLE EPISODES)

Richard Branson: Sells Joey an embarrassing Union Jack hat. (THE ONE WITH ROSS'S WEDDING, PART 1)

Sarah Ferguson: Joey meets the duchess while touring London. (THE ONE WITH ROSS'S WEDDING, PART 1)

Olivia Williams: Emily's bridesmaid, Felicity. She has a fling with Joey. (THE ONE WITH ROSS'S WEDDING, PART 2 / THE ONE AFTER ROSS SAYS RACHEL)

Hugh Laurie: He sits next to Rachel when she's on the plane to London and is annoyed by her rant about Ross. *(THE ONE WITH ROSS'S WEDDING, PART 2)*

Jennifer Saunders: Emily's stepmother, Mrs. Andrea Waltham. *(THE ONE WITH ROSS'S WEDDING, PART 2 / THE ONE AFTER ROSS SAYS RACHEL)*

Tom Conti: Emily's father, Mr. Stephen Waltham. *(THE ONE WITH ROSS'S WEDDING, PART 2 / THE ONE AFTER ROSS SAYS RACHEL)*

June Whitfield: The Waltham's housekeeper. *(THE ONE WITH ROSS'S WEDDING, PART 2)*

Iqbal Theba: Treats Joey for kidney stones. *(THE ONE HUNDREDTH)*

Gary Collins: Host of the PBS fund-raiser, where Joey is a phone operator. *(THE ONE WHERE PHOEBE HATES PBS)*

George Newbern: Danny the yeti and Rachel's love interest. *(THE ONE WITH THE YETI / THE ONE WHERE ROSS MOVES IN / THE ONE WITH THE INAPPROPRIATE SISTER)*

Bob Balaban: Phoebe's dad. She meets him at her grandmother's funeral. *(THE ONE WITH JOEY'S BAG)*

Soleil Moon Frye: Katie, the girl who hits Joey. *(THE ONE WITH THE GIRL WHO HITS JOEY)*

Michael Rapaport: Gary, Phoebe's cop boyfriend. *(MULTIPLE EPISODES)*

Steve Ireland: Mr. Zelner, Rachel's browbeaten boss. *(MULTIPLE EPISODES)*

Joanna Gleason: Rachel's boss, Kim, who works at Ralph Lauren. *(THE ONE WHERE RACHEL SMOKES / THE ONE WITH ROSS'S TEETH)*

Thomas Lennon: Joey's hand twin. *(THE ONE IN VEGAS, PARTS 1 AND 2)*

Elle Macpherson: Joey's roommate and love interest, Janine. She hates Monica and Chandler. *(MULTIPLE EPISODES)*

Missi Pyle: Ross's date. She's scared of his ultra-white teeth. *(THE ONE WITH ROSS'S TEETH)*

Ralph Lauren: He plays himself as the owner of Ralph Lauren. Phoebe thinks she had a fling with him, but it was really Kenny the copy guy. *(THE ONE WITH ROSS'S TEETH)*

Reese Witherspoon: Rachel's sister, Jill. *(THE ONE WITH RACHEL'S SISTER / THE ONE WHERE CHANDLER CAN'T CRY)*

Cole Sprouse: Ross and Carol's son, Ben. *(MULTIPLE EPISODES)*

Alexandra Holden: Elizabeth, Ross's student and girlfriend. *(MULTIPLE EPISODES)*

Bruce Willis: Elizabeth's father, Paul, hater of Ross and lover of Rachel. *(MULTIPLE EPISODES)*

Eddie Cahill: Rachel's assistant and boyfriend, Tag. *(MULTIPLE EPISODES)*

David Sutcliffe: Phoebe's boyfriend Kyle, aka Hums While He Pees. *(THE ONE WITH THE ENGAGEMENT PICTURE)*

Kristin Davis: Joey falls for her, but she dumps him. *(THE ONE WITH ROSS'S LIBRARY BOOK)*

Jason Alexander: Earl, the guy who tells Phoebe that he doesn't need toner because he's going to kill himself. *(THE ONE WHERE ROSITA DIES)*

Susan Sarandon: Joey's costar, Cecilia Monroe, on *Days of Our Lives*. *(THE ONE WITH JOEY'S NEW BRAIN)*

Gabrielle Union: Kristen Leigh, a lady who moves into Ross's apartment building and goes out with him and Joey. *(THE ONE WITH THE CHEAP WEDDING DRESS)*

Alison Sweeney: Joey's costar on *Days of Our Lives*, Jessica Ashley. She doesn't care that she won a Soapie Award. *(THE ONE WITH JOEY'S AWARD)*

Denise Richards: Monica and Ross's cousin, Cassie. Everybody has a crush on her. *(THE ONE WITH ROSS AND MONICA'S COUSIN)*

Winona Ryder: Rachel's old friend, Melissa, who once kissed her. *(THE ONE WITH RACHEL'S BIG KISS)*

Kathleen Turner: Chandler's father and Las Vegas entertainer. *(MULTIPLE EPISODES)*

Mark Consuelos: Rachel flirts with this policeman when she's pulled over. *(THE ONE WITH CHANDLER'S DAD)*

Gary Oldman: Joey's spitting, drunk costar, Richard Crosby. *(THE ONE WITH MONICA AND CHANDLER'S WEDDING, PARTS 1 AND 2)*

Chris Parnell: Chandler's colleague, who always calls him Toby. *(THE ONE WITH RACHEL'S DATE)*

Sean Penn: Ursula's boyfriend, Eric, who later dates Phoebe but can't handle that she looks like Ursula. *(THE ONE WITH THE HALLOWEEN PARTY / THE ONE WITH THE STAIN)*

Brad Pitt: He went to high school with Monica, Ross, and Rachel and cofounded the I Hate Rachel Club. *(THE ONE WITH THE RUMOR)*

Trudie Styler: Phoebe goes to her apartment to try and get Sting concert tickets. *(THE ONE WITH MONICA'S BOOTS)*

Alec Baldwin: Parker, Phoebe's too-enthusiastic boyfriend. *(THE ONE WITH THE TEA LEAVES / THE ONE IN MASSAPEQUA)*

Sasha Alexander: She's a reporter who interviews Jocy for *Soap Opera Digest*. *(THE ONE WITH JOEY'S INTERVIEW)*

Debi Mazar: Mean pregnant lady, who is in the hospital bed next to Rachel's. *(THE ONE WHERE RACHEL HAS A BABY, PART 1)*

Paul Rudd: Phoebe's boyfriend and then husband, Mike. *(MULTIPLE EPISODES)*

Freddie Prinze Jr.: Sandy, Emma's short-lived nanny. *(THE ONE WITH THE MALE NANNY)*

Christina Applegate: Rachel's sister, Amy, who takes Emma to have her ears pierced. *(THE ONE WITH RACHEL'S OTHER SISTER / THE ONE WHERE RACHEL'S SISTER BABYSITS)*

Selma Blair: Chandler's Tulsa colleague, Wendy. She tries to seduce him at Christmas. *(THE ONE WITH CHRISTMAS IN TULSA)*

Dermot Mulroney: Rachel's colleague, Gavin. He covered for her when she was on maternity leave. *(THE ONE WHERE RACHEL GOES BACK TO*

WORK / THE ONE WITH PHOEBE'S RATS / THE ONE WHERE MONICA SINGS)

Phill Lewis: Monica's old friend and Chandler's boss at the advertising agency. (THE ONE WHERE RACHEL GOES BACK TO WORK / THE ONE WITH THE MUGGING / THE ONE WITH THE LOTTERY)

Jeff Goldblum: Broadway director Leonard Hayes. Joey pees on him during an audition. (THE ONE WITH THE MUGGING)

Alex Borstein: The star of *Why Don't You Like Me?* (THE ONE WITH THE SOAP OPERA PARTY)

Aisha Tyler: Dr. Charlie Wheeler. She dates Joey and then Ross. (MULTIPLE EPISODES)

John Stamos: Zack, Chandler's colleague. Monica and Chandler think about using him as their sperm donor. (THE ONE WITH THE DONOR)

Daryl Sabara: Owen, the child who Chandler tells he's adopted. (THE ONE WHERE ROSS IS FINE)

Jennifer Coolidge: Phoebe and Monica's fake British friend, Amanda. (THE ONE WITH ROSS'S TAN)

Greg Kinnear: Charlie's ex-boyfriend, Benjamin Hobart. (THE ONE WITH ROSS'S GRANT)

Anna Faris: Erica, birth mother to Monica and Chandler's twins. (MULTIPLE EPISODES)

Danny DeVito: The aging stripper hired to dance for Phoebe. (THE ONE WHERE THE STRIPPER CRIES)

Donny Osmond: The host of the *Pyramid* game show. He's also an icon of Ross and Monica. (THE ONE WHERE THE STRIPPER CRIES)

Ellen Pompeo: Missy Goldberg, the girl Chandler and Ross had a pact not to date. (THE ONE WHERE THE STRIPPER CRIES)

Craig Robinson: He works at the courthouse and tells Phoebe she can change her name to anything. (THE ONE WITH PRINCESS CONSUELA)

Dakota Fanning: She lives in the house that Monica and Chandler are buying. (THE ONE WITH PRINCESS CONSUELA)

Jane Lynch: She is the realtor for the house next door to Monica and Chandler's. (THE ONE WHERE ESTELLE DIES)

Jim Rash: Passenger on the plane to Paris. He gets off when he hears that it's missing a phalange. (THE LAST ONE, PARTS 1 AND 2)

CHAPTER TWO:
The One about Apartments,

SERVICE

Central Perk,
and
Other Places

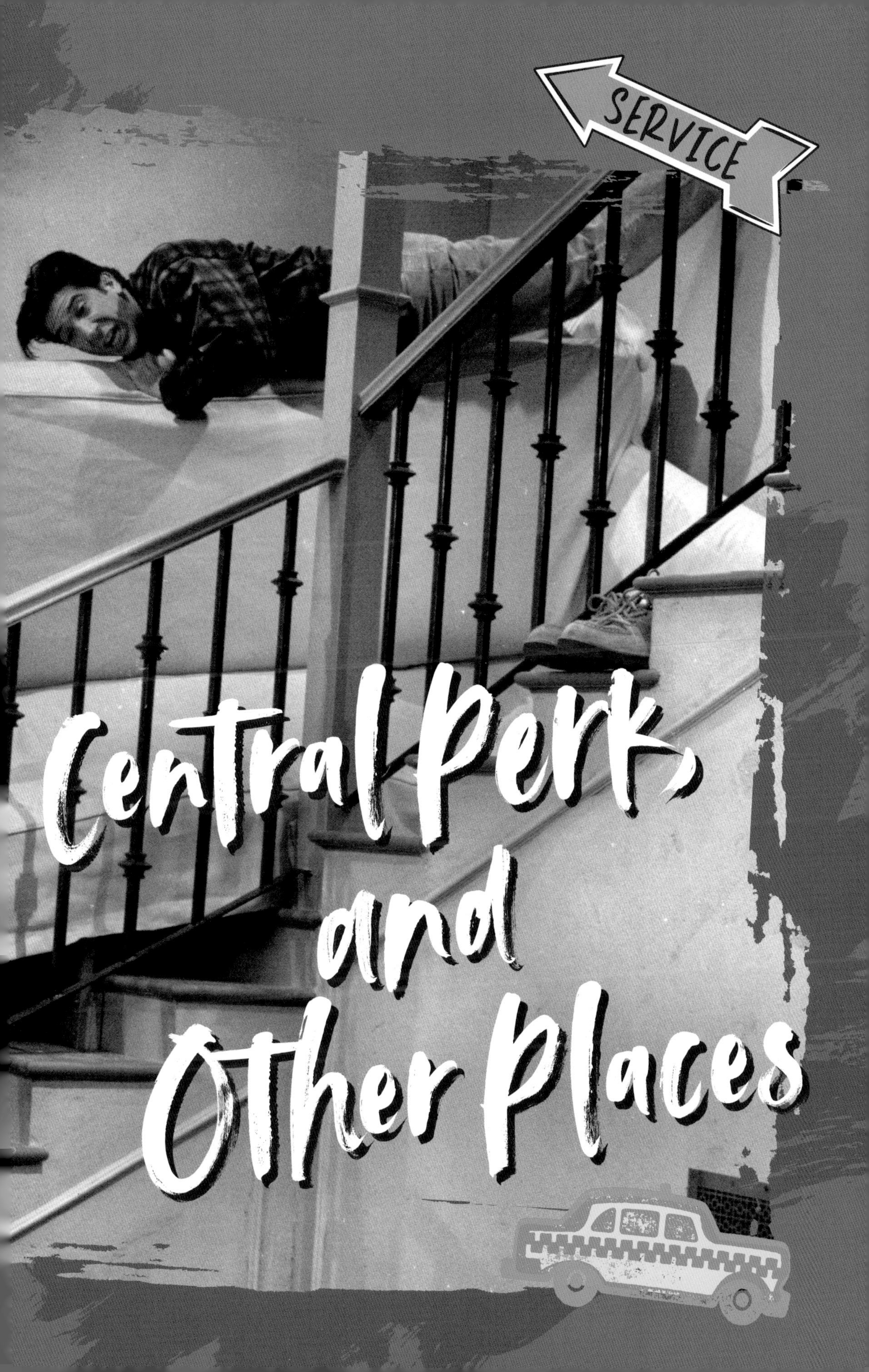

APARTMENTS

The friends' apartments play an important role in the series and are the location of many (if not most) of the dramas, plot twists, and revelations. Here is a list of who lived in each apartment throughout the series.

NUMBER 20

Ross and Monica's grandmother: Number 20 was her apartment before Monica moved in.

Monica: Lives here throughout the series, except when she and Rachel lose it to Chandler and Joey after the trivia contest. Monica and Rachel eventually move back in after they refuse to live in Chandler and Joey's apartment anymore.

Rachel: Moves in after leaving Barry at the altar. She lives here most of the time, except after the trivia contest, when she is forced to move into Chandler and Joey's apartment. Rachel and Monica eventually retake the apartment, but Rachel moves out when Chandler moves in. She returns briefly when Phoebe's apartment catches fire.

Joey: A resident of the apartment once after winning the trivia contest.

Chandler: Lives here after the trivia contest, moves back into his original apartment, and then moves in again when he and Monica decide to live together.

Phoebe: Monica's roommate before Rachel, but she eventually moves in with her grandmother because Monica is too bossy.

She returns for a short time after her apartment catches fire.

Ross: Lives here one summer as a teen, when his grandmother occupied it and he had ambitions of becoming a dancer.

Jack and Erica: Monica and Chandler's baby twins are brought to the apartment just before the family moves out.

NUMBER 19

Joey: Lives here throughout the series, except when he moves briefly into a bachelor pad after he gets into a fight with Chandler and when he temporarily occupies number 20 after Rachel and Monica lose the trivia contest.

Chandler: Lives here until he moves into number 20 after winning the trivia contest. He ends up moving out permanently and in with Monica when they decide to take their relationship to the next level.

Monica: She lives here briefly after losing the trivia contest to Joey and Chandler.

Rachel: She lives here several times, including after losing the trivia contest, after Phoebe's apartment catches fire, briefly when she's pregnant, and when Emma is a toddler.

Phoebe: She has a short stay here after her apartment catches fire.

Emma: She lives here with her mother, Rachel.

Eddie: Chandler's crazy, paranoid roommate lives here when Joey moves briefly to a bachelor pad.

Janine: Joey's dream woman moves in briefly until she tells him she hates his friends.

PHOEBE'S APARTMENT

Frances: Phoebe's grandmother lives here until her death.

Phoebe: This is Phoebe's permanent home after moving out of Monica's except when she is forced to leave after a fire.

Denise: Phoebe's possibly imaginary roommate. No one has ever actually met her.

Rachel: When Chandler moves into apartment 20 after he and Monica decide they want to live together, Rachel relocates to Phoebe's. Her stay ends when post-fire refurbishment changes the apartment from two bedrooms to one.

Mike: He moves in after his relationship with Phoebe becomes serious.

ROSS'S SECOND APARTMENT

Ugly Naked Guy: He lives here from the beginning of the series until he decides to sublet the apartment to Ross.

Ross: He moves in after impressing Ugly Naked Guy with his own naked hobby (and a basket of mini muffins!).

Rachel: She's supposed to share the apartment with Ross after moving out of Monica's, but she decides against it after finding out Ross lied about annulling their marriage. She moves in again when she's pregnant but moves out when things become difficult between her and Ross.

Phoebe: She stays here for a few days to give Monica and Chandler some privacy.

POSTS ON ROSS'S BUILDING NOTICE BOARD

When Ross talks to the hot girl in his apartment building, we get a good view of the community notice board. It gives an interesting and detailed look at the people who live there, as well as what they think about Joey!

- Are you the Hot Girl who waved at me? If so, give me a call! Joey.

- Leaflet advertising a getaway to bayou country.

- Please join us for a Nationwide Candlelight Vigil for Homeless Kids.

- Leaflet for a moving and storage company.

- Photo of a motorbike for sale.

- A flyer for veterans.

- Lost Dog—Answers to "Ben." Golden Retriever. If you have any information, please call.

- Actors Needed for Major Motion Picture—To shoot summer 99 in Manhattan.

- Leaflet for 10% off everything, including sale items.

- A flyer with a cartoon frog.

- Warning! Intruder! If you see this creep—call the cops! (Includes an artist's impression of Joey.)

- Moving!! Must Sell Everything! TV 19", VCR, Queen-size mattress and box spring, Couch, Dining room set, 2 dressers, Dough Boy 2 years old, 2 bikes men & women, 9" easel (must see to appreciate), 2 dogs, 3 cats, 1 goldfish & more.

(THE ONE WITH RACHEL'S INADVERTENT KISS)

POTTERY BARN ITEMS

When Rachel develops a love for Pottery Barn items, she has to keep it a secret from Phoebe, who dislikes large companies. Here are the "historical" items that Rachel pretends to buy from a flea market and some Ross bought as well.

PHOEBE AND RACHEL'S APARTMENT

- Apothecary table

- Room separator

- Wicker dining chair

- Sahara chest

- Parker console table

- Large ornamental birdcage

- A fan

- A lamp (bought when Rachel and Phoebe are on their way home from the flea market, after Phoebe finds out about Pottery Barn)

(THE ONE WITH THE APOTHECARY TABLE)

ROSS'S APARTMENT

- Apothecary table

- Sheets

(THE ONE WITH THE APOTHECARY TABLE)

RESIDENTS OF THE BUILDING

As with all apartment buildings, there are an assortment of interesting, hot, and just plain weird residents. Here are a few who made their presence known to the friends.

Mr. Heckles: A strange, robe-wearing whiner who constantly complains about the noise coming from the girls' apartment. He often uses a broom to knock on the ceiling and eventually dies in the middle of one knocking incident. He leaves all his worldly belongings (aka, his trash) to Monica and Rachel, who then have to clear out his apartment. *(THE ONE WHERE HECKLES DIES)*

Paolo: A cat-owning Italian who has a relationship with Rachel. He speaks very little English and once makes a pass at Phoebe while on her massage table. *(FIRST SEEN IN THE ONE WITH THE BLACKOUT)*

Sweaty Girl and Friend: They live in apartment number 5. Chandler and Joey knock on their door when Marcel escapes. The girls are hot because their radiator has broken, but the guys' attempts at flirting are thwarted when Joey asks them for pictures. *(THE ONE WHERE THE MONKEY GETS AWAY)*

Noisy Man: He lives upstairs from Monica and Rachel and is noisy because he took up all his carpets. Every time Monica tries to tell him off, he charms her and she backs down. For a while, Phoebe dates him, but then he's overheard having sex with another woman. Joey, Chandler, and Ross go upstairs to tell

him off, but they end up being charmed as well. *(THE ONE WHERE CHANDLER CAN'T REMEMBER WHICH SISTER)*

Mrs. Chatracus: Lives directly below Chandler and Joey. When Monica is living in the apartment, she knocks a hole in her floor / Mrs. Chatracus's ceiling in an attempt to find out where an electrical wire went to. *(THE ONE WITH ALL THE RUGBY)*

Danny: Has just moved into number 15 after trekking for four months in the Andes. When Monica and Rachel first encounter him, they think he's a yeti and fog him. They later try to apologize, but he keeps closing the door on them. The girls think he's rude, but then he shaves and Rachel develops a crush on him. *(THE ONE WITH THE YETI)*

Pigeon Guy: Phoebe has a secret affair with a guy who keeps pigeons on the roof. *(THE ONE WITH ROSS'S LIBRARY BOOK)*

Guy with the Moustache, Smokes-a-Lot Lady, Some Kids, Red-Haired Guy Who Does Not Like to Be Called Rusty: According to Joey, these are the neighbors he knows. *(THE ONE WITH ALL THE CANDY)*

Gary from Upstairs: Gary comes down to get candy at 4 a.m. His roommate says they taste like tiny drops of heaven. *(THE ONE WITH ALL THE CANDY)*

Noisy Sex Lady: She has people coming from out of town and needs Monica to make more candy. *(THE ONE WITH ALL THE CANDY)*

Mrs. Braverman: She lives downstairs and is the real owner of the cheesecakes that Rachel and Chandler keep eating. *(THE ONE WITH ALL THE CHEESECAKES)*

Tall Guy from the First Floor: Phoebe asks if he's the father of Rachel's baby. Rachel is not impressed, but Phoebe considers him cute. *(THE ONE WITH THE RED SWEATER)*

Couple on the First Floor: Monica questions the adoption lady about whether the couple on the first floor are trying to adopt. Apparently, the guy tried to sell her drugs. *(THE ONE WITH THE HOME STUDY)*

MR. HECKLES

The whiny neighbor downstairs may pass away in season 2, but he certainly leaves an impression on the noisy friends upstairs. When Mr. Heckles dies, the friends are in charge of clearing out his apartment. Here are all of Mr. Heckles's appearances on the show, including what they found in his book of grievances, his high school yearbook, and his list of reasons why he broke up with his girlfriends.

HECKLES'S APPEARANCES

- Mr. Heckles claims that the lost cat is his and that his name is Bob Buttons. When the cat runs away, he tells the girls that they owe him a cat. *(THE ONE WITH THE BLACKOUT)*

- Mr. Heckles arrives at Monica and Rachel's apartment to complain about the noise. He says his cats can't sleep even though he doesn't have any cats. Later, Rachel falls from the balcony and ends up dangling outside his apartment, wrapped in Christmas lights. Heckles doesn't see her but still complains about the noise. *(THE ONE WITH TWO PARTS, PART 1)*

- When Marcel escapes from the apartment, Mr. Heckles claims him, dresses him in a tutu, and buys boxes of bananas. When animal control arrives, he's quick to give the monkey back. *(THE ONE WHERE THE MONKEY GETS AWAY)*

- Mr. Heckles complains that the friends are stomping, which is disturbing his birds, which he doesn't have. He tells them off and then says he's going to rejoin his dinner party.

He then drops dead while banging his broom on the ceiling. *(THE ONE WHERE HECKLES DIES)*

- In a flashback, Mr. Heckles arrives to complain that the noise is disturbing his oboe practice. He then pretends to be Chandler's new roommate, thereby chasing the real one away. This ultimately leads to Joey moving in with Chandler for the first time. *(THE ONE WITH THE FLASHBACK)*

Heckles's Big Book of Grievances

April 17—Excessive noise. Italian guy comes home with a date.

April 18—Excessive noise. Italian guy's gay roommate comes home with dry cleaning.

(THE ONE WHERE HECKLES DIES)

Found in Mr. Heckles's High School Yearbook

"Heckles, you crack me up in science class. You're the funniest kid in school."

Heckles was voted class clown.

Heckles played clarinet in band.

Heckles was a member of the scaled modeler's club.

(THE ONE WHERE HECKLES DIES)

Reasons Why Mr. Heckles Broke Up with His Girlfriends

- Too tall

- Big gums

- Too loud

- Too smart

- Makes noise when she eats

(THE ONE WHERE HECKLES DIES)

UGLY NAKED GUY'S ACTIVITIES

The friends enjoy spying on the ugly naked guy across the way. Here are some of the activities he gets up to.

- Gets a Thighmaster. (THE ONE WITH THE SONOGRAM AT THE END)

- Lays kitchen tiles. (THE ONE WITH THE EAST GERMAN LAUNDRY DETERGENT)

- Lights a bunch of candles during the blackout and burns himself. (THE ONE WITH THE BLACKOUT)

- Takes a turkey out of the oven and then dances with a naked girlfriend. (THE ONE WHERE UNDERDOG GETS AWAY)

- Takes up the Hula-Hoop. (THE ONE WITH TWO PARTS, PART 2)

- Gets gravity boots. (THE ONE WITH THE EVIL ORTHODONTIST)

- Decorates his tree, and Phoebe is shocked by the size of his Christmas balls. (THE ONE WITH PHOEBE'S DAD)

- Plays the cello. (THE ONE WITH THE LESBIAN WEDDING)

- Was once Cute Naked Guy, but he put on weight. (THE ONE WITH THE FLASHBACK)

- Buys a hammock and, according to Joey, looks like a Play-Doh fat factory. (THE ONE WITH THE GIANT POKING DEVICE)

- Doesn't move during the entire day, and the friends think he's dead. They fashion a gigantic poking device and prod him with it through the gap between the buildings. Luckily, he's still alive, but he's now a very angry Ugly Naked Guy, showing them his own poking device . . . (THE ONE WITH THE GIANT POKING DEVICE)

- Returns to his apartment after a long absence and is packing boxes, most of which are labeled "clothes." Ugly Naked Guy is moving out, and Ross bribes him with mini muffins in an attempt to sublet his apartment. When that doesn't work, Ross joins Ugly Naked Guy in his favorite hobby—being naked! (THE ONE WHERE EVERYBODY FINDS OUT)

- Once had a trampoline but broke it. Once owned a cat but sat on it by mistake. (THE ONE WHERE EVERYBODY FINDS OUT)

WEIRD THINGS EDDIE SAYS AND DOES

**Could there *be* anyone weirder than Eddie?
When Joey moves out of the apartment he shares
with Chandler, Chandler gets a new roommate, Eddie.
Here are some of the ways he torments Chandler.**

- Spends most of the time in his room. *(THE ONE WHERE DR. RAMORAY DIES)*

- Tells a supposedly funny story about making pancakes for his ex-girlfriend, Tilly, only it turns dark when he says she broke up with him, pulled out his heart, and smeared it all over his life. *(THE ONE WHERE DR. RAMORAY DIES)*

- Accuses Chandler of sleeping with Tilly when she comes over to deliver his fish tank. *(THE ONE WHERE DR. RAMORAY DIES)*

- Says that Chandler killed his fish, Buddy. *(THE ONE WHERE DR. RAMORAY DIES)*

- Steals all the insoles from Chandler's shoes. *(THE ONE WHERE DR. RAMORAY DIES)*

- Makes cookies with black blobs that may or may not be raisins. *(THE ONE WHERE DR. RAMORAY DIES)*

- Puts a Goldfish cracker in the fish tank and names it Chandler. *(THE ONE WHERE DR. RAMORAY DIES)*

- Regularly watches Chandler while he sleeps. *(THE ONE WHERE EDDIE WON'T GO)*

- Refuses to leave—many times. *(THE ONE WHERE EDDIE WON'T GO)*

- Dehydrates fruit and vegetables. *(THE ONE WHERE EDDIE WON'T GO)*

- Displays a dehydrated tomato. *(THE ONE WHERE EDDIE WON'T GO)*

- Puts his (real) goldfish into his pocket. *(THE ONE WHERE EDDIE WON'T GO)*

- Turns up in Central Perk with a mannequin head, which he stole from Macy's. *(THE ONE WHERE EDDIE WON'T GO)*

- Tells the fake story of how he and Chandler took a road trip to Las Vegas, where Chandler won $300 and bought Eddie some shoes. *(THE ONE WHERE EDDIE WON'T GO)*

- Believes Joey and Chandler when they tell him he has never lived in their apartment. *(THE ONE WHERE EDDIE WON'T GO)*

MEMORABLE ITEMS

Here are all of the items found in the friends' apartments, as well as in Estelle's office and at Central Perk. Some of the items are plain and others are a bit bizarre, but all are memorable.

JOEY AND CHANDLER'S APARTMENT

- African art
- Bedroom doors—one cut in half
- Bicycle
- Boxing picture on the wall
- Buzzer to let people into the apartment building
- CDs
- Cereal boxes and containers above the fridge
- Clown head cookie jar and other clown ornaments
- Coffee maker
- Coffee table
- Dog ornament and books on the bookcase
- Floor lamp
- Foosball table in place of a kitchen table
- Football
- Framed photos
- French poster
- Fridge covered in magnets, notes, and pictures, with boxes and a plant pot on the top
- Globe, lamp, baseball cap, and books on desk
- Hockey mask and hockey stick
- Huge, white dog (a souvenir from Joey's bachelor pad)
- Kettle
- Kitchen appliances and utensils
- Kitchen chairs at the Foosball table
- Kitchen counter with tea towel hanging off it
- Knicks and sports memorabilia
- Large, green plant in a basket

- Laurel and Hardy picture
- Leather chair, brown sofa, and low chair (replaced with Barcaloungers and yellow sofa)
- Light switch that doesn't do anything
- Little wooden rack with condiments
- Magna Doodle on back of the front door (arrived in *THE ONE WITH THE HYPNOSIS TAPE*)
- Microwaves
- Model boat
- Native American statue
- Newspapers
- Notice board with pictures
- Oven
- Pizza boxes
- Plastic shark

- Radiator
- Shaggy, light brown carpet in the living room
- Shelving unit with glasses, drinks, sauces, tins, plates, and containers
- Stereo system
- Stools against the counter
- Telephone book
- Telephone/answering machine on top of wooden bookcase
- Television on wooden stand, with videos on the shelves underneath (replaced with Joey's gigantic media cabinet)
- Three-legged glass table with a trophy on the top
- Toaster

- Vertical blinds and plain curtains
- Wall light with a bag and boxing gloves hanging off it
- Weights and weight bench
- Wooden chair with fancy back
- Wooden desk with chair
- Wooden table next to the door, covered with chintz, including bottles and a trophy

ROSS'S SECOND APARTMENT

- 3-D artwork of a sailboat
- A notice board with postcards and notes
- Artwork on the walls, some abstract with bold colors and one of a plane
- Brown leather sofa, with checked throw and several cushions
- Burgundy/brown walls
- Coffee table (and later apothecary table) in front of the sofa, often with magazines or books, the remote, a trinket dish, phone, phonebook, and answering machine
- Cream-colored rug

- Green chair next to the desk
- Lamps on the table and wall, in shades of cream, white, and brown
- Large, red candle on a stand
- Large, round dragonfly art on the wall
- Large thermometer on the wall
- Picture of a meditating figure with chakras
- Polished, wooden desk next to the window, with photo frame, papers, and books
- Round, patterned pouf
- Several bushy plants in baskets

- Shelving units with books, CD player, and an assortment of "cheap knockoffs and dinosaur junk"—aka ornaments; wooden sculptures of figures, dinosaurs, and animals; skeletons; busts; a clock; and pictures
- Small wooden corner unit next to the front door, with photo, a small vase, and flower
- Venetian blinds and long plaid curtains at the window
- Wooden floors
- Wooden table with colorful plant and photo
- Wooden television cabinet

117

MONICA AND RACHEL'S APARTMENT

- Balcony
- Blue cabinets and shelves in the kitchen
- Books and magazines
- Brass faces on the wall beside the window
- Buzzer to let people into the apartment building
- Candlesticks and candles
- Clock cookie jar and tiger cookie jar
- Cupboard door (later revealed to house Monica's organized junk)
- Desk with globe
- Figure pictures and other artwork
- Flowers
- Frame around the peephole
- French posters
- Fruit bowl
- Glass table with a dish and trinket box

- Green ottoman
- Hanging basket on wooden post
- Kettle and coffee maker
- Kitchen appliances, utensils, plates, cups, bowls, food, and containers on the counter and on the shelves
- Large white sofa with colorful throw
- Large wooden unit with television and video
- Ornamental figures as bookends
- Pictures of fruit in the kitchen
- Pink occasional chair next to the window
- Potted plants
- Purple walls
- Radiators
- Refrigerator with magnets
- Round kitchen table with four chairs, one with a tiny picture of a vintage lady on the back

- Sink with wooden drainer and a curtain underneath
- Small, round table with a lamp and ornaments
- Small, wooden table with tissue box, ornament, and framed photo
- Square coffee table with huge dish on the top
- Stereo and CD rack
- Telephone
- Vase with a smiling face
- Wall lamps, table lamps, Mexican star lamp, and floor lamps
- White armchair
- Window seat/shelf with cushions
- Wooden food trolley

JOEY'S BACHELOR PAD

- 3-D picture of *The Last Supper*
- Barcalounger
- Ceramic flower ornament
- Colorful rotary dial phone on a fancy table
- Elvis bust lamp
- Female statues
- Fish ornament
- Funky black chair
- Furry and animal-print cushions on the sofa
- Huge mirror
- Huge panther stretching against the wall
- Modern art ornaments
- Neon Las Vegas light
- Panther coffee table
- Phone in the bathroom
- Picture on the wall with six white masks
- Plastic parrot ornament
- Potted plants
- Push-button phone
- Rain simulation ornament
- Several round tables with chairs
- Three ceramic dogs
- Uncomfortable-looking red couch with matching chair
- Various modern artworks on the wall
- Wall lights
- Wooden cabinet with plants in vases

CENTRAL PERK

- Artwork on the wall
- Bar with stools
- Cakes in glass cake stands
- Chalkboard menu
- Chandeliers
- Coat/hat rack
- Coffee machine
- Colorful rugs
- Flowers in vases
- Green posts
- Green, red, and white striped curtain
- Jars of coffee/tea
- Mugs
- Neon signs

- Plates
- Roller blinds
- Service sign on the wall
- Stage
- Tray spot

- Various tables and chairs, including the orange couch and gray/green armchair
- Waiters and waitresses
- Wall lights

PHOEBE'S APARTMENT

- Alley cat painting
- Armchair
- Beaded curtain
- Books
- Bowl of fruit on wooden table
- Clock
- Couch with cushions
- Flowers in a vase
- Gladys, Phoebe's creepy homemade art
- Green cabinet
- Lamp behind the couch
- Mermaid table (later apothecary table)
- Multiple vases on a white table
- Ornaments
- Painting of a bird
- Painting of a red flower
- Painting of a woman
- Painting of a woman dancing
- Plant in holder on the wall
- Purple curtains
- Room divider
- Sconces
- Small table next to the couch with a vase and flower on it
- Statue
- Table with plants
- Trinkets
- Wall decoration shaped like a castle
- Wall lamp
- Wooden desk chair
- Wooden table and chairs
- Writing desk

ESTELLE'S OFFICE

- Ashtray
- Basket with a plant in it
- Books all over the sofa
- Books on top of one cabinet
- Box of tissues
- Ceramic cow head
- Cigarette holder with cigarettes
- Client photos on the wall
- Clock
- Coat on the back of the door
- Coatrack
- Desk lamp
- Floral curtains
- Flowers in a vase
- Foot spa
- Framed playbills
- Fridge
- Glass jar
- Green frog figurines
- Half-eaten sandwich
- Lamp and books on top of the fridge
- Little ornamental wooden chair
- Metal tins
- Mirror on the wall
- Model car
- Mug
- Newspaper
- Newspaper clippings
- Painting of a lady
- Painting of some flowers
- Paper and files beneath the desk
- Phone
- Scripts
- Sign on the wall
- Sofa covered in paraphernalia
- Takeout boxes
- Takeout cup with cigarette butts inside
- Teeny horse and carriage
- Telegram machine
- Toaster
- Trash can next to the desk
- Trinket box
- Trinkets all over the office
- Trophy
- Two chairs, one on either side of the desk
- Two wooden filing cabinets
- Typewriter
- Wooden desk
- Wooden inbox
- Yellow flowers on the desk

BEACH HOUSE

- Beach chairs
- Beach-related artwork
- Buckets and spades
- Ceramic sun
- Cereal boxes, juice boxes, and other food and drinks
- Desk and chair
- Fire pokers
- Flowers
- Fruit bowl with oranges, pineapple, apples, and bananas
- *Happy Days* game
- Kitchen counter with utensils and appliances
- Kitchen towel
- Lighthouse
- Margarita glasses and jug
- Oars on the wall
- Ornamental boats
- Oven with checked towels
- Refrigerator
- Round table and chairs with red-and-white tablecloth
- Sand
- Skylight
- Small, green, wooden trunk
- Stools
- Striped and colorful beach towels
- Table lamp
- Telephone
- Television
- Toaster
- Umbrella stand
- Watering can

SPECIALTY DRINKS ON THE

CHALKBOARD

While Rachel finds it hard to remember drink orders at Central Perk, at least she has the chalkboard to remind her of the specials.

Cappuccino
Espresso
Café au lait
Café mocha
Mochaccino
Central Jolt Java
N.Y. Classico
Urban Tribe Java
Manhattan Mocha
Long Island Cream
Empire Roast
Ms. Liberty Blend

(THE ONE WITH THE LESBIAN WEDDING)

CHANGING ARTWORK ON THE BACK WALL OF CENTRAL PERK

The artwork in Central Perk changes regularly. Here are some of the memorable pictures that graced the back wall throughout the series.

SEASON 1

- Colorful characters (one neon) dancing in a circle.

SEASON 2

- Gigantic, orange coffee cup with diamond design on the side and neon steam coming from the top.

- A modern-art version of the Statue of Liberty holding a coffee cup in one hand and a bag of coffee beans in the other.

- Colorful artist palette with leaves, coffee cups, and other decorations.

- A multicolored character running with his arms over his head.

- King Kong, a plane, and the Empire State Building. A quote says "No More Mr. Decaf!"

- A large, green picture with the word GRIND showing a coffee cup and grinder. Two smaller pictures: a gray one with the word TICKLE, showing a red piano, and the other with a red background, the word SQUEEZE, and a picture of an accordion.

SEASON 3

- Eight small, colorful pictures with words: SQUEEZE with picture of an accordion; BANG with picture of a drum; TICKLE with picture of a piano; LICK with picture of a guitar; BLOW with picture of a saxophone; SUCK with picture of a harmonica.

- Large, round picture with orange flowers and an animal wearing clothes.

- Large, yellow picture showing toast popping out of a toaster.

- Picasso-style faces with a coffee cup.

125

- A scene including an old car, figures, and a skyline.

- Three medium-sized paintings showing colorful scenes, including figures, stars, the sea, and the moon.

SEASON 4

- Colorful characters (one neon) dancing in a circle.

- Multicolored interpretation of New York.

- A huge Christmas wreath surrounded by stockings.

- A table with a vase of flowers, a cup and saucer, and a pineapple.

- A large, orange picture showing a coffee cup with steam coming from the top.

- A blue dog with yellow background.

SEASON 5

- A man in a suit sitting on a sofa.

- Yellow, blue, and red flowers in a white vase.

- Huge, sparkly Christmas wreath.

- Close-up of the Statue of Liberty.

- Abstract painting with a giant daisy and two people.

- Four small black-and-white photographs, including several flowers.

SEASON 6

- Two large faces, one facing up, the other facing down.

- Three small neon squares above a picture of two coffee cups with steam coming from the top.

- A giant sparkly wreath.

- A blue dog with yellow background.

- One large picture composed of eight coffee cups with different patterns.

- Abstract painting of mostly geometric shapes in green, blue, and brown.

- Close-up of the Statue of Liberty.

- Two young men facing each other.

- Noah's ark, complete with animals.

SEASON 7

- A lake scene with mountains in the background.
- Dozens of red coffee cups.
- A golden picture with a blue and black triangle/pyramid.
- Star of David, large, red baubles, a sledge, and poinsettia.
- A selection of pictures, including three red canvases and one of a blue figure with flames coming out of his head.
- A blue King Kong on top of a yellow Empire State Building.
- A large picture of fruit.
- A scene with various items, including a glass door, a lamp, a mirror, and a piano.

SEASON 8

- Large Halloween-themed picture.
- An orange chair on a red and black checked floor.
- The American flag with the Statue of Liberty.
- A giant wreath with baubles and ribbons.
- A huge blue and white flower.
- An American flag.
- British bulldog in a kitchen with colorful furniture.
- Two red and white hearts with an arrow going through them.
- A red, three-legged cow.
- A close-up of the Statue of Liberty.
- Uncle Sam "I Want You!" poster.

SEASON 9

- Twelve little pictures of colorful chickens.
- Three tall pictures of New York landmarks.
- An abstract painting of one small and one large striped circle, surrounded by white squiggles.
- Nine small pictures, all connected into one large picture. Scenes include a plane, a skyline/buildings, and people.
- A close-up of the blue dog.

SEASON 10

- Multicolored doodle artwork, which includes anchors, wheels, hearts, a hand, figures, stars, the Om sign, dogs, numbers, and shapes.
- A Wall Street–inspired picture with a close-up of the Statue of Liberty.
- A map of America and the Statue of Liberty.
- Six magazine covers.
- A large cup of coffee with the word JOE running vertically at the top.

PLANES, TRAINS, AND AUTOMOBILES

The friends use various methods of transport to get from one place to another, though some are more successful than others.

- Phoebe's taxi belonged to her grandmother, and Phoebe drives it on many occasions. After her grandmother dies, her ashes are kept in a box under the front seat. There is no smoking allowed in the cab, and it has no passenger seatbelt after the paramedics cut through it after a previous collision. At one point, Phoebe terrifies Ross when she drives recklessly to the airport so that he can tell Rachel he loves her. (THE LAST ONE, PARTS 1 AND 2)

- The friends all travel to the airport to say goodbye to Marcel as he heads to the San Diego Zoo. Ross tries to give the monkey a heartfelt speech, but Marcel is more interested in humping Ross's leg. (THE ONE WITH THE FAKE MONICA)

- After Chandler announces that Ross is in love with Rachel, Rachel dashes to the airport. Unfortunately, Ross is already boarding the plane and her message accidentally goes to another man. A week later, Rachel goes to the airport to greet Ross on his return, but there's a surprise—he's with another woman. (THE ONE WHERE RACHEL FINDS OUT)

- When Rachel sees Ross with Julie at the airport, she tries to escape but falls over a chair and hits her head. She uses the flowers she bought for Ross to stop the bleeding, and then they all head for baggage claim. (THE ONE WITH ROSS'S NEW GIRLFRIEND)

- Chandler and Joey take Ben out for the day and accidentally leave him on the bus. They go to the bus depot to collect him, only to find two abandoned babies. Luckily, they choose the right one and return him to Ross. (THE ONE WITH THE BABY ON THE BUS)

- When Phoebe briefly goes into business with Monica, they buy a van that has a superhero woman holding a sword and riding a dragon creature emblazoned on the side. (THE ONE WHERE THEY'RE GOING TO PARTY!)

- Ross sees an attractive woman sitting in the same train carriage, so he sits beside the door so that she'll have to walk past him. The move pays off, and the two spend time in her hometown of Poughkeepsie. Eventually, the traveling exhausts Ross, he falls asleep on the train, and he wakes up in Montreal. Another woman speaks to him, but there's a problem—she lives in Nova Scotia. (THE ONE WITH THE GIRL FROM POUGHKEEPSIE)

- When Chandler tells Janice that he's moving to Yemen, he thinks she'll just go away. However, not only does she insist on helping him pack, but she also accompanies him and his many boxes to the airport. Not content with waving him off in the departure lounge, Janice says she's going to stay until the plane actually departs. This forces Chandler to buy a ticket for Yemen, and then he has to ask an old lady if he can stay with her when they arrive. (THE ONE WITH ALL THE RUGBY)

- On the advice of Monica, Ross rushes to the airport to see Emily before she returns to London. She is excited to see him, but when he says "I love you," she thanks him and then boards the plane. (THE ONE WITH THE FREE PORN)

- Ross is freaked out because Emily and Susan are bonding in London, and he thinks they'll end up together. He and Carol go to meet them at the airport, where he is relieved to discover that when they say goodbye, the two women don't kiss with tongue. (THE ONE WITH RACHEL'S NEW DRESS)

- Rachel arrives at the airport for a last-minute trip to London so she can stop Ross from marrying Emily, but she's forgotten her passport. Instead of canceling the trip, she rushes back to the apartment and then, once on the plane, manages to infuriate a fellow passenger by playing drums on a magazine and talking about her complicated relationship with Ross. (THE ONE WITH ROSS'S WEDDING, PART 2)

- On the way back to New York, Monica and Chandler's plans to meet up in the bathroom are thwarted by discussions of Joey's career problems. (THE ONE AFTER ROSS SAYS RACHEL)

- Ross spots Rachel at the airport while he's waiting to see if Emily will go on their honeymoon with him after saying the wrong name at the altar. When she doesn't show up, Ross and Rachel decide they'll go on the honeymoon together, but as they're boarding the plane, Emily arrives, and Rachel accidentally ends up flying off to Greece on her own. (THE ONE AFTER ROSS SAYS RACHEL)

- On her way to Las Vegas, Phoebe accidentally reveals to Chandler that Monica had lunch with Richard. This leads to a huge fight on their anniversary. *(THE ONE IN VEGAS, PART 1)*

- During a flight to Las Vegas, Rachel and Ross try to embarrass each other after Rachel says that she doesn't embarrass very easily. Their tricks include Ross pretending that Rachel is a stranger begging him for sex and Rachel throwing water over Ross and pretending he's had an accident. Finally, Ross draws on Rachel's face with permanent marker, which later won't come off. *(THE ONE IN VEGAS, PART 1)*

- When Joey finds the keys to a Porsche, his intention is to leave a note for the owner on the windshield. However, when a beautiful woman thinks that he owns it, Joey doesn't disagree. When the real owner returns, Joey dresses in Porsche gear and then builds a car out of cardboard boxes in the hope that prospective women will think he still owns a Porsche. *(THE ONE WITH JOEY'S PORSCHE)*

- When Elizabeth goes off on spring break, Ross accompanies her to the airport. He's dismayed to see that her friend group is all young men, so he ends up going, too. *(THE ONE WITH JOEY'S FRIDGE)*

- After Monica is upset that her dad used her childhood possessions to stop water from getting to his Porsche, she's given the car as an apology gift. Ross is absolutely furious. *(THE ONE WHERE ROSITA DIES)*

- When Ross turns thirty, he buys a little red sports car. Unfortunately, it's blocked in by two other cars, and the friends try but fail to get it out. When the space finally clears, Ross and Joey hop in but then see a middle-aged bald man cruising past in his own sports car. After the man comments about how hot they

are, Ross's excitement fades. *(THE ONE WHERE THEY ALL TURN THIRTY)*

- Ross borrows Monica's car, but Rachel (who is banned from driving it) decides that she wants to go, too. During the excursion, they get pulled over by two policemen, first because Rachel is speeding and then because Ross is driving too slowly. *(THE ONE WITH CHANDLER'S DAD)*

- On his way to Tulsa for the first time, Chandler talks to Joey on the phone. He assures him that everything will be okay and that he'll see him soon. Joey then hangs up before Monica can speak to her husband. *(THE ONE WITH THE PEDIATRICIAN)*

- On hearing that the Powerball lottery is now up to $300 million, Monica and Joey drive to Connecticut to buy tickets. Everyone pitches in except Ross, who thinks the whole thing is ridiculous. He relents later on, but then Phoebe drops the bowl over the balcony, sending all the tickets onto the street. They lose half of them but manage to win $3 with the rest, which Phoebe spends on a coffee and some mini muffins. Meanwhile, a random guy finds a ticket on the street and wins $10,000. *(THE ONE WITH THE LOTTERY)*

- On their way home from Barbados, Mike tells Phoebe that he's supposed to be going on a date that evening. Apparently, he's been seeing a woman named Precious for the past three months but plans to break up with her that night. Later, while Mike waits in the restaurant to break up with his girlfriend, she turns up at his apartment. Phoebe breaks up with Precious on Mike's behalf and makes her cry on her birthday. Elsewhere on the plane, Ross tries to tell Joey that he kissed Joey's ex-girlfriend Charlie, but Joey already knows. *(THE ONE AFTER JOEY AND RACHEL KISS)*

- On discovering that Emma's birthday cake is a penis instead of a bunny, Rachel borrows Monica's Porsche so that she can try to return it. She gets pulled over for speeding and has forgotten her license, so Ross goes to rescue her. On the way back, Rachel terrifies Ross with her driving skills, and then he manages to turn the penis cake into a bunny. (THE ONE WITH THE CAKE)

- When Phoebe and Rachel see Chandler getting into a car with another woman, they worry he's having an affair. They follow him to a house in Westchester and watch as he goes in for forty-five minutes. Joey knows there's something not right since he doesn't think Chandler could be with a woman for that long. He's correct, of course. It later transpires that the car belongs to Nancy—Monica and Chandler's realtor, who is helping them buy a house out of the city. (THE ONE WHERE CHANDLER GETS CAUGHT)

- Ross and Phoebe arrive at JFK airport so that Ross can declare his love for Rachel. Rachel, meanwhile, is at Newark airport about to board the plane to Paris after getting a job there. In an effort to delay take-off, Phoebe calls Rachel to say that something is wrong with the left phalange. Another passenger overhears the call and leaves the plane, which causes everyone else to get off, too. Ross arrives and tells Rachel that he loves her, but she gets on the plane anyway—until she realizes that she's in love with him, too, gets off, and goes to find him. (THE LAST ONE, PARTS 1 AND 2)

MEDICAL SCENES AND ILLNESSES

From flying hockey pucks to Phoebe's sexy phlegm, here are all the times the friends have had cause to visit medical practices or look after themselves.

- Ross and Susan accompany Carol to her sonogram, but before the procedure, the three bicker over names and the amount of involvement Ross will have in the baby's day-to-day life. *(THE ONE WITH THE SONOGRAM AT THE END)*

- Rachel goes to Barry's orthodontist practice with the intent of returning her engagement ring but is told that Barry went on her honeymoon with her maid of honor, Mindy. *(THE ONE WITH THE SONOGRAM AT THE END)*

- When Ross gets hit in the face with an ice hockey puck, Joey and Chandler take him to the hospital. A scary admittance nurse is more concerned with her unsatisfying chocolate bar and ends up being accidentally knocked out with the puck. *(THE ONE WITH GEORGE STEPHANOPOULOS)*

- After accidentally causing a guy to be hit by an ambulance, Phoebe and Monica spend a lot of time visiting him as he lies in a coma. They fantasize about what he's like and which one of them he'll go out with, but when he wakes up, he's not interested in either of them, and they give him a lecture. *(THE ONE WITH MRS. BING)*

- When Rachel hurts her ankle while taking down the Christmas lights, Monica goes with her to the hospital. Rachel has no insurance so she "borrows" Monica's. This inevitably leads to mix-ups with the forms but also to dates with Dr. Michael Mitchell and Dr. Jeffrey Rosen. Ross uses the same hospital when Marcel swallows some Scrabble tiles. *(THE ONE WITH TWO PARTS: PART 2)*

- Rachel and Barry have sex in his orthodontist chair, but their affair ends when she and Mindy have a heart-to-heart. They both go to the surgery to confront Barry, but Mindy decides to forgive him. *(THE ONE WITH THE EVIL ORTHODONTIST)*

- Carol is in labor, but her doctor, Dr. Franzblau, is more interested in flirting with Rachel. Joey accidentally becomes a single mother's birth partner, Susan and Ross almost miss the birth because of their bickering, and Chandler tells Monica that if they're both childless by forty, they'll have a baby together. (THE ONE WITH THE BIRTH)

- Ross has an allergic reaction to Monica's lime and kiwi pie. They head to the hospital, but Ross is terrified of needles. Dr. Carlin gives him a shot, while Ross squeezes Monica's hand so hard she needs an X-ray. (THE ONE WITH THE BABY ON THE BUS)

- Monica has her eyes tested shortly after catering Richard's party. There is a definite attraction, and the examination ends with the couple kissing. (THE ONE WHERE ROSS AND RACHEL . . . YOU KNOW)

- Phoebe has a toothache but is too scared to go to the dentist because every time she does, somebody dies. When she does go, she ends up thinking that she has killed Ugly Naked Guy because he's been lying beside his window all day long. Luckily, it's a false alarm. (THE ONE WITH THE GIANT POKING DEVICE)

- Ross finds a strange growth on his bottom, which is too wrinkly to be a mole but too fancy to be a pimple. Chandler sends Ross to see Dr. Rhodes, the guy who removed Chandler's third nipple. He invites his colleagues in to investigate, and they all cram into the room to take a gander at Ross's backside. (THE ONE WITH ROSS'S THING)

- When Dr. Rhodes can't decide what Ross has on his bottom, Phoebe recommends he see Guru Saj. He diagnoses the growth as a koondis and then accidentally removes it when he catches it with his watch. Joey and Chandler then take the duck to Saj when he has a cough, and Saj recommends the duck eat a bat. (THE ONE WITH ROSS'S THING)

- When a cold gives Phoebe a sexy voice, she's thrilled. When she gets better, she's determined to become ill again and does everything she can to bring on another cold. This includes licking Monica's cup, collecting her snotty tissues, and then kissing Gunther. (THE ONE WITH JOEY'S NEW GIRLFRIEND)

- When Monica strikes herself in the eye with some ice, she goes to see an on-call eye doctor, who turns out to be Richard's son, Timothy. He diagnoses a scratch to her eye and gives her a patch. He's having Thanksgiving dinner alone, so Monica invites him to her own dinner. There they form an attraction to each other until Monica freaks out when Timothy kisses just like his dad. (THE ONE WITH CHANDLER IN A BOX)

- Phoebe goes to the hospital to have Frank Jr. and Alice's embryos transferred into her womb. There's a lot of pressure on Phoebe since this is their only chance, so Phoebe talks to the potential babies while they're in the petri dish and asks them to hold on tight. (THE ONE WITH THE EMBRYOS)

- Phoebe (accompanied by Rachel) goes for a routine scan and freaks out when she discovers that she's pregnant with triplets. (THE ONE WITH THE FREE PORN)

- When Joey's snoring gets out of control, Chandler insists that he attend a sleep clinic. It is at this clinic that Chandler meets Marjorie, who is being treated for sleep-talking. The doctor gives Joey a mouth guard, and it tastes so good that he wears it to Central Perk. *(THE ONE WITH ALL THE WEDDING DRESSES)*

- After the duck swallows Ross's grandmother's wedding ring, he is rushed to the vet. As the doctor works on his patient, the boys think back to the happy times they've shared together, and then Ross decides that Joey and Chandler should both be his best men. *(THE ONE WITH THE WORST BEST MAN EVER)*

- When Phoebe goes into labor, she is attended to by Dr. Harad, a huge fan of *Happy Days* and Fonzie. She then gets Dr. Oberman, a first-year resident who looks like a kid. Phoebe makes him cry, and then Dr. Harad returns with more Fonzie trivia. Meanwhile, Joey is struck down with kidney stones and passes them as Phoebe gives birth. *(THE ONE HUNDREDTH)*

- During a flashback, twenty-year-old Chandler is rushed to the hospital after Monica accidentally drops a knife on his foot, slicing off the tip of his toe. Monica thinks she has the toe on ice—only she's picked up a carrot by mistake. *(THE ONE WITH ALL THE THANKSGIVINGS)*

- When Rachel has a suspected eye infection, Monica takes her to the eye doctor. Rachel is terrified so the examination is stressful, but the doctor gives her some eyedrops and jokingly warns that if she doesn't use them, she'll need a glass eye. Back at home, the friends have to wrestle Rachel to the ground every time she needs her eyedrops. *(THE ONE WITH JOEY'S BIG BREAK)*

- Chandler comes home to find Joey writhing on the floor after collapsing while lifting weights. It turns out that he has a hernia, but his lack of health insurance stops him from getting treated. Instead, he puts his hernia to good use by showing it to a child actor to provoke him to cry during a scene. *(THE ONE WHERE JOEY LOSES HIS INSURANCE)*

- Monica is sent home sick from work, but she's determined that everything is fine . . . *d.* Instead of resting, she wants to have sex with Chandler to prove that she's not unwell. At first he resists, but then Monica starts rubbing on vapor rub. Chandler finds it erotic and changes his mind, with painful results. *(THE ONE WITH RACHEL'S SISTER)*

- To earn extra money, Joey tries to get into an identical twin study by hiring "look-alike" Carl to act as his brother, Tony. When the doctor tells them that they're not identical twins, Joey blames Carl. *(THE ONE WITH UNAGI)*

- A pregnant Rachel goes for her first ultrasound, and Ross turns up to discuss whether or not they should get married. When she's shown the sonogram, Rachel is upset that she can't see which part is her baby, so Ross tries to help. *(THE ONE WHERE RACHEL TELLS . . .)*

- Rachel visits Dr. Schiff but seems to forget that she's there for an examination. Instead, she giggles, flirts, and even puts her pinkie finger in his chin dimple. *(THE ONE WITH ROSS'S STEP FORWARD)*

- When Rachel goes for her prenatal examination, Ross tells the doctor that they don't want to know the sex of the baby. While Ross is distracted by baby pictures, Rachel takes a peek at the file but doesn't get to see anything interesting. Ross mistakenly thinks Rachel knows what gender they're having, so he ends up calling the doctor so he can find out, too. It turns out Rachel doesn't actually know the gender, but it's too late now—Ross tells her they're having a girl. *(THE ONE WHERE CHANDLER TAKES A BATH)*

- Rachel is taken to the hospital with stomach pains, but they turn out to be Braxton Hicks contractions. Ross is concerned that he's missing out on too much of Rachel's pregnancy, so Joey suggests that Rachel move out of his place and move in with Ross even though—as it turns out—Joey is secretly in love with Rachel. *(THE ONE WITH THE SECRET CLOSET)*

- Rachel is eight days past her due date for her baby, so she and Ross visit the doctor's office. The doctor recommends some home remedies for bringing on labor, such as herbal tea, castor oil, spicy foods, taking a long walk, and sex. *(THE ONE WHERE RACHEL IS LATE)*

- When Rachel goes to the hospital to have her baby, the hospital only has semiprivate rooms, and a variety of strange couples pass through. The couples include a man and woman who want to share every detail of their labor; a couple who hate each other; a woman who can hardly feel her contractions; a woman who doesn't even make it to the bed; and Janice! Meanwhile, Chandler and Monica decide to have a baby, and Phoebe meets a patient she wants to date. When Rachel is taken to the delivery room, complications arise when it's discovered that the baby is breach. However, the baby is born safely and is named Emma. *(THE ONE WHERE RACHEL HAS A BABY, PARTS 1 AND 2 / THE ONE WHERE NO ONE PROPOSES)*

- When Ross accidentally punches a post while aiming for Joey, he breaks his thumb. Joey has to help him fill in some forms at the hospital and wonders what Ross is short for. Rossell? Rosstopher? He then writes dinosaurs as Ross's occupation and draws a doodle to go with it. (THE ONE WHERE EMMA CRIES)

- Rachel keeps bothering Emma's doctor with every little ailment and is finally told to find a new doctor when she calls him at 3 a.m. because of hiccups. She gets him back by making a crank call to him. (THE ONE WITH THE PEDIATRICIAN)

- When Rachel is looking for a new pediatrician for Emma, Ross assures her that his own childhood doctor is dead. However, it turns out that he is very much alive, and what's more, Ross is still one of his patients. (THE ONE WITH THE PEDIATRICIAN)

- After Monica and Chandler try for a year to conceive without any luck, they visit a fertility clinic. Chandler is anxious that his test will be filmed and shared on the Internet, and if that isn't worrying enough, Janice shows up just as he's about to give his specimen. When the test results come in, it turns out that Chandler's sperm have low motility and Monica's uterus is an "inhospitable environment." This realization leads the couple to think first about a sperm donor and then about adoption. (THE ONE WITH THE FERTILITY TEST)

- Chandler and Monica visit the fertility doctor, who talks to them about their options. He recommends surrogacy or a sperm donor, and when he mentions adoption, Chandler jokes that the doctor wants them to adopt him. (THE ONE WITH THE DONOR)

- Monica and Chandler go to visit Erica, the pregnant lady who wants them to adopt her baby. She is under the impression that Monica is a reverend and Chandler is a doctor. When they come clean, the guy at the agency refuses to believe there's been a mistake, so Chandler jokingly offers to perform surgery on him to prove that he is not in the medical profession. (THE ONE WITH THE BIRTH MOTHER)

- Rachel's father has a heart attack, so she and Ross go to visit him in the hospital. That night, they stay in the old Green family home, but when Rachel tries to have sex with Ross, he says no. This leads to a confrontation at the hospital, which Rachel's father overhears. (THE ONE WHERE JOEY SPEAKS FRENCH)

- Monica and Chandler support Erica as she gives birth. A boy is born, and then the doctor announces that another is on the way—this time a girl. The couple is shocked—they were only expecting to adopt one baby! (THE LAST ONE, PARTS 1 AND 2)

BATHROOMS

From Chandler and Monica's bubble bath to Phoebe discovering a pregnancy test in the trash can, here are some of the most memorable bathroom scenes.

- Chandler accidentally walks in on Rachel when she's just left the shower. Rachel decides the only way to get back at him is to walk in on *him* in the shower. However, her attempts at revenge lead to a string of disasters. First, she walks in on Joey in the shower, then Joey walks in on Monica, and Monica walks in on Joey Sr. *(THE ONE WITH THE BOOBIES)*

- At Jack Geller's birthday party, Monica and Richard have a private moment in the bathroom. When Richard goes to leave, Judy arrives, forcing Monica to hide behind the shower curtain. Unfortunately for her, Jack comes in seconds later, and she overhears her parents making out. *(THE ONE WHERE JOEY MOVES OUT)*

- When Chandler and Joey buy a chick and duck, they pop the duck in the tub for a swim. Joey wonders if the chick can swim, so he pops him in, too. Not surprisingly, the chick sinks, so Chandler pulls him out and Joey switches on the hairdryer. *(THE ONE WITH A CHICK AND A DUCK)*

- In the midst of pregnancy cravings, Phoebe follows a yummy smell into the bathroom and discovers that the smell is Joey's baloney sandwich, which he's eating in the shower. *(THE ONE WITH THE FAKE PARTY)*

- While secretly enjoying a bubble bath together, Chandler and Monica are interrupted by Joey. Monica is forced to hide under the bubbles while Chandler tries to get rid of his roommate. *(THE ONE WITH ALL THE KISSING)*

- While on a date with Elizabeth Hornswoggle, Ross's leather pants cause him to burn up. He goes to the bathroom to cool down but then can't get the pants up again. After taking advice from Joey, Ross ends up with his legs covered in lotion and powder (which creates a paste), accidentally slaps himself in the face, and still can't get the leather pants back on. *(THE ONE WITH ALL THE RESOLUTIONS)*

- While Rachel and Phoebe are in the bathroom discussing Chandler's disappearance, Phoebe comes across a pregnancy test in the trash and assumes it belongs to Monica. *(THE ONE WITH MONICA AND CHANDLER'S WEDDING, PART 1)*

- Monica draws Chandler a bath to show him that baths are nice, which includes candles, music, bath salts, bubble bath, and a little navy ship to make it manly. Chandler gets addicted to taking baths, and he's even taking one when Ross and Rachel pop in to tell everyone they're having a girl. *(THE ONE WHERE CHANDLER TAKES A BATH)*

- Joey tries to go to the bathroom, but Rachel has had everything baby-proofed, and he can't open the toilet lid. *(THE ONE WITH THE BOOB JOB)*

- Monica may love her cornrows, but during a bathroom song and dance, she gets one stuck on the shower curtain and tries (and fails) to gnaw her way out of the problem. Chandler says he'll untangle her but only if she agrees to get rid of the cornrows altogether. *(THE ONE AFTER JOEY AND RACHEL KISS)*

138

SPORTS AND EXERCISE

Whether the friends are playing sports, watching sports, or just trying to get out of exercising, there's no denying that sports activities play a pivotal role in the series.

- The gang wins a game of softball, thanks to Monica's boyfriend, Alan. *(THE ONE WITH THE THUMB)*

- Chandler and Joey take Ross to an ice hockey match at Madison Square Garden, but Ross gets hit in the face with the puck and ends up in the hospital. *(THE ONE WITH GEORGE STEPHANOPOULOS)*

- When Chandler puts on a little weight, Monica offers to help him work out. She becomes so obsessed that Chandler labels her insane and wishes he'd never agreed to it. *(THE ONE WHERE ROSS FINDS OUT)*

- Joey and Chandler can't decide who to take to the Knicks game. Monica convinces them to take Richard, and they become inspired by his tipping skills, cigars, and moustache. Joey and Chandler love spending time with Richard, but then he realizes that they see him as a dad figure and the friendship fizzles out. *(THE ONE WHERE OLD YELLER DIES)*

- In *THE ONE WITH RACHEL'S PHONE NUMBER*, Joey has courtside tickets to see a Knicks game with Chandler, but it clashes with the only night Monica has off from the restaurant. To avoid conflict, Chandler says that he has to stay in Tulsa, but secretly he heads home to be with Monica. Joey finds out the truth, and then it's revealed that the tickets were for the next night anyway.

- In *THE ONE WHERE RACHEL'S SISTER BABYSITS*, Phoebe and Mike go to a Knicks game for their one-year anniversary.

- Chandler and Ross should be playing racquetball, but they go to Central Perk instead. They soon wish they hadn't skipped the game when they encounter two bullies who steal Chandler's hat. For the next few days, the boys are bullied every time they go to Central Perk. This ends when Chandler, Ross, and the bullies all have their belongings stolen while contemplating a fight outside Central Perk. *(THE ONE WITH THE BULLIES)*

- In *THE ONE WITH PHOEBE'S COOKIES*, Jack invites Chandler to play racquetball with him shortly after his engagement to Monica.

- During Rachel's birthday party, Joey sets up a volleyball court in Chandler's room and breaks his lamp. *(THE ONE WITH THE TWO PARTIES)*

- Chandler has three tickets to a Rangers game and offers one to Joey. There's only one problem—Janice is going, too. (THE ONE WITH THE PRINCESS LEIA FANTASY)

- In THE ONE WITH THE LATE THANKSGIVING, Joey and Ross go to a Rangers game at Madison Square Garden, but it makes them late for Monica's Thanksgiving dinner.

- Phoebe is showing off her boxing skills to Joey and punches him so hard that he bleeds. While Phoebe is putting ice on the wound, Monica's new bed arrives. Phoebe is so preoccupied that she doesn't realize that they're delivering a race car bed. (THE ONE WITH THE RACE CAR BED)

- The friends want to play a game of football during Thanksgiving. However, Monica and Ross are hesitant because their parents haven't let them play ever since Monica broke Ross's nose during their regular Geller Cup tournament. The football match does occur, but the siblings' competitive streak strikes again, and they're the last ones on the field, arguing over who will win the Geller Cup trophy—a troll doll nailed to a piece of wood. (THE ONE WITH THE FOOTBALL)

- Phoebe's boyfriend, Robert, teaches her to play basketball. She says she's allowed a

23-pointer instead of a 3-pointer because she's dainty. (THE ONE WHERE MONICA AND RICHARD ARE FRIENDS)

- In THE ONE ON THE LAST NIGHT, Ross claims that he gave up a career in basketball to become a paleontologist, and in THE ONE WITH THE MEMORIAL SERVICE, Joey comes home from a game with Chandler and Ross and reports that Chandler poked himself in the eye.

- When Phoebe suggests that the staff wear roller skates at the Moondance Diner, Monica is forced to learn how to skate. She ends up falling in a heap outside Central Perk, and Rachel hurts her side during the collision. (THE ONE WITH A CHICK AND A DUCK)

- In THE ONE WHERE JOEY DATES RACHEL, Ross has to roller-skate to his new NYU class, which is located off campus.

- Monica's boyfriend, Pete, enters an anything-goes fighting match in THE ONE WITH ROSS'S THING. Ross and Monica go to the first match in THE ONE WITH THE ULTIMATE FIGHTING CHAMPION, but Pete is beaten up pretty badly. That's nothing compared to the next fight, however, when his entire upper body ends up in plaster.

- Having not used the gym in years, Chandler attempts to close his gym account. He takes Ross along for backup, but then Ross ends up joining the gym. The boys then try to close their bank accounts (cutting the gym payments off at the source), but instead they end up with a joint account. (THE ONE WITH THE BALLROOM DANCING)

- Ross accepts an invitation to play rugby with Emily's British friends, but he's awful at it. He decides that he'll have to go Red Ross (how Ross describes himself when he loses his temper), but even that doesn't help. In the end, Emily gives him some tips on the players' weaknesses, and he manages to survive the match—just about. *(THE ONE WITH ALL THE RUGBY)*

- According to Rachel, Ross got hurt playing badminton with her dad, but Ross insists it was just because her mom's dog kept looking at him. *(THE ONE WITH ALL THE RUGBY)*

- Monica and Chandler play tennis with Chandler's boss, Doug, and his wife, but Monica is so competitive that Chandler begs her to let his boss win one game. She responds by breaking her racket. *(THE ONE WITH CHANDLER'S WORK LAUGH)*

- Monica gives Chandler a massage, but it turns out that she's terrible at it. When Phoebe, Ross, and Rachel all agree, Monica is upset. She questions Chandler when they're alone, then cries when he confirms his view of her massage technique. She mellows when Chandler says that she gives the best bad massages and that if there were an award for it, Monica would win all the votes. The award could even be called the Monica. *(THE ONE WITH JOEY'S BAG)*

- When Rachel and Phoebe go running together, Rachel is embarrassed by Phoebe's weird moves and makes an excuse as to why she can't exercise with her again. Phoebe eventually persuades Rachel to let go of her inhibitions, and she then runs in her own crazy way. *(THE ONE WHERE PHOEBE RUNS)*

SCORE!

GO LONG!

A-WOO-HOO!

- Ross says that toward the end of his marriage to Carol, he was doing a lot of kar-a-tay. *(THE ONE THAT COULD HAVE BEEN, PART 1)*

- After Rachel and Phoebe go to self-defense class, Ross brings up the concept of unagi, which he tells them is a state of total awareness, although Phoebe and Rachel are convinced it's sushi. According to Ross, only by achieving true unagi can you be prepared for any danger that might befall you. Determined to show that the girls don't have unagi, Ross spends lots of time trying—and mainly failing—to scare them. *(THE ONE WITH UNAGI)*

- After Joey buys a boat, Rachel offers to teach him to sail. Unfortunately for Joey, Rachel is the scariest sailing teacher ever. When she realizes that she's behaving just like her father, they give up and eat sandwiches and drink beer instead. *(THE ONE WITH PHOEBE'S COOKIES)*

- It is revealed that Ross goes to the same yoga class as Mr. Treeger. *(THE ONE WHERE RACHEL TELLS . . .)*

- In *THE ONE WITH THE BIRTHING VIDEO*, Chandler mentions that he and Monica have seen Ross doing yoga in his underwear.

- In *THE ONE WITH RACHEL'S OTHER SISTER*, Rachel says that she does Pilates while Amy claims to do yoga. The peaceful practice does nothing to quell their anger toward each other, however, and when they fight, Rachel ends up breaking one of Monica's fancy plates.

AHH SALMON SKIN ROLL

DANGER

DANGER!

Unagi!

FUNERALS AND MEMORIALS

There are a few memorial services and funerals that take place during the series, but perhaps none as memorable as Ross's memorial service—for himself.

- **Nana's funeral:** When Ross and Monica's nana dies, Ross is in charge of finding a funeral outfit but instead finds her secret stash of Sweet'n Low. At the funeral, Ross falls into an empty grave, Monica is criticized by her mother, and Joey is more interested in the Giants vs. Cowboys game. Nana's funeral inspires Jack Geller to tell Monica he wants to be buried at sea because it "looks like fun." *(THE ONE WHERE NANA DIES TWICE)*

- **Phoebe's grandmother's funeral:** Phoebe and her grandmother were shopping at the market when Grandma bent down to get some yogurt and never came back up. The memorial service includes a 3-D section with 3-D glasses, but before the program starts, Phoebe's dad appears and then runs away when he sees Phoebe's reaction to him. *(THE ONE WITH JOEY'S BAG)*

- **Ross's memorial service:** When Chandler and Ross find their college alumni website, they use it to spread rumors about each other, including that Ross cloned a dinosaur in his lab and she's now his girlfriend. Things become competitive, and Chandler spreads the rumor that Ross was hit by a blimp and died. Unfortunately for Ross, nobody comments about his "death" on the website, so he organizes his own memorial service at Monica's. There are only two mourners at the get-together—a man who fancies Chandler and a woman who once had a crush on Ross. On hearing this, Ross sprints out of the bedroom, but now the woman thinks he's a freak for organizing his own memorial, and she storms off. *(THE ONE WITH THE MEMORIAL SERVICE)*

TRIPS

From England to Barbados and everywhere in between, here are all of the trips taken, talked about, or canceled.

- Rachel wants to go skiing in Vail at Thanksgiving, but her tickets get locked in the apartment. *(THE ONE WHERE UNDERDOG GETS AWAY)*

- Rachel and Paolo are supposed to go to the Poconos for the weekend, but then Paolo makes a pass at Phoebe, and the trip is off. *(THE ONE WITH THE DOZEN LASAGNAS)*

- Ross travels to San Diego to see Marcel. A zoo manager tells Ross that Marcel has died, but a janitor tells him the truth—there was a break-in a few months back, and the monkey was taken. He's now working in the entertainment business. *(THE ONE AFTER THE SUPERBOWL, PART 1)*

- Rachel invites her friends to stay at her sister's ski cabin. Since it's only been a week since her breakup with Ross, he's not invited. However, when Phoebe's cab runs out of gas at a rest stop, Ross borrows Carol's car to rescue them, much to Rachel's disgust. He delivers the gas, and the gang goes on their way, but just as they pull out of the rest stop, Ross discovers that Carol's car battery is now dead. *(THE ONE WITHOUT THE SKI TRIP)*

- When Monica agrees to go on a date with Pete, he asks if she likes pizza. He then flies them both to Italy for dinner. *(THE ONE WITH THE HYPNOSIS TAPE)*

- When Phoebe decides to visit her mother's best friend, the friends all travel to Montauk and stay in a beach house full of sand. While Phoebe investigates her childhood, Ross and Rachel flirt, and Chandler wonders if he could ever be Monica's boyfriend. When Ross's girlfriend, Bonnie, turns up, Rachel encourages a breakup, reunites with Ross, and writes a long letter—eighteen pages, front and back, asking Ross to accept full responsibility for everything that went wrong in their relationship. The letter is so long that he falls asleep while reading it and tells Rachel that he agrees with it, even though he doesn't know what he's agreeing to. When Ross later discovers the truth, he is enraged. Rachel is also furious that he fell asleep while reading her letter. Meanwhile, Joey digs a gigantic hole, Monica gets stung by a jellyfish, and Chandler pees on her after seeing it on a Discovery documentary. (THE ONE AT THE BEACH / THE ONE WITH THE JELLYFISH)

- When Ross and Chandler's friend Gandalf plans a trip to New York, they envision a night of partying and adventure. When Gandalf cancels, they go partying with Joey instead but get so tired, they decide to have an early night. (THE ONE WHERE THEY'RE GOING TO PARTY!)

- After hitting it off on their first night together, Emily and Ross check into a bed-and-breakfast in Vermont. He calls Monica to let her know and then has to hang up because there is a deer just outside, eating fruit from the orchard. (THE ONE WITH JOEY'S DIRTY DAY)

- After finding out that Emily can't choose between him and another man, Ross rushes to London to win her love, but unknown to him, Emily is making her way back to New York to talk to him. While Ross sits outside her flat in the pouring rain, Emily calls her answering machine in the hope that Ross can hear her voice from outside. After he hears Emily declare her love, Ross calls her from an old-fashioned London telephone box. (THE ONE WITH THE FREE PORN)

- Joey, Chandler, Monica, and Ross head to London for Ross's wedding, while a pregnant Phoebe and ex-girlfriend Rachel stay in New York. The trip is full of drama—Joey and Chandler bicker while out on a sightseeing trip, Ross's and Emily's families fight over the wedding costs, Monica and Chandler sleep together, Rachel arrives unexpectedly, and the wedding goes disastrously wrong. (THE ONE WITH ROSS'S WEDDING, PARTS 1 AND 2)

- When Ross doesn't think that Emily will show up for their honeymoon, he invites Rachel to go with him to Greece. She boards the plane, but then Emily arrives and Ross stays behind. (THE ONE AFTER ROSS SAYS RACHEL) On her return to New York in THE ONE WITH ALL THE KISSING, Rachel assures Ross that she had a fantastic time. After he leaves, she furiously tells Monica that she had to stay in the honeymoon suite, and people kept asking why she was crying.

- When pregnant Phoebe is frustrated because the friends continually talk about London, they suggest a trip to Atlantic City. Phoebe is excited to go, but on the way out the door, her water breaks and they go to the hospital instead. (THE ONE WITH ALL THE KISSING)

- In an attempt to gain some privacy, Monica and Chandler plan a trip to New Jersey. They both give different reasons why they're going away but then spend the weekend arguing. On their return, Chandler is relieved to discover that they haven't split up, and Joey works out that the couple are dating. (THE ONE WITH THE KIPS)

- The friends head to Las Vegas to surprise Joey while he's there working on a movie, or so they think. It's an eventful trip—Monica and Chandler fight on their anniversary, Phoebe is asked to leave the casino, Joey finds his "hand twin," and Ross and Rachel get drunk and then married. (THE ONE IN VEGAS, PARTS 1 AND 2)

- When Ross and Elizabeth go on a trip to a cabin, they don't expect Rachel and Paul to show up, too. In an effort to avoid Paul, Ross is forced to hide underneath the sofa and then under Paul's bed. There he observes Paul telling himself that he's a neat guy and a love machine. (*THE ONE WHERE PAUL'S THE MAN*)

- Monica takes Chandler to Las Vegas to speak to his dad about coming to their wedding. Chandler doesn't want to have anything to do with him at first, but they eventually make peace and Charles receives an invitation. (*THE ONE WITH CHANDLER'S DAD*)

- Monica and Chandler head to the Bahamas for their honeymoon but are annoyed by another couple who keep getting free stuff. (*THE ONE WHERE RACHEL TELLS . . .*) On their flight home in *THE ONE WITH THE VIDEOTAPE*, they meet another married couple called Greg and Jenny, who they're determined to hang out with in New York. When it looks as though the couple gave them false names and

a wrong number, Monica tracks them down and demands they meet up again.

- Chandler makes a reservation for himself and Monica to take a trip to Vermont. However, Monica can't go because she has to work at the restaurant, and the hotel won't accept cancellations. In the end, Chandler and Ross go together, but the trip is not exactly relaxing. Ross is wired on maple candy, and the hotel loses the reservation, forcing Chandler to pay for a deluxe room. Still, Ross has an idea—they can get the money back from taking everything they can, including apples, shampoo, tampons, toilet rolls, newspapers, lightbulbs, and even loose salt. (*THE ONE WITH RACHEL'S DREAM*)

- The friends head to Barbados, where Ross is a key speaker at a paleontology conference. The trip is terrible—the rain is torrential, David plans to propose to Phoebe but Mike shows up and gets back together with Phoebe, Ross kisses Charlie, Rachel declares her love for Joey, Monica and Mike get into a Ping-Pong battle, Chandler accidentally erases Ross's speech on the computer, and Monica gets a frizzy hairdo and shell-covered cornrows. (*THE ONE IN BARBADOS, PARTS 1 AND 2 / THE ONE AFTER JOEY AND RACHEL KISS*)

CLASSES

From Lamaze to guitar lessons, here are all the classes the friends took or taught.

- Ross attends Lamaze class with Carol and Susan. Carol can't attend the next class, so Susan and Ross argue over who should be the woman giving birth during their relaxation exercises. When Carol does attend, she freaks out about the birth, which leads to Ross stressing about his abilities as a father. (THE ONE WITH TWO PARTS, PART 1)

- Monica, Rachel, and Phoebe join a tap-dance class to track down Fake Monica, the woman who has stolen Monica's credit card. Rachel picks up the routine immediately, Phoebe does her own thing, and Monica ends up dancing with Fake Monica. (THE ONE WITH THE FAKE MONICA)

- Joey's acting for soap operas class—See Jobs: Joey (Non-acting), page 13.

- Phoebe takes a literature class at the New School and invites Rachel to come along. When Rachel arrives late, she hasn't read the book and then steals Phoebe's excellent summary. Phoebe takes revenge when she tells Rachel that Jane Eyre is a robot, and then she compares the book to *RoboCop*. In the end, Rachel drops out and Monica steps in—as the mega-bossy student who demands tests and drives everybody crazy. (THE ONE WITH ROSS'S SANDWICH)

- When Joey wants to learn to play guitar, Phoebe offers to be his teacher but won't let him touch the instrument. When Joey touches some guitars in a music shop and then learns the names of the chords, Phoebe is furious and accuses him of questioning her techniques. He then fires Phoebe and hires a real teacher but eventually asks Phoebe to teach him again. He then tries to play her guitar and drops it onto the floor. (THE ONE WITH ALL THE RESOLUTIONS)

- When Ross buys Phoebe a bicycle, she doesn't mention that she can't ride it. Ross tries to teach her in the park, but eventually the bike gets fitted with training wheels. (THE ONE WITH ALL THE CANDY)

- After confronting a critic who gave her restaurant a terrible review, Monica and Joey stumble across a cooking class at the New School. They decide to stay, and it's only minutes before Monica becomes the teacher's pet and gets jealous when the teacher prefers Joey's cookies. Monica admits that she's a professional chef, but she hasn't paid for the class, so she and Joey take off. They then find a beginner's acting class, but Joey can't answer the simplest question. (THE ONE WITH THE COOKING CLASS)

CHAPTER THREE:
the One about

Love, Weddings, and Kids

LOVE INTERESTS

The friends all have more than their share of relationships over the years. Some are amazing, some are odd, and some just won't go away.

CHANDLER

Janice: Janice is known for her catchphrase "Oh my God!" and her whiny nature. Chandler spends much of the time trying to dump Janice while going back to her again and again. For a short time, Chandler does fall in love with her, but then she goes back to her estranged husband and the relationship ends. Janice's status as Chandler's on-again, off-again girlfriend finally ends when he pretends to move to Yemen. *(THE ONE WITH ALL THE RUGBY)* After that, Janice turns up at the most random and awkward moments, like when she dates Ross, when Rachel gives birth, when Monica and Chandler go for fertility tests, and when she is interested in buying the house next door to the one Monica and Chandler are buying. *(THE ONE WITH THE EAST GERMAN LAUNDRY DETERGENT ONWARD)*

Aurora: An Italian woman who was in the Israeli army. Chandler meets Aurora at Joey's play, and they date for a while but break up when she is unwilling to give up her husband and boyfriends for him. *(THE ONE WITH THE BUTT)*

Jill Goodacre: During a blackout, Chandler is locked in an ATM vestibule with the famous model. The awkward encounter leads to a flirtation, which ends when the power comes back on. *(THE ONE WITH THE BLACKOUT)*

Lowell: Colleague Shelley mistakenly thinks that Chandler is gay and wants to set him up with Lowell from Financial Services. Chandler is not gay, but if he was, he'd be interested in Brian from Payroll. *(THE ONE WHERE NANA DIES TWICE)*

Andrea: Chandler attempts to flirt with Andrea at Phoebe's Nana's funeral, but Ross ruins it when he tells Chandler that it's okay to be gay. *(THE ONE WHERE NANA DIES TWICE)*

Danielle: Chandler is crazy about his new date, but when she doesn't call him back, he becomes obsessed with the phone. However, when Danielle arrives in Central Perk to look for him, Chandler decides she's too needy and is no longer interested in her. *(THE ONE WITH THE EVIL ORTHODONTIST)*

Joan: Chandler breaks up with Joan because her nostrils are too big. He claims that when she leaned back, he could see her brain. (THE ONE WHERE HECKLES DIES)

Maureen Rasillo: Ross says that Chandler broke up with Maureen because she didn't hate Yanni. (THE ONE WHERE HECKLES DIES)

Allison: She works at Chandler's company and is pretty and smart. Chandler hasn't asked her out due to her unusually large head, and when he does, he still can't get past how big it is. (THE ONE WHERE HECKLES DIES)

Jade: A mystery woman named Jade calls Chandler, thinking she's talking to someone called Bob. Jade arranges a date with "Bob," and Chandler schemes so that when that guy doesn't show, he'll be there to comfort her. The plan works, and he sleeps with her. She then calls "Bob," and Chandler impersonates him once again. Jade tells him that she had sex with her new guy (Chandler), and he wasn't very good. (THE ONE WITH FIVE STEAKS AND AN EGGPLANT)

Girls on the Bus: Chandler and Joey flirt with two girls, but their planned date is canceled when they realize they've left baby Ben on the bus. (THE ONE WITH THE BABY ON THE BUS)

Susie Moss: In fourth grade, Chandler pulled up Susie's skirt during a school play, and she was labeled Susie Underpants until she was eighteen. She takes her revenge years later by getting Chandler to wear her underwear, pretending she wants sex, having him undress in a restaurant bathroom, and then stealing his clothes. (THE ONE AFTER THE SUPERBOWL, PART 2)

Gail: Gail stares at Chandler in Central Perk, but when he goes over to talk to her, she sees the gaudy bracelet he's wearing from Joey, makes an excuse, and leaves. After that, Chandler christens the bracelet the Woman Repeller. (THE ONE WITH THE PROM VIDEO)

Kissing Girl: At Rachel's birthday party, Chandler tells Joey that a woman just walked up to him, said "I want you, Dennis," and then stuck her tongue down his throat. She can then be heard calling "Dennis" from the bathroom. (THE ONE WITH THE TWO PARTIES)

Margha: See Love Interests: Joey, page 159. (THE ONE WITH THE FOOTBALL)

Mary-Angela: Chandler kisses Mary-Angela, one of Joey's sisters, when he's drunk at a party, but the next day, he can't remember which sister he made out with. Joey tells him that it was Mary-Angela, but Chandler still doesn't know who that is. During a visit to the Tribbiani home, one of the sisters asks him to accompany her to the bathroom and then kisses him in the hallway. Chandler thinks she must be Mary-Angela (because according to him, the sisters all look alike), but she is actually Mary-Therese. This mistake leads to Chandler being told off by Joey and punched by another sister, Cookie. (THE ONE WHERE CHANDLER CAN'T REMEMBER WHICH SISTER)

Ginger: Chandler meets Ginger, a former girlfriend of Joey's, while he's waiting to use the Central Perk bathroom. Her relationship with Joey broke down when he accidentally threw her false leg into a fire. When Chandler finds out about the leg, he freaks out, but ultimately decides he'll be cool with it. However, when Ginger discovers he has a third nipple, she runs away, and Chandler ends up getting it removed. *(THE ONE WITH PHOEBE'S EX-PARTNER)*

Chloe: See Love Interests: Ross, page 153. *(THE ONE WHERE ROSS AND RACHEL TAKE A BREAK)*

Joanna: Joanna is Rachel's boss at Bloomingdale's. She and Chandler go on a date, but Chandler thinks Joanna is a big dull dud with mascara goop in her eyes. He refuses to go out with her again, but she makes Rachel's life miserable until he does. *(THE ONE WITH THE DOLLHOUSE)* Joanna eventually sleeps with Chandler and then leaves him handcuffed in her office. Rachel and Sophie find him seminaked, and then Chandler takes revenge on Joanna by locking her to a chair. After that, the two break up for good. *(THE ONE WITH THE CUFFS)*

Kathy: Kathy is Joey's girlfriend, but Chandler is in love with her. *(THE ONE WITH JOEY'S NEW GIRLFRIEND)* They kiss, and Joey is furious. Chandler buys new furniture for the apartment in an attempt to apologize for his indiscretion *(THE ONE WHERE CHANDLER CROSSES THE LINE)* and even spends some time trapped in a box, contemplating what he's done. *(THE ONE WITH CHANDLER IN A BOX)* The guys make up, and Chandler dates Kathy, but their relationship ends when he accuses her of sleeping with an actor and then she does. *(THE ONE WITH RACHEL'S CRUSH)*

Marjorie: While visiting a sleep clinic with Joey, Chandler meets Marjorie, who is there to be treated for sleep-talking. She's a beautiful woman, but when she stays over, she screams in her sleep and wakes up both Chandler and Joey. *(THE ONE WITH ALL THE WEDDING DRESSES)*

Monica: See Love Interests: Monica, page 165.

Julie Graff: When Julie overhears Monica talking about her wedding to Chandler, she wishes her good luck but not in a positive way. It later transpires that she was Chandler's camp girlfriend, but he dumped her when she gained 145 pounds in a year. He apologizes to her, and she reveals that his name in camp was Skidmark. *(THE ONE WITH THE NAP PARTNERS)*

Adrienne Turner: While at college, Chandler had a crush on Adrienne, but Ross kissed her at a pregraduation party. *(THE ONE WHERE THE STRIPPER CRIES)*

Rachel: It's revealed that while at college, Chandler kissed Rachel to take revenge on Ross, who had just kissed Chandler's crush Adrienne Turner. *(THE ONE WHERE THE STRIPPER CRIES)*

 ROSS

Carol Willick: Ross's ex-wife and mother of his child, Ben. She was the first woman Ross ever slept with, but after years of marriage, Carol announced that she was in love with a woman named Susan Bunch, and the marriage ended. *(THE ONE WITH THE SONOGRAM AT THE END ONWARD)*

Susan Sallidor: Ross fancied her in college and told her that Chandler was gay just so that she wouldn't like Chandler. *(THE ONE WHERE NANA DIES TWICE)*

Nora Tyler Bing: Chandler's mother kisses Ross in a restaurant when he's upset about Italian guy Paolo. *(THE ONE WITH MRS. BING)*

Kristen: Ross takes a woman who lives in his building on a Valentine's Day date, but when he spends most of the evening talking to his ex-wife Carol, his date leaves. (*THE ONE WITH THE CANDY HEARTS*)

Celia the Bug Lady: Ross takes the curator of insects at the museum to dinner, but when they go back to his apartment, she's tormented by Marcel. When she asks Ross to talk dirty to her, he needs some coaching from Joey. (*THE ONE WITH THE STONED GUY*)

Linda: Ross dates Linda but decides not to call her again. Chandler wonders if it's because she said that the Flintstones could have really happened. (*THE ONE WITH ALL THE POKER*)

Julie: Ross arrives home from China with Julie, an old friend from grad school. For a time, the two get along famously until Ross discovers that Rachel is actually in love with him, and he decides to explore a relationship with Rachel. (*THE ONE WHERE ROSS FINDS OUT*) Julie is last seen entering the coffee shop, where she falls in love with Russ—a Ross look-alike. (*THE ONE WITH RUSS*)

Rachel: Ross has loved Rachel since high school, and after a few missteps, they finally kiss in *THE ONE WHERE ROSS FINDS OUT* and become a couple in *THE ONE WITH THE PROM VIDEO*. Their relationship is on and off throughout the series and includes Ross sleeping with someone else because he thought they were on a break. (*THE ONE WHERE ROSS AND RACHEL TAKE A BREAK*) In the years ahead, Ross and Rachel

drunkenly get married in Vegas (*THE ONE IN VEGAS, PART 2*), get divorced (*THE ONE WITH JOEY'S PORSCHE*), have a baby (*THE ONE WHERE RACHEL HAS A BABY, PART 2*), and then reunite in the final episode (*THE LAST ONE, PARTS 1 AND 2*).

Moth Lady: Ross tells Rachel that he might ask out the curator of moths at the museum. (*THE ONE WITH RUSS*)

Chloe: She works at the Xerox place and has a bellybutton ring. She's first mentioned when Chandler and Ross are talking about

fantasies. (THE ONE WITH THE PRINCESS LEIA FANTASY) Then in THE ONE WITH THE JAM, Chandler asks Joey if he'd prefer a naked Chloe or a big tub of jam. Joey thinks both would be good together. The guys go to the copy shop, and Chloe invites them to a nightclub. At the club, all Chloe wants to talk about is copying, and then she makes a play for Ross, who has just had a massive fallout with Rachel. They end up in bed, and the next morning Ross realizes he's made a dreadful mistake, especially when Rachel turns up at his apartment and Chloe hides behind the door. Rachel soon finds out about Ross's other woman, and the infamous "We were on a break!" quote is born. (THE ONE WHERE ROSS AND RACHEL TAKE A BREAK)

Cailin: Cailin is Ross's date on the night of Joey's play, *Boxing Day*. Unfortunately for her, Ross is obsessed with watching Rachel's date Tommy, so she leaves. Ross is too obsessed with Tommy to care. (THE ONE WITH THE SCREAMER)

Bonnie: Phoebe sets Ross up with Bonnie in THE ONE WITH THE ULTIMATE FIGHTING CHAMPION, and Rachel is fine with it since she remembers Bonnie as a weird bald girl. However, she now has long, blonde hair and is beautiful and really gets along with Ross. The relationship ends when Rachel encourages Bonnie to shave her head again and then admits to Ross that she still loves him. (THE ONE AT THE BEACH)

Amanda: While Ross thinks that Amanda is into him, she actually just wants a baby-sitter. He takes revenge by making some long-distance calls, and then Amanda's date tips him $10. (THE ONE WITH JOEY'S NEW GIRLFRIEND)

Cheryl: A paleontologist doctoral candidate, Cheryl seems perfect, but her apartment is filthy. There are clothes on every surface, junk all over the floor, flies, a hamster and rat roaming around, strange goo on the sofa, and slices of meat and empty food containers everywhere. Ross hates hanging out there, but Cheryl won't go to his apartment because she thinks it has a weird smell. When he breaks up with her, Monica asks if she can clean her apartment. (THE ONE WITH THE DIRTY GIRL)

Girl from Poughkeepsie and Uptown Girl: Ross meets the Girl from Poughkeepsie on a train. She is pretty, smart, and a lot of fun but lives over two hours away. Then he meets Uptown Girl, a woman who lives close by and is pretty, not fun, and maybe even stupid. Based on location only, Ross can't decide which woman to date, so Phoebe recommends he not date either woman. (THE ONE WITH THE GIRL FROM POUGHKEEPSIE)

Emily Waltham: Rachel's boss asks her to take his niece to the opera, but Rachel convinces Ross to go instead. They hit it off and, despite only knowing each other for a few weeks, decide to get married. (THE ONE WITH JOEY'S DIRTY DAY) However, the London wedding is called off when Ross says Rachel's name at the altar instead of Emily's, and then she instructs him never to see Rachel again, which Ross decides he can't agree to. They separate, and Emily later remarries but not before leaving a message on Ross's answering machine saying that she keeps thinking about him. (THE ONE WITH THE RIDE-ALONG)

Elizabeth Hornswoggle: Ross arranges a date with Elizabeth while in Central Perk. They watch a movie in her apartment, but when Ross's new leather pants cause him to burn up, he disappears into the bathroom to take them off. He can't get the too-tight pants on again, and his long absence freaks out Elizabeth. When Ross eventually returns, it's with his pants scrunched up under his arm. (THE ONE WITH ALL THE RESOLUTIONS)

Jen: See Love Interests: Joey, page 160. (THE ONE WITH RACHEL'S INADVERTENT KISS)

Caitlin: Caitlin is a pizza delivery woman who Ross attempts to flirt with by making terrible puns and sharing trivia about the smell of gas. She does eventually give Ross her number but only because Rachel steps in to help. (THE ONE WHERE ROSS CAN'T FLIRT)

Girls in Central Perk: In order to convince Ross that he's still dateable after three divorces, Phoebe recruits the help of three women in Central Perk. He explains his divorce stories, and the women are sympathetic, but then he throws a tantrum and is branded "creepy" by one and "attractive" by another. (THE ONE WHERE ROSS HUGS RACHEL)

Janine: When Janine moves in with Joey, Ross develops a crush on her. (THE ONE WHERE PHOEBE RUNS) It comes to nothing, however, and she ends up dating Joey in THE ONE WITH THE ROUTINE.

Hillary: In preparation for a date with Hillary, Ross whitens his teeth to a spectacular brightness. While having dinner with her, he is too embarrassed to show his mouth but relaxes when she turns off the lights—until the black light turns his teeth fluorescent. (THE ONE WITH ROSS'S TEETH)

Jill: Rachel's spoiled sister Jill comes to stay with her after her dad cuts her off. (THE ONE WITH RACHEL'S SISTER) After accidentally giving her blessing, Rachel is disturbed to discover that Ross and Jill are going on a date. According to Ross, they got along well, especially when he showed her slides of his favorite fossils. Rachel asks him not to go out with Jill again, so Jill takes revenge on her sister by kissing Ross and then breaking his slide projector when he stops her. (THE ONE WHERE CHANDLER CAN'T CRY)

Elizabeth: When Ross starts dating twenty-year-old student Elizabeth, he believes they're a perfect match. However, their relationship is forbidden by the university (THE ONE WHERE ROSS DATES A STUDENT) and frowned upon by her father (THE ONE WHERE ROSS MEETS ELIZABETH'S DAD / THE ONE WHERE PAUL'S THE MAN). They sneak around for a while and even go on spring break together. (THE ONE WITH JOEY'S FRIDGE) In the end, their age difference is too much of a deterrent and they separate, but Elizabeth still manages to deal the final blow when she throws a water balloon at Ross's head. (THE ONE WITH THE PROPOSAL, PART 1)

Whitney: See Phoebe's Love Interests: Kyle, page 172 (THE ONE WITH THE ENGAGEMENT PICTURE)

Library Woman: While guarding the make-out section of the university library, Ross bumps into a woman who previously checked out his dissertation. They end up making out, too, and get caught by security. *(THE ONE WITH ROSS'S LIBRARY BOOK)*

Joan: Joan (often known for her broad back) from the linguistics department is supposed to be Ross's date to Cousin Franny's wedding until Monica insists that he take her instead. *(THE ONE WITH ALL THE CHEESECAKES)*

Kristen Leigh: When Ross sees a woman moving in across the road, he helps by carrying her boxes and gives her a history of the area's sewage system. Despite this, Kristen goes on a date with him but not before she also agrees to go out with Joey. When the guys find out, they both try to impress her but then spend so much time dissing each other that Kristen leaves. *(THE ONE WITH THE CHEAP WEDDING DRESS)*

Cassie: When Ross and Monica's cousin Cassie comes for a visit, she's so beautiful that Chandler, Ross, and Phoebe can't take their eyes off her. However, Cousin Ross is the only one who tries to kiss her! *(THE ONE WITH ROSS AND MONICA'S COUSIN)*

Mona: Mona works at Monica's restaurant and meets Ross at Monica and Chandler's wedding. *(THE ONE AFTER "I DO")* The two go out for a while (and she even loves his semiprecious stone collection), but then Ross freaks out when Mona wants to send out a holiday card with him and asks where the relationship is going. Ross then gives her a key to his apartment and changes the locks. *(THE ONE WITH ROSS'S STEP FORWARD)* Although Mona is okay with Rachel and Ross having a baby, she can't cope with Rachel moving in with Ross (especially because Ross didn't tell her), so she dumps him. *(THE ONE WITH THE BIRTHING VIDEO)*

Kristen: Ross recalls going on a date with a woman called Kristen (not Kristen Leigh), where he tries out Joey's romantic backpacking story. Unfortunately for him, she keeps interrupting, so his seduction attempt goes nowhere. *(THE ONE WITH THE VIDEOTAPE)*

Mrs. Anita Altman: When they were in high school, Rachel saw Ross and the fifty-year-old librarian making out behind the card catalog and created a rumor about it. Ross

was working late in the library when Mrs. Altman needed help with her word jumble, and one thing led to another. Ross describes Anita Altman as being very gentle and tender—may she rest in peace. *(THE ONE WITH THE RUMOR)*

Katie: Ross and Rachel go to a baby store to find everything they need for the baby. Ross picks out a lot of dinosaur items, which impresses Katie the store assistant, who describes him as Indiana Jones. Rachel is furious that the woman was so brazen, but when she turns up at the apartment, Ross is keen to get coffee with her. When Ross returns to the apartment, Rachel describes Katie as a little slutty and asks him not to go out with her—or anyone—again. *(THE ONE WITH THE COOKING CLASS)*

Michelle: After unsuccessfully trying to pick up women in Central Perk, Ross meets newly dumped Michelle. He takes her back to his apartment because she needs to use the toilet but is terrified of going in public. While in the bathroom, the ditzy woman looks through Ross's cabinets and then questions him about the medicines. When she wants to give Ross her phone number, he tells her that if it's meant to be, he'll guess it. Then he and Rachel have an argument about boundaries, and it's revealed that Ross threw away a guy's phone number when he called looking for Rachel. This leads to her moving out of the apartment and back in with Joey. *(THE ONE WHERE MONICA SINGS)*

Boring/Perfect Lady: Joey and Phoebe set up dismal blind dates for Ross and Rachel so that they can see how awful it is in the dating world and then end up with each other. Joey's idea of a bad date is a teacher who is into books, history, foreign movies, and puzzles— in other words, Ross's perfect woman. They decide to cancel the date but not tell Ross, so he ends up being stood up and alone in a restaurant. The waiters all make bets on how long he'll wait before he goes home, and although Ross is insulted, he ends up with some free crab cakes. *(THE ONE WITH THE BLIND DATES)*

Charlie Wheeler: Ross meets Charlie when he's asked to show her and another professor around the campus. He develops a crush on her, but she goes out with Joey after kissing him at a soap opera party. *(THE ONE WITH THE SOAP OPERA PARTY)* Charlie and Ross eventually get together while in Barbados, but then Charlie dumps Ross for her old boyfriend, Benjamin Hobart. *(THE ONE WITH ROSS'S GRANT)*

Joan: After a mix-up with some shopping bags, Ross ends up wearing a woman's shirt. Joey tries to warn him, but Ross reckons he's just jealous and goes on a date with Joan. It ends before it even starts when it's discovered that they're both wearing the same top. *(THE ONE WITH THE BIRTH MOTHER)*

Missy Goldberg: When Chandler and Ross go to their college reunion party, they see Missy Goldberg, a woman they had both liked in college and had a pact not to go out with. Ross arranges a date with her, but when he mentions the pact, she admits that she and Chandler actually used to make out a lot when they were in college—and in the science lab. Ross's turf no less. *(THE ONE WHERE THE STRIPPER CRIES)*

 JOEY

Angela Del Vecchio: A former girlfriend of Joey's, Angela makes a nibbling sound when she eats. She starts dating Bob, and Joey decides to split them up with Monica's help. *(THE ONE WITH THE EAST GERMAN LAUNDRY DETERGENT)* When the guys' kitchen table collapses, Chandler says it was fine until Joey and Angela had sex on it. *(THE ONE WITH THE DOZEN LASAGNAS)* Later, Joey calls Angela to see if he can meet up with her and her boyfriend (because he wants to learn how to kiss men for an acting role). *(THE ONE WITH BARRY AND MINDY'S WEDDING)* Angela is mentioned again when Joey says that she never had a birthday when they were going out—for three years! *(THE ONE WITH THE DIRTY GIRL)*

Obsession Girl: Joey flirts with her on the subway, but it ends in disaster when she sees his City Free Clinic VD poster. *(THE ONE WHERE UNDERDOG GETS AWAY)*

Lorraine: Joey goes on a Valentine's date with Lorraine, a woman who wants to slather his body with chocolate mousse and lick it off. Lorraine brings a friend for Chandler, who turns out to be Janice. *(THE ONE WITH THE CANDY HEARTS)*

Ursula: Joey dates Phoebe's twin sister, Ursula, after meeting her in a restaurant. She ends up ghosting him, and Phoebe steps in to break up with Joey on her sister's behalf. *(THE ONE WITH TWO PARTS, PARTS 1 AND 2)*

Melody: She makes fruit baskets for a living and wants to sleep with Joey, but Joey's taking part in a fertility study and is on a sex ban. Monica encourages Joey to "be there for her," which he does—and then gets bombarded by deliveries of fruit baskets. *(THE ONE WHERE RACHEL FINDS OUT)*

Annabel: She works in the department store where Joey is the Bijan for Men Guy. He asks Annabel out for coffee, but she already has plans with the Hombre Man. However, when Hombre Man is fired, Joey gets his coffee date after all. *(THE ONE WITH THE BREAST MILK)*

Adam's Apple Lady: Joey says that when he first moved to the city, he went out with a great girl, but she had an Adam's apple. *(THE ONE WHERE HECKLES DIES)*

Girls on the Bus: See Love Interests: Chandler, page 151. *(THE ONE WITH THE BABY ON THE BUS)*

Lori: The casting lady for *Days of Our Lives*. She persuades Joey to sleep with her for a guaranteed major role in the soap. (THE ONE WITH RUSS)

Denise DeMarco: Joey says he promoted his penis from a major to a general after sleeping with Denise. (THE ONE WITH RUSS)

Erika Ford: Erika writes a fan letter to Dr. Drake Ramoray and encloses fourteen eyelashes. Even though Erika is a crazy stalker and fully believes she's dating Dr. Ramoray, Joey dates her anyway because he's attracted to her. When she freaks out after seeing Drake kissing a woman on the show, Erika turns up at Joey's apartment. The friends concoct a wild story to get her out of the building and their lives. (THE ONE AFTER THE SUPERBOWL, PART 1)

Shannon Cooper and Stacy Roth: Joey doesn't want to invite Shannon or Stacy to Rachel's birthday party because they steal stuff. In reality, he slept with them but didn't call them back. (THE ONE WITH THE TWO PARTIES)

Margha: Joey meets Margha while the friends play football. A rivalry breaks out between Joey and Chandler, who argue over who will "get her." While she initially chooses Chandler, the fight leads Margha to decide that she wants neither of them. (THE ONE WITH THE FOOTBALL)

Catherine and Donna: Joey mentions that when he first saw ex-girlfriend Catherine walking with her friend Donna, he felt heartbroken because they were laughing. Chandler reminds him that he had sex with them that same afternoon. (THE ONE WHERE CHANDLER CAN'T REMEMBER WHICH SISTER) Chandler mentions a time when Joey broke up with Donna and was upset when they bumped into each other at the supermarket. (THE ONE WHERE PHOEBE RUNS)

Ginger: See Love Interests: Chandler, page 151. (THE ONE WITH PHOEBE'S EX-PARTNER)

Chloe: See Love Interests: Ross, page 153. (THE ONE WHERE ROSS AND RACHEL TAKE A BREAK)

Kate Miller: Kate is an actress who plays Adrienne in one of Joey's plays. At first Joey hates her because she makes fun of his milk spout commercial, but then he realizes he likes her. (THE ONE WITH THE TINY T-SHIRT) Kate is the only person Joey's ever wanted who doesn't want him back, but during a private rehearsal, they sleep together. She could be the person Joey finally falls in love with, except that Kate is also seeing the director and thinks of sleeping with Joey as being caught up in the moment. (THE ONE WITH THE DOLLHOUSE) When the bad reviews come in, the director dumps Kate and Joey takes her home, but then she leaves the city after getting a job on *General Hospital*. (THE ONE WITH THE SCREAMER)

Lauren: Lauren is Kate's understudy. She has a crush on Joey and used to schedule her classes so that she could watch him on *Days of Our Lives*. Joey goes out with her when Kate shows no interest in him, but the short relationship ends when Joey sleeps with Kate and Lauren calls him a pig. When Rachel recognizes her, Lauren tells her that they ran into each other in the hallway after she slept with Joey and then he dumped her the next day. (THE ONE WITH THE DOLLHOUSE)

Beth: After feeling used by Kate, Joey calls an old girlfriend named Beth to apologize for his past behavior. He also wants to apologize to a woman named Jennifer—and her mother. (THE ONE WITH THE DOLLHOUSE)

Kathy: Joey's actress girlfriend who also works for a medical researcher. The two meet in acting class when they're teamed up as partners. Joey is convinced that Chandler doesn't like Kathy, but in reality, he's madly in love with her. (THE ONE WITH JOEY'S NEW GIRLFRIEND / THE ONE WITH THE DIRTY GIRL) The relationship ends when Kathy realizes that she's in love with Chandler. (THE ONE WHERE CHANDLER CROSSES THE LINE)

Casey: Joey cheats on Kathy with a woman he meets in Central Perk. He plans an early dinner with her and a late dinner with Kathy, but then his car breaks down on the parkway. Back at the apartment, Chandler and Kathy grow close and then kiss. (THE ONE WHERE CHANDLER CROSSES THE LINE)

Stripper: Joey sleeps with the stripper hired for Ross's bachelor party, and then the next morning she's gone—and so is the antique wedding ring Ross was going to give to Emily. Thinking that the stripper has stolen it, the boys hire her again to confront her, but she denies knowing anything about the ring. The actual ring thief is the duck, who swallowed it. (THE ONE WITH THE WORST BEST MAN EVER)

Felicity: In London, Joey is approached by bridesmaid Felicity while he's homesick for New York. He and Felicity kiss while he's supposed to be on the lookout for Rachel arriving at the church, and then he misses her storming through the door. (THE ONE WITH ROSS'S WEDDING, PART 2) The next day, Joey interrupts Chandler and Monica by wanting the hotel room so that he can entertain Felicity. (THE ONE AFTER ROSS SAYS RACHEL)

Cynthia: Joey brings Cynthia back to his apartment after their first date. Unfortunately for him, Monica and Chandler have been making out in front of a video camera, and Cynthia mistakenly thinks it's been set up for her. She is last seen sprinting from the apartment, witnessed by Rachel. (THE ONE WITH ROSS'S SANDWICH)

Katie: Joey's new girlfriend is tiny and sweet, but she has a habit of punching him "playfully." Joey finds her punches painful, and when he complains about it, she thinks he's making fun of her and punches him again. In the end, Joey dresses up in several sweaters to break up with Katie, but before he can tell her, she punches Rachel and Rachel kicks her. Katie then dumps Joey and he's thrilled. (THE ONE WITH THE GIRL WHO HITS JOEY)

New Friend: Rachel tells Joey that he should become friends first with potential girlfriends before asking them out. The theory accidentally becomes a pickup line, and when he meets a new friend and her roommate, he sleeps with both. (THE ONE WITH THE COP)

Jen "Hot Girl": Jen lives in Ross's building across from the main apartments. When she waves Joey over, he calculates which apartment she lives in but surprisingly finds himself in Ross's apartment. When he tries again, he faces Ross once more and then gets a reputation as a prowler. Meanwhile, Ross asks Jen out and picks her up for their date. Joey appears again and is so frustrated that he gives up ever being able to find the Hot Girl. (THE ONE WITH RACHEL'S INADVERTENT KISS)

Janine: Janine is an Australian dancer who moves in with Joey after Chandler moves out. (THE ONE WHERE PHOEBE RUNS) At first the relationship is platonic, but they eventually get together during THE ONE WITH THE ROUTINE. Joey loves having Janine as his girlfriend, but she can't stand Monica and Chandler, so Joey breaks it off and she leaves in THE ONE WITH THE APOTHECARY TABLE.

Dry Cleaner Lady: In an effort to get his headshot on the wall of the local dry cleaner's, Joey goes on a date with the assistant. When he returns, his picture is up but with an insult written across it. It turns out that the woman Joey went out with was the wife of the store owner. (THE ONE WHERE PAUL'S THE MAN)

Erin: Joey sleeps with Erin but leaves Rachel to break up with her on his behalf. However, Rachel and Phoebe get along so well with Erin that they don't give her Joey's message, and they persuade him to go out with her again. He ends up falling for her, but Erin doesn't see a future for them and leaves Phoebe and Rachel to break the news to Joey. (THE ONE WITH ROSS'S LIBRARY BOOK)

Cancellation Date: Joey cancels his dinner with Phoebe so that he can go on a date, but

she's furious and lectures him on the values of friendship. Then David comes back from Minsk, and Phoebe wonders if she should change her beliefs. (THE ONE WITH ALL THE CHEESECAKES)

Cecilia Monroe: Cecilia is an actress on *Days of Our Lives* whose character is about to be killed off to give Dr. Drake Ramoray a new brain. Before she leaves, however, Cecilia has time to have a fling with Joey. (THE ONE WITH JOEY'S NEW BRAIN)

Kristen Leigh: See Love Interests: Ross, page 156. (THE ONE WITH THE CHEAP WEDDING DRESS)

Steak Waitress: When Joey complains that the guys went to a steak restaurant instead of having a bachelor party for Chandler, Chandler reminds him that he went home with the waitress. (THE ONE WITH THE STRIPPER)

Mabel: A giggly woman who goes on a date with Joey. Thinking that he's falling in love with Rachel, Joey asks Mabel if she's ever started to look at someone in a different way, and she thinks he means from behind. She then goes into a story about once catching a glimpse of actor Stephen Baldwin. (THE ONE WHERE JOEY DATES RACHEL)

Rachel: When Joey suspects that he's falling in love with Rachel, he's terrified. (THE ONE WHERE JOEY DATES RACHEL) Monica, Chandler, and Phoebe are sympathetic, but when Joey admits his feelings to Ross, Ross is shocked. (THE ONE WITH THE BIRTHING VIDEO) Joey eventually tells Rachel that he's in love with her, but it's not the right time and nothing comes of it. (THE ONE WHERE JOEY TELLS RACHEL) Later, Rachel realizes that she might have a crush on Joey, and they finally share a kiss in Barbados. (THE ONE IN BARBADOS, PARTS 1 AND 2) Although Ross assures them that it's fine, they can't move past their friendship and into a real relationship, so they break up but remain great friends and roommates. (THE ONE WITH ROSS'S TAN)

Jane: When Phoebe tells Joey that she got him a real-life furry playmate, she means a dog, but Joey thinks she's talking about her friend Jane, who he refuses to sleep with again. (THE ONE WITH THE BIRTHING VIDEO)

The Interviewer: When Joey is asked to do a feature for *Soap Opera Digest*, he vows not to say anything career-destroying like he did during another interview. He manages to say all the right things for most of the interview, but when the interviewer comes back into Central Perk to ask what his favorite soap opera is, Joey says that he doesn't watch any because he has a life. Afterward, he contacts her to retract the comments and ends up sleeping with her "a little bit" so she won't print his negative comment. (THE ONE WITH JOEY'S INTERVIEW)

Mary-Ellen: Mary-Ellen is described as smart, funny, and not opposed to threesomes. Phoebe sets Joey up with her at the same time that he's supposed to find a friend for Phoebe. After a disastrous restaurant date, she gets up to leave and tells Joey that she'll stay if he can remember her name. He wishes her good night. (THE ONE WITH THE PEDIATRICIAN)

Hayley: Joey meets Hayley in Central Perk, but when they go back to her apartment, he knows he's been there before. Joey concludes that he and Hayley once had sex, but neither of them can remember. He tries to get past

it but then demands to know why she can't recall their time together. Just then, Hayley's roommate comes home, and he realizes he had sex with the roommate. (THE ONE WITH THE SHARKS)

Molly: When Joey meets Ross and Rachel's nanny, he's immediately attracted to her but is warned against doing anything about it for fear that she'll leave when it all goes wrong. This revelation makes Joey want her even more, so Chandler is enrolled to keep him away. In the end, despite Joey getting some alone time with Molly, he's not destined to win her over since she has a girlfriend and isn't interested in him or men. (THE ONE WITH PHOEBE'S RATS)

Yucky Girl: Joey tells Phoebe that he went out on a date the night before with a woman who was "yuck." Then he decides that they should keep their voices down, because she's still in his bedroom. (THE ONE WITH THE BLIND DATES)

Charlie: Joey meets Charlie when Ross brings her to a rooftop soap opera party. (THE ONE WITH THE SOAP OPERA PARTY) They're not exactly suited for each other because she's an intellectual and he's . . . Joey. Still, they go out with each other until a trip to Barbados, when they break up and Joey gets together with Rachel and Charlie goes out with Ross. (THE ONE IN BARBADOS, PARTS 1 AND 2)

Laura: Laura is Monica and Chandler's social worker when they want to adopt a child. Unfortunately, she once spent the night with Joey, he never called her again, and she's still furious. When Joey knocks on the door, Monica and Chandler try to keep him out, but he climbs up the fire escape, is seen by Laura, and fabricates a story about how she never called him back and broke his heart. *(THE ONE WITH THE HOME STUDY)*

Mandy: Phoebe says that Joey slept with her friend Mandy and then forgot she existed. *(THE ONE WITH THE BIRTH MOTHER)*

Sarah: Phoebe does not want Joey to date Sarah, but he persuades her to introduce them. The day after the date, Joey refuses to call Sarah because she took some fries off his plate. Apparently, Joey doesn't share food. When he goes out with her again, he orders more food for the table, but she still tries to take his, and it ends up all over the floor. When Sarah leaves to call her office, Joey steals the dessert from her plate and tells her he's not even sorry. *(THE ONE WITH THE BIRTH MOTHER)*

MONICA

Paul the Wine Guy: Monica sleeps with Paul after he tells her he's been impotent since his wife left. Afterward, she finds out that he also slept with her colleague, so she stamps on his watch. *(THE ONE WHERE MONICA GETS A ROOMMATE)*

Steve: The friends make fun of Monica's ex-boyfriend Steve, who has a lisp. *(THE ONE WITH THE THUMB)*

Alan: Alan is Monica's new boyfriend whom her friends are obsessed with. The group plays sports with Alan, rows on the lake with him, and thinks he's the best date Monica has ever had. Unfortunately, Monica is not too keen on Alan. When she breaks up with him, he's relieved because he can't stand her friends. *(THE ONE WITH THE THUMB)*

Jason Hurley: Monica once dated Jason, but he slept with Phoebe a couple of hours later. It's brought up again during the *Be Your Own Windkeeper* quiz, when Rachel says that Phoebe actually waited just one hour. *(THE ONE WITH GEORGE STEPHANOPOULOS / THE ONE WHERE EDDIE WON'T GO)*

Bob: Joey wants to get back together with ex-girlfriend Angela, but first he needs Monica's help to break up Angela and her new beau Bob. Joey tells Monica that Angela and Bob are siblings. Monica likes Bob until she witnesses his "sister" kissing his ear. Joey comes clean about Angela and Bob not being related and they work together to split the couple up. *(THE ONE WITH THE EAST GERMAN LAUNDRY DETERGENT)*

Fun Bobby: Monica invites Fun Bobby to a holiday party, but Bobby is depressed because his grandfather just died. *(THE ONE WITH THE MONKEY)* Phoebe tells everyone that the underwear on the telephone pole outside is Monica's after Monica and Fun Bobby had sex on the terrace. *(THE ONE WITH PHOEBE'S HUSBAND)* Fun Bobby returns another time but has now given up alcohol and is the most boring boyfriend ever. Monica turns to alcohol to cope with their dates, and Bobby thinks she has a problem and breaks up with her. *(THE ONE WITH RUSS)*

Coma Guy: Monica says "woo-hoo!" to a guy on the street who she thinks is cute, which causes him to get distracted and be hit by an ambulance. Monica and Phoebe then argue over who will look after him in the hospital. When he wakes up, he's not interested in either of them. *(THE ONE WITH MRS. BING)*

Howard: Nicknamed the "I Win Guy" because he would shout "I win" every time he and

Monica had sex. They dated for two months. (*THE ONE WITH THE CANDY HEARTS*)

Scotty Jared: He's so hairy that when Monica burns his photo during the Valentine's Day cleansing ritual, the other girls think he's wearing a sweater. (*THE ONE WITH THE CANDY HEARTS*)

Dr. Michael Mitchell and Dr. Jeffrey Rosen: While pretending to be each other for insurance purposes, Monica and Rachel date the doctors. The girls' paranoia and bickering make them look crazy. (*THE ONE WITH TWO PARTS, PART 2*)

Ethan: A young man who tells Monica he's a virgin college student. She sleeps with him and then confesses that she lied about her age—she isn't twenty-two; she's twenty-six. That's okay with Ethan because he lied, too—he's not a college student; he's actually a high school senior. (*THE ONE WITH THE ICK FACTOR*)

Jean-Claude Van Damme: Rachel and Monica fight over who will go out with Jean-Claude while he's making a movie in New York. Rachel goes out with him once and then reluctantly asks him to date Monica, but she

also tells him that Monica wants a threesome with him and Drew Barrymore. (*THE ONE AFTER THE SUPERBOWL, PART 2*)

Roy Gublick: Roy saw *Star Wars* 317 times, and his name was in the paper. He is seen as Monica's prom date in a home movie. (*THE ONE WITH THE PROM VIDEO*)

Dr. Richard Burke: Eye doctor Richard is the divorced friend of Monica's parents. He has known Monica since she was a kid, but when she caters a party for him, he starts to see her in a different way. (*THE ONE WHERE ROSS AND RACHEL . . . YOU KNOW*) Richard is one of the great loves of Monica's life, but when he's reluctant to have any more children, the couple part. (*THE ONE WITH BARRY AND MINDY'S WEDDING*) He returns briefly for a fling in *THE ONE WHERE MONICA AND RICHARD ARE FRIENDS* and then tries to win Monica back when she's about to become engaged to Chandler. (*THE ONE WITH THE PROPOSAL, PARTS 1 AND 2*)

Julio: A waiter at the Moondance Diner, who Monica starts to date. Julio writes her a poem called "The Empty Vase," which Phoebe translates to mean that he thinks Monica is empty. When confronted, Julio claims the poem is about all American women, so Monica breaks up with him and hires a barbershop quartet to sing an insulting song for him. (*THE ONE WITH ALL THE JEALOUSY*)

Mischa: Phoebe introduces Monica to Mischa, the interpreter for her own date, Sergei. They get along so well that Mischa barely has time to translate anything, and he and Sergei have a falling-out. The translator then resigns and takes Monica to the Rainbow Room to spend his diplomatic coupons. (*THE ONE WHERE ROSS AND RACHEL TAKE A BREAK*)

Pete Becker: Pete is a customer at the
Moondance Diner. When Pete leaves
Monica a $20,000 tip with his phone
number, she thinks it's a joke—until
Chandler reveals that Pete is the megarich
inventor of Moss 865, a computer program
used around the world. (THE ONE WITH
THE HYPNOSIS TAPE) Monica continues to
turn Pete down but then falls for him in
THE ONE WITH A CHICK AND A DUCK. Pete
decides he wants to be the Ultimate Fighting
Champion in THE ONE WITH ROSS'S THING, but
after seeing him continually injured, Monica
calls the relationship off in THE ONE WITH THE
ULTIMATE FIGHTING CHAMPION.

Chip Matthews: Chip is the popular guy from
high school who took Rachel to the prom.
Monica goes on a date with him, but he
hasn't changed at all. Chip rides the same
motorbike, hangs with his old friends, still
plays childish jokes, lives with his parents,
and still works at the movie theater. After
he offers her posters for her room, Monica
dumps him. (THE ONE WITH THE CAT)

Dr. Timothy Burke: Timothy is Richard's son,
who Monica invites to Thanksgiving dinner.
They're attracted to each other, but when
Monica kisses him, she discovers that he's
just like his dad. (THE ONE WITH CHANDLER
IN A BOX)

Chandler Bing: Monica first gets together
with Chandler while they're in London for
Ross's wedding to Emily. (THE ONE WITH
ROSS'S WEDDING, PART 2) Looking for a
distraction after being mistaken for Ross's
mother, Monica goes to Chandler's hotel
room looking for Joey, as revealed in THE
ONE WITH THE TRUTH ABOUT LONDON. Only
he's not there, and she and Chandler end up
in bed together. The couple stays together

for the rest of the series and eventually gets
married, buys a house, and, in THE LAST
ONE, PARTS 1 AND 2, adopts two babies, Jack
and Erica.

Dan: While Phoebe gives birth at the hospital,
Rachel arranges a date for herself, as well
as a date for Monica, with a nurse called
Dan. Dan is working as a nurse to help pay
for medical school and was also involved
in the Gulf War. Monica is already dating
Chandler, but when he describes their
relationship as "just goofing around," she tries
to make him jealous by flirting with Dan. It
works, and Monica and Chandler become
exclusive. (THE ONE HUNDREDTH)

Stuart: Monica wonders why she wasn't invited
to Cousin Franny's wedding, but when she
turns up anyway, she discovers that she once
went out with Stuart, the groom. (THE ONE
WITH ALL THE CHEESECAKES)

RACHEL

Barry Farber: Rachel's former fiancé, whom she left at the altar in the first episode. Described as looking like Mr. Potato Head, he appears first in *THE ONE WITH THE SONOGRAM AT THE END* and recurs several times, including when he and Rachel embark on a fling even though he's engaged to her friend Mindy. *(THE ONE WITH THE EVIL ORTHODONTIST)* Later, Rachel reluctantly acts as Mindy's bridesmaid. *(THE ONE WITH BARRY AND MINDY'S WEDDING)*

Tony DeMarco: Monica mentions that Rachel once dated Tony DeMarco. Monica's current relationship with Paul is "like that with feelings." *(THE ONE WHERE MONICA GETS A ROOMMATE)*

Paolo: First appears as the owner of a lost cat in *THE ONE WITH THE BLACKOUT*. Rachel and Paolo enjoy a passionate relationship (much to the disgust of a jealous Ross) until Paolo makes a pass at Phoebe when she gives him a professional massage. *(THE ONE WITH THE DOZEN LASAGNAS)* Rachel and Paolo later have a one-night stand when Rachel is upset about Ross and Julie's relationship, before finally calling off their relationship for good. *(THE ONE WITH ROSS'S NEW GIRLFRIEND)*

Pete Carney: Mentioned as the Weeper, a guy who cried every time he had sex with Rachel. *(THE ONE WITH THE CANDY HEARTS)*

Adam Ritter: Rachel throws his boxer shorts into the fire during the Valentine's Day cleansing ritual. *(THE ONE WITH THE CANDY HEARTS)*

Dr. Michael Mitchell and Dr. Jeffrey Rosen: See Love Interests: Monica, page 164.

Billy Dreskin: Rachel once had sex on her parents' bed with Billy Dreskin, a boy whose father tried to put Dr. Green out of business. *(THE ONE WITH TWO PARTS, PART 2)*

Carl: A boring man Rachel met at Central Perk. She's on a date with him when Ross announces he's taking a trip to China. The next time we see Carl, he's lecturing Rachel on the balcony, and Rachel has an imaginary conversation with Ross before he heads to the airport. *(THE ONE WHERE RACHEL FINDS OUT)*

Ross: See Love Interests: Ross, page 153.

Michael: Rachel goes out with Michael, and it's the first date he's had since his divorce. Unfortunately, drunken Rachel is more interested in talking about Ross, and Michael gets through the date by playing the movie *Diner* in his head. *(THE ONE WHERE ROSS FINDS OUT)*

Russ: Russ is a Ross look-alike who even has the same personality and style. Everyone except Rachel can see just how close the two guys are, and she ends up dating Russ. She eventually sees the similarities and breaks up with him, and then he meets Julie. *(THE ONE WITH RUSS)*

Jean-Claude Van Damme: See Love Interests: Monica, page 164.

Casey: A guy Rachel meets at the movies. Ross takes a message for Rachel from Casey, but he hides it in the cupboard so that she doesn't see it. *(THE ONE WITH THE PROM VIDEO)*

Chip Matthews: Chip is a popular guy in high school. He takes Rachel to the prom and then has sex with Amy Welsh. *(THE ONE WITH THE PROM VIDEO)* Also see page 165.

Mark: Mark is Rachel's colleague at Bloomingdale's and Ross's nemesis—Ross has always suspected Mark of liking Rachel when Ross was going out with her. *(THE ONE WHERE CHANDLER CAN'T REMEMBER WHICH SISTER ONWARD)* After Rachel's breakup with Ross, Mark tells Rachel that he has a crush on her, and they go on a date. Ross sees them leaving and then spends hours spying from Chandler's apartment. Rachel realizes that she's just dating Mark to take revenge on Ross, so she asks him to leave. *(THE ONE WITH THE TINY T-SHIRT)*

Tommy: Tommy seems sweet on the outside but screams at people for no reason. Ross is the first to witness Tommy's temper when they discover a couple sitting in their seats at the movie theater and Tommy loses it. Ross tells Rachel, but he's branded jealous, and then Tommy screams again when Ross bumps into him while holding hot coffee. The mean guy finally gets caught when the friends walk in on him screaming at the chick and duck. *(THE ONE WITH THE SCREAMER)*

Josh: In an attempt to make Ross jealous, Rachel dates a college guy. He steals money and a leather jacket from Rachel, but she's thrilled when he gives her a bracelet—one

that he stole from Monica. *(THE ONE WITH JOEY'S NEW GIRLFRIEND)*

Patrick: Chandler sets Rachel up with Patrick but makes the mistake of telling him that she's only looking for a fling. When she finds out, Rachel is concerned that Patrick will get the wrong impression, especially since she slept with him on the first date. Chandler tries to make things right by telling Patrick that Rachel is looking for a serious relationship, so he dumps her. *(THE ONE WITH THE GIRL FROM POUGHKEEPSIE)*

Joshua: Joshua is a newly divorced customer at Bloomingdale's who asks Rachel for her help picking out a new wardrobe. Rachel is besotted but is frustrated when he doesn't show much interest in her. *(THE ONE WITH RACHEL'S CRUSH)* They do eventually get together in *THE ONE WITH THE FAKE PARTY*, but Rachel scares him off by suggesting marriage after four dates. *(THE ONE WITH ALL THE WEDDING DRESSES)*

Dave: Monica decides that Rachel should talk to Dave, a customer in Central Perk, but Gunther is so upset that he bans him from the coffee shop. The date goes well but ends early when Rachel decides to console Ross instead of inviting Dave in. *(THE ONE WITH ALL THE KISSING)*

Dan: See Love Interests: Monica, page 165. *(THE ONE HUNDREDTH)*

Danny: While looking for a waffle iron, Rachel and Monica encounter a yeti in the storage room and throw a bug bomb at it. In reality, the yeti is a guy named Danny, who has just moved in downstairs. *(THE ONE WITH THE YETI)* Rachel develops a crush on him but is sure he's playing hard to get. When they do organize a date, Rachel is disturbed by his inappropriate interaction with his sister and decides not to go on the date after all. (THE ONE WITH THE INAPPROPRIATE SISTER)

Patrick and Eldad: When Rachel needs a date, Phoebe finds Patrick, a chin-dimpled lawyer who does volunteer work, while Chandler and Monica find Eldad, a sweet-smelling guy who is smart, funny, and a great dancer. When they all meet at Central Perk, Phoebe tells Patrick to give Rachel some money, while Chandler demands Eldad dance for her. In the end, Rachel feels too much pressure from Phoebe, Monica, and Chandler to pick the guy they chose for her, so she chooses neither of them but is interested in what conditioner Eldad uses. (THE ONE WITH JOEY'S FRIDGE)

Sebastian: While Monica, Chandler, and Phoebe fight over whose guy is best for Rachel, Rachel meets Sebastian at the newsstand. The friends grill him so much that they scare him off, and he even refuses to give Rachel his phone number. (THE ONE WITH JOEY'S FRIDGE)

Paul: When Ross dates his student Elizabeth, he's forced to meet her scary dad, Paul. (THE ONE WHERE ROSS MEETS ELIZABETH'S DAD) Paul may dislike Ross, but he takes an immediate liking to Rachel, and they start seeing each other—that is, until Rachel tries to get him to open up by talking about his childhood memories, and he can't stop crying. (THE ONE WITH THE RING)

Charlie: While arguing about Rachel stealing Monica's thunder during her engagement celebrations, Monica mentions that at her sweet sixteen, Rachel went to third base with Cousin Charlie. Rachel assures her she only

did that because the party was so boring. (THE ONE WITH MONICA'S THUNDER)

Tag: Rachel employs Tag as her assistant because she has a crush on him. (THE ONE WITH RACHEL'S ASSISTANT) Even though it's against company rules, the two begin dating in THE ONE WHERE CHANDLER DOESN'T LIKE DOGS. He's younger than Rachel, and although she really likes him, their romance is doomed when she turns thirty and decides she needs to find a serious relationship. (THE ONE WHERE THEY ALL TURN THIRTY) Tag returns when Phoebe thinks he's the father of Rachel's baby. (THE ONE WITH THE RED SWEATER)

Matt Wire, Mark Lynn, Ben Wyatt: According to Monica, Rachel slept with these men on the first date. (THE ONE WITH ALL THE CANDY)

Cell Phone Guy: See Love Interests: Phoebe, page 172. (THE ONE WITH JOEY'S NEW BRAIN)

Former Teacher: Rachel reveals that she once had a crush on a teacher. When Joey asks how she got over him, she replies that she didn't—she got under him instead. (THE ONE WITH JOEY'S AWARD)

Melissa Warburton: Rachel claims that she once made out with former college friend and party planner Melissa, but Phoebe doesn't believe her. At first Melissa denies all knowledge but then admits the kiss and reveals that she's still in love with Rachel. (THE ONE WITH RACHEL'S BIG KISS)

Cash: A pregnant Rachel meets actor Cash on the set of *Days of Our Lives*. They go on a date, which freaks Ross out, especially when he discovers that his unborn child will be going on a ferry. In the end, Cash bolts when

Rachel tells him she's pregnant, and she has a heartfelt chat with Ross. (THE ONE WITH RACHEL'S DATE)

Billy Trat: When Rachel discovers that Ross and his high school friend Will Colbert created a rumor in high school about her having a tiny penis, she surmises that this is why Billy Trat never strayed past her upper body. (THE ONE WITH THE RUMOR)

Roger: When Rachel's pregnancy is making her hormones crazy, Phoebe brings home Roger, a bespectacled virgin who has agreed to have sex with her. Rachel turns down the offer, and Phoebe is furious, demanding that she tell Roger herself, since he was really looking forward to it. (THE ONE WITH ROSS'S STEP FORWARD)

Joey: See Love Interests: Joey, page 161.

Timmy: While arguing during Thanksgiving, Rachel's sister Amy accuses her of stealing Timmy from her twenty years ago. Rachel claims that he was her boyfriend first and Amy made out with him. (THE ONE WITH RACHEL'S OTHER SISTER)

Bill: Rachel and Phoebe go out for the evening for the first time since the birth of Emma. While in a bar, Bill and his friend send over drinks, and then the four get talking. It turns out that Bill lives in the same building as Rachel's grandmother and that he calls her Spuds. On discovering that she's single, Bill asks for Rachel's number, but when he calls later in the evening, Ross answers, writes down the message, and hides it. (THE ONE WITH RACHEL'S PHONE NUMBER)

Gavin: When Rachel first met her new colleague Gavin, she thought he was pompous and obnoxious, but now she decides to take the high road and be nice to him. Even though she doesn't really want him at her birthday party, he comes anyway and gifts her a scarf. They kiss on the balcony—in full view of Ross from across the street. (THE ONE WITH PHOEBE'S RATS) Later, Rachel pretends she's sick so that she doesn't need to go to work and face Gavin. He turns up at her apartment with soup, but nothing can ever happen between them since Rachel still has issues with Ross. (THE ONE WHERE MONICA SINGS)

Steve: Joey and Phoebe set up awful blind dates for Rachel and Ross so that they'll see how awful it is in the dating world and then end up with each other. Phoebe sends Rachel on a date with Steve, an ex–massage client who is creepy and weird. During the evening, he tells Rachel that he's not good-looking, rich, or funny; lost his restaurant to drugs; lives in a studio apartment with two other guys; and is pretty sure he's infertile. At the end of the evening, Steve asks Rachel if she'd like to make love to him, and when she says no, he's relieved because "it doesn't work anyway." He gifts her a T-shirt that has "FBI—Female Body Inspector" emblazoned on the front, which Ross is happy to take. (THE ONE WITH THE BLIND DATES)

  PHOEBE

Carl: Phoebe mentions that she once dated Carl, a man who ate chalk. (THE ONE WHERE MONICA GETS A ROOMMATE)

Tony: Phoebe breaks up with Tony because it's no longer fun, particularly because of his hunger strike. (THE ONE WITH THE EAST GERMAN LAUNDRY DETERGENT)

David: A scientist and Phoebe's first true love. They meet in Central Perk while Phoebe is singing, but David ends up moving to Minsk to work on a three-year research grant. *(THE ONE WITH THE MONKEY)* He returns for a quick visit in *THE ONE WITH ALL THE CHEESECAKES*, and then in *THE ONE WITH THE MALE NANNY*, David turns up at Phoebe's apartment and asks if she's seeing anyone. Despite currently dating Mike, Phoebe says "no" at first and then later kisses David just as Mike walks in. By the end of the season, David is back from Minsk and planning to propose until Mike returns and reunites with Phoebe. *(THE ONE IN BARBADOS, PARTS 1 AND 2)*

Coma Guy: See Love Interests: Monica, page 163. *(THE ONE WITH MRS. BING)*

The Puppet Guy: When Joey's dad is introduced to Phoebe's new boyfriend, he asks what happened to the Puppet Guy, but it's a sore subject. *(THE ONE WITH THE BOOBIES)* Later, the girls take the *Be Your Own Windkeeper* quiz, and Rachel and Monica remind Phoebe that not only did the Puppet Guy wash his feet in the pool of her inner power, but his puppet did, too. *(THE ONE WHERE EDDIE WON'T GO)*

Roger: A psychiatrist who psychoanalyzes everyone, causing them to hate him. Phoebe thinks Roger is great until he goes on a rant about how the whole group is dysfunctional. *(THE ONE WITH THE BOOBIES)* Phoebe contemplates going back out with him but then admits that he was mean and creepy. *(THE ONE WITH THE CANDY HEARTS)*

Nokululu Oonk Ah Ah: During the Valentine's Day cleansing ritual, Phoebe burns a receipt from a dinner she had with Nokululu. *(THE ONE WITH THE CANDY HEARTS)*

Jason Hurley: Phoebe admits to sleeping with Jason just a couple of hours after he and Monica had broken up. It's later revealed that it was actually just an hour after they broke up. *(THE ONE WITH GEORGE STEPHANOPOULOS)*

Randy Brown: Phoebe's childhood boyfriend. Phoebe's sister, Ursula, stole him from her and broke his heart, and then Randy hated both of them. *(THE ONE WITH TWO PARTS, PART 1)*

Duncan: Phoebe's gay ice-skater husband, who she was madly in love with. Phoebe married Duncan six years ago because he needed a green card, and then he moved away. He returns to tell her he wants a divorce and is actually straight and wants to marry somebody else. *(THE ONE WITH PHOEBE'S HUSBAND)*

Scott: A guy who won't sleep with Phoebe because he apparently understands how emotional sex can be for a woman, so he doesn't want to rush things. Phoebe begs him to sleep with her and says he doesn't have to call her again if he doesn't want to. Joey says this guy is his God. *(THE ONE WHERE ROSS FINDS OUT)*

Rob Donan: He kisses Phoebe after he schedules her to perform in a children's library. *(THE ONE AFTER THE SUPERBOWL, PART 1)*

Ryan: A military man who surfaces from his submarine every couple of years. Phoebe met him while she was playing guitar in Washington Square Park, when Ryan threw saltwater taffy in her tip bucket because he didn't have any money. Ryan visits Phoebe while she has chicken pox and then catches it himself. *(THE ONE WITH THE CHICKEN POX)*

Malcolm: An ex-boyfriend of Ursula's who follows Phoebe, thinking she's Ursula. Phoebe dates him but then finds out that he's still stalking Ursula. *(THE ONE WITH THE JAM)*

Noisy Man: Phoebe tells off the noisy man upstairs but ends up falling for him. They have a short but noisy fling, which ends when the friends hear him having sex with another woman. *(THE ONE WHERE CHANDLER CAN'T REMEMBER WHICH SISTER)*

Robert: Phoebe meets Robert in the park. He jogs and swims and offers to teach Phoebe how to play various sports. He's a great guy with a big problem—he wears loose shorts and no underwear, causing Chandler and Ross to get an eyeful. In the end, Gunther is the only one brave enough to tell Robert to "put the mouse back in the house." *(THE ONE WHERE MONICA AND RICHARD ARE FRIENDS)*

Sergei: A foreign diplomat who Phoebe meets while giving free massages outside the UN. He's dashing, sophisticated, and speaks no English so he comes with an interpreter, Mischa. Phoebe invites Monica along on their date. Monica and Mischa get along so well that he doesn't have time to tell Phoebe what Sergei is saying. When they leave, Phoebe tries to teach Sergei some basic English. *(THE ONE WHERE ROSS AND RACHEL TAKE A BREAK)*

Vince and Jason: Vince is a burly fireman, while Jason is a sensitive kindergarten teacher. Phoebe secretly dates both of them at the same time because she can't decide who she prefers better. In the end, the decision is made for her when the men bump into each other in Central Perk. Jason is upset that Phoebe slept with Vince and not him, while Vince the fireman is furious that she made a candlelight dinner in the park for Jason. *(THE ONE WITH ROSS'S THING)*

Rick: One of Phoebe's massage clients and a Greenpeace supporter. Phoebe has a crush on Rick, and during one treatment she bites him. Joey recommends that she think of something boring while massaging him, but she gets so carried away that the hours pass by. Phoebe then admits to Rick she has a crush on him, and they make out, only to be caught by Phoebe's boss. The would-be fling ends when it's revealed that Rick is married and Phoebe gets fired. *(THE ONE WITH THE BALLROOM DANCING)*

Phil Huntley: After falling in love with a fur coat, Phoebe says it's the best thing she's ever had wrapped around her—including Phil Huntley, who she considers to be "fine." *(THE ONE WITH THE YETI)*

Larry: Phoebe meets Larry when he's doing a health inspection at Monica's restaurant. Phoebe loves his power and the way he can shut down a restaurant over the slightest violation. However, it soon gets annoying, especially when Larry spies a carton of milk sitting on the counter at Central Perk and sees Gunther walking through with bags of trash. (THE ONE WHERE ROSS MOVES IN)

Gary: Phoebe meets Gary after finding his police badge in Central Perk. (THE ONE WITH THE COP) They date for a while, but when Gary wants to move in together, Phoebe hesitates. Eventually, she decides to take the chance, but then Gary shoots a bird that's singing outside the window, and the relationship is over. (THE ONE WITH THE BALL)

Mysterious Husband: When talking about weddings, Phoebe seems shocked to discover that if you marry in Las Vegas, your marriage is legitimate outside Vegas, too. She then shrugs and says, "Oh well," implying that she may have once been married in Vegas but had decided it wasn't legal. (THE ONE AFTER VEGAS)

Kenny the Copy Guy: While using the photocopier at Ralph Lauren, Phoebe makes out with someone she thinks is Ralph Lauren himself. She then finds out that her new love is actually Kenny the copy guy, but she sleeps with him again anyway. (THE ONE WITH ROSS'S TEETH)

Kyle: Also known as Cute Coffee House Guy and Hums While He Pees, Kyle dates Phoebe while in the middle of a divorce from his wife, Whitney. When Whitney turns up at Central Perk, Ross is persuaded into talking to her, and they hit it off. The new relationships lead to arguments between Ross and Phoebe, with Ross defending Whitney and Phoebe defending Kyle. In the end, Kyle and Whitney decide to get back together. (THE ONE WITH THE ENGAGEMENT PICTURE)

Cell Phone Guy: When a cute guy leaves his cell phone in Central Perk, Rachel and Phoebe argue over who will answer it when he calls. When an older gentleman shows up at their door and it turns out the cute guy was just his assistant, Phoebe is even more attracted to the older gentleman. Rachel gives her blessing for Phoebe to go out with him. (THE ONE WITH JOEY'S NEW BRAIN)

Jake: Phoebe meets Jake in Central Perk and gets along so well with him that an engaged Monica freaks out that she'll never have a new boyfriend again. (THE ONE WITH JOEY'S AWARD) Later, Jake wears Phoebe's panties, which inspires Joey to try out female underwear for himself. (THE ONE WITH CHANDLER'S DAD)

Tim: Phoebe meets Tim at Monica's restaurant. At first, she thinks he's really nice, but then his sweetness starts to drive her crazy. She wants to dump him but gets angry that Monica is also planning to fire him, because that means she can't dump him. They end up firing him and dumping him, but then Monica takes pity and rehires him. (THE ONE WITH RACHEL'S DATE)

Eric: Phoebe meets second-grade teacher Eric at Monica's Halloween party. Eric is Ursula's fiancé, but they break up when Phoebe tells him that Ursula has been lying to him about a lot of things. Eric and Phoebe date for a short time, but he can't get over the fact that she looks so much like Ursula—especially when he sleeps with Ursula by mistake, thinking she's Phoebe. (THE ONE WITH THE HALLOWEEN PARTY / THE ONE WITH THE STAIN)

Don: Phoebe dates Don, but she thinks he might actually be Monica's soul mate (even though Monica is married to Chandler) because they have a lot in common. When questioned as to why she would go out with someone she thought was better suited to somebody else, Phoebe reckons it's okay because a girl needs to eat. (THE ONE WHERE JOEY TELLS RACHEL)

Jim Nelson: Phoebe keeps seeing the same man everywhere she goes, so when he finally asks her out, she says yes. They go out for dinner, but he is weird and creepy, comments on Phoebe's breasts, and wants to know if she is wild and loves to party. Jim writes wildly unpopular erotic novels for children and has a PhD—a Pretty Huge . . . Phoebe doesn't stay to learn more. (THE ONE WITH THE TEA LEAVES)

Parker: Phoebe meets Parker at the dry cleaner. (THE ONE WITH THE TEA LEAVES) At first, she thinks he's perfect, with an incredible zest for life, but her friends think he's too annoying. When Phoebe catches Ross making fun of him, she lectures everyone about their judgment and then describes their collective dating record as a who's who of human crap. Despite her enthusiasm, however, Phoebe breaks up with Parker because he's too positive about everything, and she can no longer bear him acting like Santa Claus on Prozac. At Disneyland. Getting laid. (THE ONE IN MASSAPEQUA)

Cliff: While Rachel is in labor, Phoebe meets a man with a broken leg. She wants to know more about him, so she enlists Joey (as Dr. Drake Ramoray) to help. Cliff is a widower, and he and Phoebe get along really well—until he realizes that Phoebe got Joey to play a fake doctor to interrogate him. (THE ONE WHERE RACHEL HAS A BABY, PART 1) In an effort to help, Joey tells Cliff about Phoebe's past, including that she was once married

to a gay ice dancer; she gave birth to her brother's triplets; and her twin sister used to do porn. (THE ONE WHERE RACHEL HAS A BABY, PART 2)

Mike: Phoebe meets Mike through a blind date set up by Joey (not that Joey knew him—he was a stranger who happened to be in Central Perk at the right time). Mike is a lawyer, but just before he meets Phoebe, he gives up his practice to become a pianist. After a shaky start, Mike becomes the love of Phoebe's life, although having just divorced his first wife, he doesn't think he'll ever marry again. They break up for a time but then get back together, Mike proposes, and the two have a romantic outdoor winter wedding. (THE ONE WITH THE PEDIATRICIAN ONWARD)

Vikram: When Ross compliments Phoebe for never having a serious relationship, she is so upset, it ruins her first date with Mike. To try and persuade him that Phoebe isn't normally so neurotic, Ross visits Mike but accidentally tells him that Phoebe has never had a serious boyfriend. He then backtracks and tells Mike that she was once in a six-year relationship with a guy named Vikram, a kite designer who used to date Oprah. When Phoebe finds out, she's furious but ends up playing along with the story. Phoebe finally admits that her former boyfriend is imaginary, but then the phone rings and it's Ross—acting as Vikram. (THE ONE WITH THE SHARKS)

Pablo Diaz, Brady Smith, Guy in Van, Bob Greenmore, Jethro Tull: Men mentioned in Phoebe's little black book. Guy in Van was her first love, Jethro Tull is a rock band, and Bob has passed away having lived a full life, which included being in the first wave at Omaha Beach. (THE ONE WITH ROSS'S GRANT)

THINGS THAT HAPPEN WHILE MONICA AND CHANDLER ARE HIDING THEIR RELATIONSHIP

Monica and Chandler don't want anyone to know they're dating yet, though this decision leads to more than a few dramas and misunderstandings.

- Monica has to hide from Joey under the water during a bubble bath with Chandler. *(THE ONE WITH ALL THE KISSING)*

- Chandler accidentally kisses Monica in front of the girls, so he has to kiss them, too. *(THE ONE WITH ALL THE KISSING)*

- Rachel walks in on Monica in a compromising position while Monica is waiting for Chandler. This leads to Monica pretending that she's dating a waiter at work. *(THE ONE WHERE PHOEBE HATES PBS)*

- Monica and Chandler do it in a closet at Central Perk. *(THE ONE WHERE PHOEBE HATES PBS)*

- When Joey walks in on Monica and Chandler in the middle of the night, Monica and Chandler tell him that it's really 9 a.m. *(THE ONE WITH THE KIPS)*

- Chandler loses his underwear in the back of Monica's sofa. Phoebe finds them, and Joey has to pretend they're his. *(THE ONE WITH ROSS'S SANDWICH)*

- Rachel finds a female razor in Chandler's bathroom, so Joey has to pretend he's playing a woman in a play and ends up with his legs shaved. *(THE ONE WITH ROSS'S SANDWICH)*

- When Monica and Chandler set up a video camera to record themselves having sex, Joey's date thinks that he's set up a video camera so that he can tape *them* having sex, so he has to pretend to Rachel that he makes low-budget adult movies. (THE ONE WITH ROSS'S SANDWICH)

- Monica gives Chandler a nude Polaroid of herself, which Joey finds. When Rachel sees Joey looking at it, she assumes that he has a peephole from which he takes secret pics of them. (THE ONE WITH ROSS'S SANDWICH)

- When Joey rebels against telling lies, he invents a story where he slept with Monica in London and now she's obsessed with him. The story develops into everyone thinking that Monica has stolen Joey's underwear, given him naked pictures, and tried to entice him with a video camera. (THE ONE WITH ROSS'S SANDWICH)

- Rachel hears Monica calling Chandler "Mr. Big," which forces Monica to lie that she was actually calling him "Mr. Bigot" because he tells racist jokes. (THE ONE WITH ALL THE RESOLUTIONS)

- Monica pretends that she's Chandler's cleaning lady when Rachel catches her in his apartment. (THE ONE WITH CHANDLER'S WORK LAUGH)

- Rachel, Phoebe, and later Ross see Monica and Chandler doing it against the window. (THE ONE WHERE EVERYBODY FINDS OUT)

- Monica and Chandler pretend to do laundry when they're really meeting each other. This leads to Rachel giving them a huge bag of dirty clothes and Phoebe handing over a bag of change for the machine. (THE ONE WHERE EVERYBODY FINDS OUT)

ITEMS THAT RACHEL HAS BEEN COLLECTING FOR MONICA'S WEDDING

Rachel really wants to be Monica's maid of honor so, in preparation, she has been collecting a few sentimental items since before Monica was even engaged.

A book of poetry that Monica loves.

A picture from Halloween, where Monica is a bride and Rachel is Wonder Woman.

A pink satin purse for the rings.

Vintage handkerchiefs.

A blue garter that Rachel was saving for her own wedding.

(THE ONE WITH THE NAP PARTNERS)

CHANDLER'S TOP FOUR REASONS TO GET MARRIED

Chandler isn't the most knowledgeable when it comes to relationships, but he does have pretty strong ideas on why people decide to get married.

Pregnancy

Being ready

Actually wanting to get married

Being sorry

(THE ONE WITH THE GIRL WHO HITS JOEY)

ROSS'S PROS AND CONS LISTS FOR RACHEL AND JULIE

When Ross tries to decide between dating Rachel or Julie, he makes the catastrophic mistake of making a pros and cons list.

Rachel Cons

Kind of ditzy

Too into her looks

Spoiled

Just a waitress

Chubby ankles

Rachel Pros

The way you cry at game shows

How much you love your friends

The way you play with your hair when you're nervous

How brave you are for starting your life over

How great you are with Ben

The way you smell

Julie Cons

She's not Rachem
(Chandler made a typographical error when transcribing the list)

(THE ONE WITH THE LIST)

RACHEL'S CONS LIST FOR ROSS

After reading Ross's pros and cons list, Rachel decides to make one for him.

Whiny

Obsessive

Insecure

Gutless

Never seizes the day

Wears too much gel
in his hair

(THE ONE WITH PHOEBE'S DAD)

WEIRDEST PLACES THE FRIENDS HAVE HAD SEX

To keep themselves entertained during a blackout, the friends share the weirdest places they've gotten it on.

Monica:
Senior year of college on a pool table.

Joey:
The women's room on the second floor of the New York City Public Library.

Phoebe:
Milwaukee.

Ross:
Disneyland 1989, "It's a Small World After All."

Rachel:
The foot of the bed.

Chandler can't answer because he's locked in an ATM vestibule with Jill Goodacre.

(THE ONE WITH THE BLACKOUT)

9

6

OBSERVATIONS RACHEL WRITES ON TAG'S EVALUATION

Rachel is having a secret affair with her assistant, Tag, but her funny evaluation comments threaten to reveal their relationship to her boss.

EVALUATION FORM

- She calls him Sweet Cheeks.

- She says he's a good kisser.

- She likes his teeny, tiny tushy.

- He's able to unhook her bra with minimum supervision.

- She hopes there are no problems with performance.

- Smiley face.

- Small pornographic sketch.

(THE ONE WITH ALL THE CANDY)

MEMORABLE PROPOSALS

From romantic to desperate and everything in between, here are the memorable proposals from the series.

- Despite only knowing her for a short time, Ross proposes to Emily shortly before she leaves for England, and she says yes. (THE ONE WITH ALL THE HASTE) It is this proposal that prompts Rachel to suggest marriage to the newly divorced Joshua, ultimately scaring him off. (THE ONE WITH ALL THE WEDDING DRESSES)

- After Monica and Chandler have an argument about their relationship, he proposes in front of everyone. The reason he's proposing? Because he's sorry. Not surprisingly, Monica turns him down. (THE ONE WITH THE GIRL WHO HITS JOEY)

- In Las Vegas, Chandler says that if Monica rolls a hard eight, they'll get married. She does, and they head to the chapel but are beaten to it by Ross and Rachel. (THE ONE IN VEGAS, PART 2)

- When Monica puts her name down at a prestigious wedding venue, Chandler finds out accidentally and freaks out. (THE ONE WHERE PAUL'S THE MAN) While Monica worries what his reaction will be, Chandler secretly buys a ring (THE ONE WITH THE RING) and plans to propose. However, his attempt is thwarted when they bump into Richard at the restaurant where Chandler was going to propose. (THE ONE WITH THE PROPOSAL, PART 1) Chandler decides to pretend like he's not interested in marriage at all, which is terrible timing because now Richard wants to marry Monica. She turns him down, finds out about Chandler's secret plans when Joey tells her what happened, and then they get engaged by candlelight in Monica and Chandler's apartment. (THE ONE WITH THE PROPOSAL, PART 2)

- When Joey thinks that Phoebe is pregnant, he tells her it's a scary world out there and then asks her to marry him. He presents her with a ring, but when he later finds out it's Rachel who is actually pregnant, he asks Phoebe for the ring back and proposes to Rachel. *(THE ONE WITH THE RED SWEATER)*

- After giving birth to baby Emma, Rachel is upset that she might be left alone. She pours her heart out to Joey, and he promises he'll always be there for her. He then knocks Ross's jacket on the floor and finds the engagement ring that Judy Geller gave Ross. When Joey opens it, Rachel thinks that he is proposing, and she says yes. *(THE ONE WHERE RACHEL HAS A BABY, PART 2)* Of course, it's all a gigantic misunderstanding, which causes stress and confusion for everyone involved—especially when Ross sees Rachel wearing his ring even though he can't remember proposing. *(THE ONE WHERE NO ONE PROPOSES)*

- After asking for advice from Chandler, David decides that he must propose to Phoebe in order to make her forget about Mike. Knowing that Phoebe will say yes even though she's not in love with David, Monica calls Mike, and he shows up in Barbados to make a proposal of his own. In the end, Phoebe turns them both down but does get back together with Mike. *(THE ONE IN BARBADOS, PARTS 1 AND 2)*

- Phoebe and Mike go to see a Knicks game for their one-year anniversary. When a man proposes to his girlfriend on the big screen, Phoebe makes fun of him but then realizes that Mike was going to do the same thing. Worried that he might not do it, Phoebe proposes to Mike on the big screen herself, only the commentator makes a snide remark, and the crowd boos her. Afterward, they go to a restaurant, and Phoebe makes a comment about lame guys who hide the engagement ring in a cake, not knowing that Mike has done exactly that. Problems aside, Mike gets down on one knee, declares his love for Phoebe, and proposes. *(THE ONE WHERE RACHEL'S SISTER BABYSITS)*

WEDDINGS

Everybody loves a good wedding, and there are more than a few in *Friends*. Although everything seemed to work out for the best in the end, there were more than a few wedding hiccups and mishaps along the way.

Ross and Carol (before the series): Ross and Carol met when they were in college and then experienced a fairly short and frustrating marriage. By the time we meet Ross, the marriage is over and Carol has left him for Susan Bunch. However, by this time, Carol and Ross have already conceived their baby, Ben.

Barry and Rachel: Rachel rushes into Central Perk after jumping out of a window during her wedding to orthodontist Barry Farber. Rachel realized she didn't love Barry and now wants to create a new life for herself. (THE ONE WHERE MONICA GETS A ROOMMATE)

Carol and Susan: When Ross's ex-wife Carol announces her marriage to Susan Bunch, Ross wants nothing to do with it. Monica is stressed while catering the event, but when Carol's parents refuse to attend, the wedding may be called off. Ross steps up, insists that the day go ahead as planned, and then walks Carol down the aisle. (THE ONE WITH THE LESBIAN WEDDING)

Barry and Mindy: Rachel's ex-fiancé, Barry, marries Mindy, and Rachel is maid of honor, wearing a huge pink dress (tucked into her underwear) and a lacy, floppy hat. Barry's parents have told friends and family that Rachel left Barry at the altar because she's insane from contracting syphilis. She's then humiliated during the wedding speeches. She decides to leave but not before singing "Copacabana" on stage! (THE ONE WITH BARRY AND MINDY'S WEDDING) Later, Rachel tells her friends that Barry and Mindy are divorcing. (THE ONE THAT COULD HAVE BEEN, PART 1)

Frank Jr. and Alice: Phoebe is excited that her eighteen-year-old brother, Frank, is getting married—until Frank Jr. reveals that his fiancée is his much-older teacher, Alice Knight. Ross and Joey are tasked with talking sense into Frank Jr., but they end up as part of the wedding party. When Phoebe tries to break up the couple, all she does is break Frank Jr.'s heart and then realizes that she can't keep them apart. (THE ONE WITH THE HYPNOSIS TAPE)

Ross and Emily: When Ross and Emily decide to get married in Emily's native London, their wedding is full of drama. The chapel has been partly torn down; the families don't get along; Rachel arrives with the intention of declaring her love for Ross; and then Ross says the wrong name during his wedding vows—Rachel! (THE ONE WITH ROSS'S WEDDING, PART 2)

Ross and Rachel: Chandler and Monica decide to get married while they're in

Chandler and Monica: Known for his fear of commitment, Chandler disappears on the day of his wedding to Monica. He eventually makes it to the hotel, where he overhears a rumor that his bride is pregnant. At the ceremony, Chandler tells Monica that he knows about the baby. Monica is confused because she's not pregnant—but Rachel is. *(THE ONE WITH MONICA AND CHANDLER'S WEDDING, PARTS 1 AND 2)*

Phoebe and Mike: Phoebe regrets having a bossy Monica as her wedding planner and fires her at the rehearsal dinner. However, when Phoebe can't cope with the last-minute arrangements, she rehires Monica. When snow hits Manhattan, it looks as though the ceremony will be canceled until Monica organizes a small but beautiful wedding in the snowy street outside Central Perk. Joey marries the happy couple while Ross is in charge of Chappy—the stinky canine groomsman. *(THE ONE WITH PHOEBE'S WEDDING)*

Las Vegas, but there's another wedding taking place in the chapel. The happy (and drunk) couple are Ross and Rachel, and the impulsive wedding later leads to Ross's third divorce. Meanwhile, Monica and Chandler have to decide whether they should get married in secret *(THE ONE IN VEGAS, PART 2)*, but in the end they decide they're not ready and opt to move in with each other instead. *(THE ONE AFTER VEGAS)*

Cousin Franny: Ross is invited to Cousin Franny's wedding reception, but Monica isn't invited. However, Monica insists on being Ross's plus-one to find out why she didn't receive an invitation. After bombarding guests at the wedding with questions on how they know the couple, Monica confronts the bride, only to find out that it's not what she did but who—Franny's new husband, Stuart, is Monica's ex-boyfriend. *(THE ONE WITH ALL THE CHEESECAKES)*

WEDDING EXPENSES THAT THE WALTHAMS WANT THE GELLERS TO PAY FOR

When Ross marries Emily in London, her parents expect the Gellers to pay for all kinds of things, some of which have nothing to do with the wedding.

Flowers

Liquor

Recarpet first floor

New guest bathroom

Landscaping

Built-in barbeque

Gazebo

New lawn

Lawn ornaments

Wine cellar

(THE ONE WITH ROSS'S WEDDING, PART 2)

BABY NAMES CONTEMPLATED BY PHOEBE

When Frank Jr. and Alice ask Phoebe to choose a name for one of their babies, she has some spectacular suggestions.

Cougar

Exxon

The Hulk

Joey

Chanoey (a combination of Joey and Chandler)

Chandler (the chosen name, even though the baby is a girl)

(THE ONE WITH RACHEL'S NEW DRESS)

NAMES DISCUSSED FOR ROSS AND RACHEL'S BABY

Ross and Rachel discuss what they should name their baby, and end up vetoing most of each other's suggestions.

Boy

Phoebo (Phoebe's suggestion)

Darwin (Ross's suggestion)

Thatcher (Ross's suggestion)

Dayton (Rachel's suggestion)

Stuart (Ross's suggestion)

Sawyer (Rachel's suggestion)

Heath (suggested sarcastically by Ross)

Blaine (suggested sarcastically by Ross)

Sequoia (suggested sarcastically by Ross but Rachel likes it)

Girl

Phoebe (Phoebe's suggestion)

Sandrine (Rachel's suggestion)

Rain (Rachel's suggestion)

James (Rachel's suggestion)

Ruth (Ross's suggestion)

Helen (Ross's suggestion)

Isabella (Ross's suggestion)

Delilah (Ross's suggestion)

Emma (Monica's favorite girl's name and the name they choose)

(THE ONE WHERE CHANDLER TAKES A BATH)

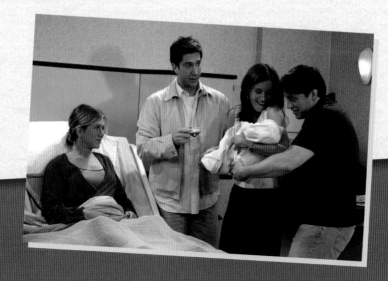

CHILDREN

There are many children featured throughout the series, both the friends' kids and others.

- After being treated for a broken nose, Ross argues with a cheeky boy over who owns the hockey puck. This fight leads to a nurse being knocked out by the puck. *(THE ONE WITH GEORGE STEPHANOPOULOS)*

- Ben is the son of Ross and Carol. He lives with Carol and her wife, Susan, but Ross shares custody. Ben is sweet and friendly but goes through a cheeky stage when Rachel teaches him practical jokes along with an accidental swear word or two. *(THE ONE WITH THE BIRTH ONWARD)*

- When Phoebe is employed to sing at a children's library, her songs are deemed inappropriate by the parents. However, the children love her because she tells the truth. *(THE ONE AFTER THE SUPERBOWL, PART 1)*

- After spending the night together in a caveman display at the museum, Ross and Rachel wake up to find a group of visiting children staring at them. *(THE ONE WHERE ROSS AND RACHEL . . . YOU KNOW)*

- After splitting with Richard because he doesn't see more kids in his future, Monica contemplates having a baby with a sperm donor. She doesn't go through with it when Joey tells her a story of how he thought her future life would go. *(THE ONE WITH THE JAM)*

- While demonstrating how to use a tennis racket in the apartment stairwell, Ross

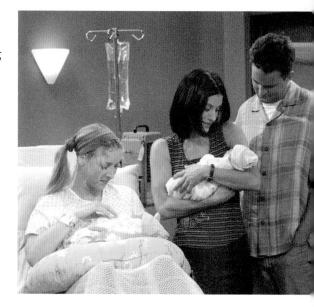

accidentally knocks Brown Bird Sarah Tuttle down the stairs, breaking her leg in the process. She was selling cookies in the hope of winning a trip to Space Camp, so Ross takes over the job. He sells most of the boxes to himself, his friends, and students with the munchies. He's now known as Cookie Dude and sells cookies by the case, but it still isn't enough to win the trip. In the end, Ross, Chandler, and Joey create their own space camp so that Sarah can go after all. *(THE ONE WHERE RACHEL QUITS)*

- When Joey auditions for a dad role in a soup commercial, he's paired up with a little boy named Raymond—a famous child actor in the advertising world. When Joey keeps flubbing his lines, Raymond shouts at him. *(THE ONE WHERE RACHEL SMOKES)*

- During an audition for an acting role, Joey has to interact with a little boy who is playing his son, Timmy. He's supposed to be surprising Timmy with a swing set, but his reaction to hernia pain causes Joey to come across as a weirdo. (THE ONE WHERE JOEY LOSES HIS INSURANCE)

- When Joey wins the role of a dying man in a TV show, his son is played by Alex. Unfortunately, the little boy finds it difficult to cry on camera; that is, until Joey shows him his hernia, and he bawls his eyes out. (THE ONE WHERE JOEY LOSES HIS INSURANCE)

- Leslie, Frank Jr. Jr., and Chandler are Frank and Alice's triplets. When Phoebe volunteers to look after them, she enrolls Chandler and Monica to help out. Unfortunately, Chandler has to go to the ER after getting a sonic blaster toy gun stuck in his throat. Phoebe ends up tearing the apartment to pieces while looking after the babies on her own. (THE ONE WITH JOEY'S PORSCHE)

- Melinda, Ashley, and Gert are little girls who dance on Ross's feet at Monica and Chandler's wedding. By the end of the night, he's in so much agony that he has to be escorted off the dance floor. (THE ONE AFTER "I DO")

- Rachel wants to hand out candy to the kids who come to the door for Halloween but ends up giving away all of the candy to a ballerina. She then gives out cash until more sweets arrive, but a little boy would prefer the cash. He brands her mean and cries, so she has to pay him $50 and agree to visit some houses with him. (THE ONE WITH THE HALLOWEEN PARTY)

- Emma is Ross and Rachel's baby. She lives primarily with Rachel, though she and Ross share parental responsibilities. In THE ONE WITH THE MEMORIAL SERVICE, Emma falls in love with Joey's toy penguin, Hugsy. Hugsy is Joey's favorite stuffed toy, and he's horrified that Emma has taken it. To get it back, he buys a second penguin, but Emma doesn't like it and neither does Joey. In THE ONE WHERE RACHEL'S SISTER BABYSITS, Rachel's sister Amy takes Emma to get her ears pierced without permission from Rachel or Ross. (THE ONE WHERE RACHEL HAS A BABY, PART 2, ONWARD)

- While Ross is waiting for his pediatrician, he helps a little girl with her *Where's Waldo?* book and flirts with her mother. When the nurse calls Ross into the room, he's embarrassed and pretends that a nearby child is his son. The little boy gets scared and runs to his mother, who just happens to be the woman Ross was chatting to in the waiting room. (THE ONE WITH THE PEDIATRICIAN)

- Monica and Chandler visit Phoebe's friends Bill and Colleen, who have an adoption story to tell. Colleen thrills Monica when she gives her a file of information, while Chandler accidentally tells their son, Owen, that he's adopted and tries to bribe him with $50 not to tell. Before they leave, Chandler also reveals that Santa isn't real. (THE ONE WHERE ROSS IS FINE)

- Phoebe and Mike decide not to spend a lot on their wedding and instead donate it to the New York City Children's Fund. They give them a check, but then Phoebe tries on a wedding veil and realizes she does want a big wedding. They make so many U-turns on whether or not to give the money to charity that, in the end, the assistant refuses their money and asks them to consider the returned check as a donation to their wedding. (THE ONE WITH THE HOME STUDY)

- Rachel does not approve of Ross taking Emma to play on the swings because of a "traumatic incident" she had as a child. She goes along with them to supervise, and then Ross ends up being knocked over by a little boy on the next swing over. (THE ONE WITH THE HOME STUDY)

- Phoebe and Rachel enter Emma into a Thanksgiving Day beauty pageant, and Phoebe becomes obsessed with putting down the other kids, who apparently don't hold a candle to Emma. Dressed in the clothes from Joey's Cabbage Patch Kid, Emma wins a trophy and $1,000, but the pageant makes them late for Monica's Thanksgiving dinner. (THE ONE WITH THE LATE THANKSGIVING)

- When Joey visits Monica and Chandler's new house, he encounters Mackenzie, a little girl who currently lives there with her parents. Joey tries to convince the eight-year-old to tell his friends that the house is haunted, but she thinks that's too childish and that Joey should just let the move happen. (THE ONE WITH PRINCESS CONSUELA)

- Chandler and Monica can't have children of their own so they adopt twins Erica and Jack. Erica is named after the birth mother and Jack after Monica's dad. (THE LAST ONE, PARTS 1 AND 2)

CHAPTER FOUR:
the One about

ANIMALS

Marcel, the chick, and the duck are perhaps the most famous animal characters featured on *Friends*, but there were many that appeared in the series.

- See Marcel the Monkey Appearances, page 197.

- See Chick and Duck Appearances, page 198.

- Chi-Chi is a childhood dog belonging to Monica and Ross, first mentioned in *THE ONE WITH THE THUMB*. When the pet died, their parents concocted a story that the dog moved to the Milners' farm in Connecticut. Monica mentions Chi-Chi during the terrible speech she gives for her parents' anniversary. Her dad can't even remember them owning the dog. (*THE ONE IN MASSAPEQUA*)

- Phoebe says that she was the last to know when Chandler was bitten by the peacock at the zoo. Chandler also mentions the incident. (*THE ONE WITH THE BLACKOUT*)

- Paolo's cat appears on the girls' balcony during a blackout. They search the building to find the owner, which leads Rachel to discover her next love interest, Paolo. (*THE ONE WITH THE BLACKOUT*)

- When Chandler contemplates being a lonely old man, he says he'll have to buy some snakes. He'll be known as Crazy Snake Man. Kids won't walk past his place—they'll run! (*THE ONE WHERE HECKLES DIES*)

- A pigeon flies in through the window while Rachel is talking to her mother on the phone. She traps it in a saucepan but accidentally releases it when Phoebe's ice-skater husband turns up. (*THE ONE WITH PHOEBE'S HUSBAND*)

- Monica mentions her old cat, Fluffy. When Ross decides to buy a cat with Julie, he wants to borrow Fluffy's old cat toys. (*THE ONE WHERE ROSS FINDS OUT*)

- Phoebe is determined that Ross will finally win over Rachel because he is her lobster and it's a known fact that lobsters fall in love and mate for life. (*THE ONE WITH THE PROM VIDEO*)

- When Phoebe tries to meet her dad, she encounters the family's ferocious Jack Russell terrier Schnoodle. She accidentally runs the dog over, and when she returns it, she meets her half-brother, Frank Jr. (*THE ONE WITH THE BULLIES*)

- When Phoebe brings over a bag with turtles all over it, Rachel reveals that they scare her. (*THE ONE WITH ALL THE JEALOUSY*)

- Monica is stung by a jellyfish while at the beach. Joey heard on a documentary that the ammonia in urine neutralizes the sting.

from her mother announcing the news of her dog's death. Apparently, LaPooh was hit by an ice-cream truck and dragged for nineteen blocks. *(THE ONE WITH THE KIPS)*

• When her birth mother sends her a fur coat, Phoebe is appalled but then tries it on and falls in love. Her obsession stops when she encounters a judgmental squirrel at the newsstand, which forces her to give up the coat. *(THE ONE WITH THE YETI)*

Monica tries to pee on herself but can't, so Joey tries but gets stage fright. Finally, Chandler is the one who relieves Monica's pain, much to the embarrassment of all three friends. *(THE ONE WITH THE JELLYFISH)*

• A male cat named Julio runs into Central Perk, and Phoebe thinks that it is the reincarnation of her mother, Lily. Rachel discovers that the cat is actually Julio and belongs to a little girl, but Ross is the only one brave enough to tell Phoebe. While Phoebe still believes the cat is her mother, she agrees to give him back. *(THE ONE WITH THE CAT)*

• When Phoebe contemplates being a surrogate for Frank and Alice, Phoebe Sr. lends her a puppy to see how hard it is to give up something you love. However, Phoebe doesn't realize that the dog belongs to her mother, and she gifts it to Frank and Alice. *(THE ONE WITH PHOEBE'S UTERUS)*

• While Ross tries to tell Rachel that he can't see her anymore because of Emily, she is more concerned with a letter she receives

• Rachel buys a hairless sphinx cat for $1,000 because it reminds her of the one her grandmother used to own. Mrs. Whiskerson starts attacking her, so Rachel sells the cat to Gunther. He pays $1,500 for it, thinking it's a snake. *(THE ONE WITH THE BALL)*

• Ross and Chandler argue over who made up a joke about "Doctor Monkey," which *Playboy* just printed. Each is determined that he is the author, until Monica says that the joke is not funny; it's insulting to women, doctors, and monkeys; and it sucked. Chandler and Ross then both disown the joke. *(THE ONE WITH THE JOKE)*

• Phoebe has been secretly looking after a dog named Clunkers in Monica and Chandler's apartment, and when they find out, Chandler insists he is extremely allergic. Really, he hates dogs because, according to him, they are needy and jumpy, and it scares him that you can't tell what they're thinking. *(THE ONE WHERE CHANDLER DOESN'T LIKE DOGS)*

• When Phoebe thinks that Rachel is having too much fun at Joey's and won't want to move back into her apartment after the fire, she buys Joey a tarantula so that Rachel will be so scared she'll want to move back in with Phoebe. In reality, Joey is terrified of it while Rachel loves it. *(THE ONE WITH THE HOLIDAY ARMADILLO)*

- Mozzarella (not his real name but the one Joey gives to him) is the happiest dog in the world. Phoebe brings him over to cheer up Joey after Rachel moves out, but his broken heart makes the dog depressed. *(THE ONE WITH THE BIRTHING VIDEO)*

- When Joey misses being on the *Days of Our Lives* float in the Thanksgiving parade, he needs a good lie as to why he wasn't there. Phoebe tries to coach him, but every story he comes up with has a raccoon at the center of it. *(THE ONE WITH RACHEL'S OTHER SISTER)*

- Chandler is planning to go down the fire escape to trick Joey into thinking he just got home from Tulsa. There's only one thing stopping him—the huge, scary pigeon out on the balcony. *(THE ONE WITH RACHEL'S PHONE NUMBER)* Later, Phoebe drops the bowl of lottery tickets after the pigeon flies at her on the balcony. *(THE ONE WITH THE LOTTERY)*

- Mike finds a rat in Phoebe's cupboard, but he's just Bob, an occasional visitor that Phoebe puts food out for. Mike is appalled but eats a box of crackers that belongs to Bob. In the hunt for the rat, it's discovered that "he" had babies. Unfortunately, the critter then gets caught in Mike's trap, leaving Phoebe to raise Bob's orphans in a shoebox. *(THE ONE WITH PHOEBE'S RATS)*

- Mike wants his old, stinky dog, Chappy, to be one of the groomsmen at his wedding to Phoebe, so Ross is in charge of walking down the snowy aisle with him. By the end of the ceremony, Ross asks Joey to wrap things up because Chappy's heartbeat "has slowed way down." *(THE ONE WITH PHOEBE'S WEDDING)*

- Joey buys Monica and Chandler a chick and duck as housewarming gifts. As he's about to give the birds to them, Joey realizes that they're missing. They're actually in the Foosball table, which Monica smashes to pieces in an effort to find them. *(THE LAST ONE, PARTS 1 AND 2)*

marcel the monkey

MARCEL THE MONKEY APPEARANCES

He may not have been around for the entire series, but Marcel the monkey certainly left an impression on us all.

- Ross adopts Marcel after he's rescued from a lab, but he almost immediately complains that the monkey is shutting him out. Ross takes him to Monica's New Year's Eve party, where once again, Marcel ignores him. (*THE ONE WITH THE MONKEY*)

- Ross takes his date (Celia the Bug Lady) back to his apartment, but Marcel terrifies her by swinging on her hair. (*THE ONE WITH THE STONED GUY*)

- Ross thinks that Marcel is out of control. He erases the messages on Ross's answering machine and pees all over the newspaper crossword. Later, he steals Monica's television remote and manages to turn the language to Spanish. (*THE ONE WITH TWO PARTS, PART 1*)

- Marcel steals Monica's remote again and then eats some of the Scrabble tiles while Chandler and Ross are playing. They take him to the hospital, where the doctor extracts a *K*, an *M*, and an *O*. Chandler thinks he must have been trying to spell *monkey*. (*THE ONE WITH TWO PARTS, PART 2*)

- Marcel is obsessed with the song "The Lion Sleeps Tonight." He insists on playing it over and over, and when Ross turns the stereo off, Marcel storms into the bedroom and slams the door. (*THE ONE WITH ALL THE POKER*)

- Rachel accidentally lets Marcel out of the apartment and then calls Animal Control to find him. The woman is determined to report Marcel as being an illegal pet until Rachel threatens to tell the woman's supervisor that she shot Phoebe in the bottom with a tranquilizer dart. (*THE ONE WHERE THE MONKEY GETS AWAY*)

- Marcel reaches sexual maturity, and it is impossible for Ross to keep him in his apartment. After a few failed attempts to get the monkey into a good zoo, San Diego finally accepts him, and the friends say farewell at the airport. (*THE ONE WITH THE FAKE MONICA*)

- Ross discovers that Marcel is now a movie star and is making *Outbreak 2: The Virus Takes Manhattan*. The friends all go down to the set, where they sing "The Lion Sleeps Tonight" to Marcel. (*THE ONE AFTER THE SUPERBOWL, PART 1*)

- Marcel is too busy making a movie to spend time with Ross—until he turns up at Central Perk and the two go around New York together. (*THE ONE AFTER THE SUPERBOWL, PART 2*)

CHICK AND DUCK APPEARANCES

Who would keep a chick and a duck in their apartment?
Joey and Chandler, of course.

- Joey buys a chick after watching a news report about how poultry should not be kept as pets. The responsibility of caring for the bird causes an argument between the guys, so Chandler takes it to a rescue center and ends up bringing home a duck. *(THE ONE WITH A CHICK AND A DUCK)*

- The friends are going to see Joey's play, and Chandler wonders if the duck and chick are allowed in the theater. Later, Rachel's new boyfriend Tommy picks up the chick while he's in Joey and Chandler's apartment. When the bird poops on his hand, Tommy screams at him and then calls the duck names. *(THE ONE WITH THE SCREAMER)*

- Joey thinks it would be cool if the chick and duck had a baby. They could call it Chuck . . . or Dick. Later, they take the duck to see Guru Saj to treat his bad cough. Saj wonders if the guys could get the duck to eat a bat. *(THE ONE WITH ROSS'S THING)*

- When Chandler insists that Joey should sell his huge media cabinet, Joey opens the door to reveal that the chick and the duck are living in there. Their home even has multicolored lights and a disco ball. *(THE ONE WITH THE CAT)*

- After all of their furniture is stolen, Joey and Chandler are left with a canoe and a filthy picnic set. When the chick and duck wander into the room, Chandler wonders if he and Joey could *be* more white trash. *(THE ONE WITH THE CUFFS)*

- Chandler watches television with Joey's girlfriend Kathy, the chick, and the duck. Later, Chandler plays hide-and-seek with the birds, though they don't fully grasp the concept. *(THE ONE WITH JOEY'S NEW GIRLFRIEND)*

- While Chandler watches *Baywatch* in the canoe, the duck paddles in a large bucket. Meanwhile, the chick hangs out on the picnic table. *(THE ONE WHERE CHANDLER CROSSES THE LINE)*

- While Joey and Chandler discuss Chandler's indiscretion with Kathy, the chick and the duck wander in from the bathroom. Joey wants to leave, but Chandler asks if he'll stay for the birds. *(THE ONE WITH CHANDLER IN A BOX)*

- Monica and Rachel are rudely awakened by a loud crowing. Joey and Chandler tell the girls that the chick is going through some changes. Primarily, she's becoming a rooster. It is this development that leads to the competition between the girls and boys: If Chandler and Joey win, they'll get the number 20 apartment, and if Monica and Rachel win, the guys will give up their birds.

The boys win and move into the apartment with the chick and the duck. *(THE ONE WITH THE EMBRYOS)*

- Chandler goes to the bathroom, and the chick and duck follow him in. A moment later, he shoos them out and demands they give him one minute (of peace). *(THE ONE WITH JOEY'S DIRTY DAY)*

- Rachel has a special dinner planned for her new crush, Joshua. Unfortunately, Joshua is terrified of farm birds, and Rachel has to shoo them back over the hall toward their apartment. *(THE ONE WITH RACHEL'S NEW DRESS)*

- It's Ross's bachelor party, and Joey introduces the chick and duck to the stripper. Later, the wedding ring disappears, and the boys suspect that the stripper stole it. In reality, the duck ate it, and a trip to the vet is in order. The ring is retrieved, but not before the boys think back on their memories of the duck. *(THE ONE WITH THE WORST BEST MAN EVER)*

- The chick and duck watch a cooking show on television until Chandler quickly turns it off. *(THE ONE WHERE PHOEBE HATES PBS)*

- Chandler is in a bad mood after an argument with Monica and is not impressed by the duck's constant happiness. *(THE ONE WITH ALL THE THANKSGIVINGS)*

- While Joey has his eyes shut, Chandler picks up the rooster, which flaps his wings and terrifies Joey. *(THE ONE WITH ALL THE RESOLUTIONS)*

- The chick and duck have apparently had a disagreement, and the duck is telling Phoebe all about it. Ross complains that the duck has pooped on his letter to Emily, but he then decides that the accident has made the letter better. Later, Joey and Phoebe have a contest to see which one of the birds can find a tasty treat first. The duck wins. *(THE ONE WITH CHANDLER'S WORK LAUGH)*

- To prevent his grandmother from noticing that he's been cut out of a TV show, Joey creates his own scene in his apartment. While filming, he's disturbed by the duck quacking, and his character then holds the duck for ransom. *(THE ONE WHERE ROSS CAN'T FLIRT)*

- When Rachel brings her sphinx cat into Joey and Chandler's apartment, the duck and chick aren't pleased. Joey assures them he doesn't think it's a cat. *(THE ONE WITH THE BALL)*

- Chandler thinks that the duck and chick are angry with him for moving across the hall. He tells them that Monica is allergic to them but then admits that she really hates them. *(THE ONE WITH MAC AND C.H.E.E.S.E.)*

- Joey tells his friends that he's napping on Monica's sofa because of the duck. When Rachel demands to know what the bird has done now, it's revealed that he ate Rachel's face cream and was sick. *(THE ONE WITH RACHEL'S BOOK)*

ENTERTAINMENT

Whether it was Joey teaching Mr. Treeger to dance or Officer Goodbody entertaining Phoebe at her bachelorette party, the friends sure had a lot of fun together.

- Ross is first seen playing his keyboard during the prom video. (THE ONE WITH THE PROM VIDEO) He digs it back out in THE ONE WHERE CHANDLER CROSSES THE LINE, when Phoebe insists on hearing his "'sound." Ross insists that his music is about communicating very private emotions and everyone should think of his work as wordless sound poems. In reality, it's a bunch of animal sounds, demos, doorbells, construction noise, and breaking glass.

- In exchange for not evicting the girls, Joey teaches Mr. Treeger to dance so that he can impress his crush, Marge. On the first attempt, he swings Joey around so quickly that he slams into the door. Joey soon loves the lessons, and he and Treeger use the roof of the apartment building as a rehearsal space. (THE ONE WITH THE BALLROOM DANCING)

- When Chandler is getting over Kathy, the girls take him to a strip club. They love chatting with the exotic dancers (and Monica even encourages one to quit to become a teacher), but Chandler feels as though he's on an outing with his mother. (THE ONE WITH JOEY'S DIRTY DAY)

- After finding out that Monica and Chandler are going out, Rachel and Phoebe decide to have a little fun with them. Phoebe pretends that she's lusting after Chandler and creates a rather scary dance to try and seduce him. Of course, the couple already know they know, and after Chandler declares his love for Monica, they come clean. *(THE ONE WHERE EVERYBODY FINDS OUT)*

- When Monica, Chandler, and Phoebe head to Las Vegas, Rachel is alone in the apartment. She celebrates by doing a naked dance, which is overseen by Ross from across the street. He assumes she's trying to seduce him, but Rachel has no idea that he even saw her. *(THE ONE IN VEGAS, PART 1)*

- Janine invites Joey, Ross, and Monica to the filming of *Dick Clark's New Year's Rockin' Eve*. While there, Joey is paired with a wild girl, but he wants Janine, and Ross and Monica perform a dance routine that they made up when they were teenagers. *(THE ONE WITH THE ROUTINE)*

- When Phoebe thinks that Rachel is having too much fun at Joey's and won't want to move back into her apartment, she buys Joey some drums. Trouble is, Rachel loves them, too, and Joey keeps poking himself in the eye with the drumsticks. *(THE ONE WITH THE HOLIDAY ARMADILLO)*

- When Monica and Chandler hear a dreadful sound coming from across the street, they realize that Ross has taken up the bagpipes. What's more, he intends on playing them at their wedding. They call the cops and then tell Ross that they hate the bagpipes, but regardless, he insists on giving everyone a painful demonstration. *(THE ONE WITH JOEY'S NEW BRAIN)*

- Chandler takes dance lessons so that he can impress Monica at their wedding. Unfortunately, the floor is too shiny for his shoes, which leads Jack Geller to comment that Chandler has stolen his moves. *(THE ONE AFTER "I DO")*

- When Monica's attempts at hiring Chandler a stripper go awry, she tries to strip herself but talks too much, gets her jacket stuck on her arm, and breaks an ornament when she kicks off her tennis shoe. *(THE ONE WITH THE STRIPPER)*

- When Officer Goodbody arrives to strip for Phoebe's bachelorette party, everyone is shocked. He can hardly breathe, he's much older than they expected, and his dance just involves some bottom shaking, a few kicks, and a flash of his chest. *(THE ONE WHERE THE STRIPPER CRIES)*

- Chandler tells Joey and Ross that he once did a naked dance for Monica with scarves. *(THE ONE WITH RACHEL'S GOING AWAY PARTY)*

PARTIES

There's always time for a party on *Friends*, though some end up creating more drama than joyful celebration.

ATTENDED

- Monica invites Fun Bobby to a holiday party that turns out to be torturous—Fun Bobby is depressed; Chandler breaks up with Janice; Ross is ignored by Marcel; Rachel gets into a fight with a woman while waiting for no-show Paolo at the airport; Joey's date brings her kids; and Phoebe and David break up. *(THE ONE WITH THE MONKEY)*

- Phoebe's surprise birthday party starts with Ross dropping the cake onto the floor when everyone shouts "surprise" at him. Phoebe is sad to discover that Joey has gone on a date with Ursula. *(THE ONE WITH TWO PARTS, PART 2)*

- The friends host a birthday barbeque for Rachel, but Ross can't make it because he's going to China for a work conference. When Rachel opens Ross's gift, an expensive pendant, Chandler blurts out that the paleontologist is in love with her. *(THE ONE WHERE RACHEL FINDS OUT)*

- A holiday party turns tropical when the knob on the radiator breaks off. Ross obsesses that Rachel called him obsessive; Mr. Treeger wants to kiss Rachel under the mistletoe; and the only reliefs from the heat are ice cubes and a few seconds standing in front of the open refrigerator. *(THE ONE WITH PHOEBE'S DAD)*

- At Jack Geller's birthday party, Monica over-hears her mother and friend talking about Richard finding a "twinkie in the city." Monica decides her parents should know the truth about her and Richard, but just as they're digesting the news, Jack's guests appear, singing "Happy Birthday" and carrying the cake. *(THE ONE WHERE JOEY MOVES OUT)*

- When Rachel's dad turns up unexpectedly to her surprise birthday party, the friends are forced to hold a second party for her across the hall so that he doesn't run into Rachel's mother. Chandler sends all the men

to Monica's party and keeps the women for himself. Chandler's party is a riot, while Monica tortures her guests by making them play boring games and insisting they place the tops back on the marker pens until they click. Rachel is upset that her parents can't be in the same room together, and Monica is furious when her guests escape and join the cool party across the hall. (THE ONE WITH THE TWO PARTIES)

- Joey's birthday party is held in his and Chandler's apartment. Chandler gets drunk on Jell-O vodka shots and ends up kissing one of Joey's sisters in the storage room—but he has no idea which one. When Chandler explains the dilemma to his friends, it turns out that he also tried to kiss Monica, Rachel, Phoebe, and Ross. (THE ONE WHERE CHANDLER CAN'T REMEMBER WHICH SISTER)

- Rachel hosts a surprise goodbye party for Emily, but it's actually a ploy to get Joshua to come to her apartment. After playing hard to get, Rachel ends up choking on a cherry while trying to flirt. She then organizes a game of spin the bottle, kisses the back of Joshua's knee, injures herself while performing a cheerleading skit, and then attempts to take off her bra under her dress. Her efforts are rewarded when Joshua finally admits that he likes her. Meanwhile, Ross is desperate to leave with Emily, as he already had plans for a last-evening dinner. Phoebe caves in to her pregnancy meat cravings. (THE ONE WITH THE FAKE PARTY)

- When Joey wins the role of best man at Ross and Emily's wedding, he throws a bachelor party consisting of the guys, museum geeks, Gunther, and a stripper. The party favors are T-shirts with "Ross Geller Bachelor Bash 1998" on one side and a photo of Joey on the other. As Gunther leaves, he thanks Ross for not marrying Rachel, and then Joey tells the museum geeks to get back to their parents' basement. He then hooks up with the stripper. (THE ONE WITH THE WORST BEST MAN EVER)

- Rachel and Monica throw Phoebe a baby shower but don't want to buy her baby items since she's a surrogate for her brother and won't get to keep the babies. Instead, they gift her leather pants, which she hates because she won't be able to wear them for two months. In fact, she rages so much that all the other guests hide their gifts so that they don't get shouted at. (THE ONE WITH THE WORST BEST MAN EVER)

- When Rachel's crush Danny has a housewarming party, she decides that the reason he hasn't invited her is that he's interested in her and he's playing hard to get. That theory is proven wrong when he comes by to invite her and Monica, so she has to pretend that she's going to a regatta instead. When she does arrive at the party, Danny tries to set her up with his friend Tom, which she sees as another sign of Danny liking her. (THE ONE WHERE ROSS MOVES IN)

- Joey finds a way for Monica and Chandler to share a kiss at the New Year's Eve party, and then Ross vows to have no divorces during 1999—until Rachel reminds him that his divorce from Emily is not yet final so he'll have at least one. (THE ONE WITH ALL THE RESOLUTIONS)

- Monica and Chandler attend an office party, and Monica thinks it is cool that they don't have to hide their relationship. When Chandler reveals his work laugh, Monica tries one, too. (THE ONE WITH CHANDLER'S WORK LAUGH)

- When Ross moves into Ugly Naked Guy's old apartment, Steve—a member of the tenants committee—arrives to ask if he'll contribute $100 to Howard the handyman's retirement collection. Ross refuses to donate since he's only just moved in, and then Steve tells everyone he's a cheapskate. To counteract the hostility, Ross throws a party for the residents, but they're already having one for Howard, and Phoebe is in attendance. Ross decides to join the party himself, and when Phoebe tries to stand up for him, she makes things even worse. (THE ONE WITH THE GIRL WHO HITS JOEY)

- Monica and Phoebe decide to be joint hosts at a party for Rachel. Monica takes over all of the preparations, which leaves only cups and ice for Phoebe to organize. Phoebe goes all out on the arrangements, making cup hats, cup banners, cup chandeliers, cup decorations, and crushed, cubed, and dry ice. Monica is jealous that Phoebe's snow cones are more popular than her food and even tells Chandler to go out with Phoebe when he dares to say that she did a great job. (THE ONE WHERE RACHEL SMOKES)

- Rachel's thirtieth birthday is celebrated with a breakfast party in Joey's apartment. Unfortu-

nately, she's so depressed that she can't get into the spirit, and things are made worse when Chandler buys her a "Happy Birthday, Grandma" card. During the party, Rachel decides that she wants to settle down and have a baby, which means she'll have to break up with her much younger boyfriend Tag. (THE ONE WHERE THEY ALL TURN THIRTY)

- Joey is too busy crying about turning thirty to enjoy his party. While Chandler is trying to blow out his own thirtieth birthday candles, Joey is crying again and demanding to know why God is doing this to them. (THE ONE WHERE THEY ALL TURN THIRTY)

- On Monica's thirtieth birthday, the friends throw her a formal surprise party. However, she turns up drunk and has to pretend to her parents that she's sober. When Monica makes a speech, she announces that she's drunk and then passes out. (THE ONE WHERE THEY ALL TURN THIRTY)

- Rachel and Phoebe are forced into hosting a "surprise" bridal shower for Monica, but they forget to invite the bride! When she eventually arrives, Monica is happy that everyone has gone home and says that she didn't like the guests anyway—but then they all pop up to surprise her! (THE ONE WITH ROSS AND MONICA'S COUSIN)

- Monica and Chandler host a costume party for Halloween, where Phoebe meets new love Eric and argues with her sister. Ross has a date with Mona, Monica wonders who would win in a fight—Catwoman or Supergirl—and Chandler and Ross arm wrestle to prove who is stronger. (THE ONE WITH THE HALLOWEEN PARTY)

- Monica feels bad that she didn't let Chandler have a bachelor party, so he has a belated one for just him and Joey. There are party hats, streamers, chips, and beer—and a naked hooker in the bedroom. (THE ONE WITH THE STRIPPER)

- It's Judy and Jack's thirty-fifth wedding anniversary party, and Jack and Judy have told their guests that Ross and Rachel are now married, which infuriates them—until they start receiving checks. They then make up an elaborate story of how the proposal and wedding happened. Meanwhile, Monica gives a dreadful speech, mentioning her dead grandmother, dead dog, tragic films, and neglected orphans of Romania. Phoebe thinks the party sucks, while Joey slips on an oyster but thinks it's a huge booger. (THE ONE IN MASSAPEQUA)

- Monica and Phoebe host a baby shower for Rachel, but the fact that they forgot to invite Rachel's mother, Sandra Green, creates an awkward atmosphere for Monica. Phoebe doesn't care if Mrs. Green likes her or not— she's more excited about the stripper she hired. Opening the presents should be a joyful part of the party, but first Mrs. Green is embarrassed because she didn't have time to buy a gift, and then the rest of the gifts make Rachel feel as though she'll be a terrible mother. (THE ONE WITH THE BABY SHOWER)

- Phoebe is invited to a dinner party at Mike's parents' house. Trying to make a good impression, she ditches her normal clothes and personality and arrives in a twinset and pearls with matching posh accent. The evening is a disaster when she tells Theodore, Bitsy, and their snooty friends all about her early life in the city; punches Theodore in the stomach; and tells Bitsy that Mike is a gentle lover but knows how to rattle a headboard. They then serve veal to vegetarian Phoebe, and she throws up in the coat closet while they gossip about her. Regardless, Mike declares his love for her. (THE ONE WITH ROSS'S INAPPROPRIATE SONG)

- It's Rachel's birthday, and Monica throws her a party. When Monica finds a shoebox, she assumes somebody has bought Rachel some shoes. Actually, it's a box full of Phoebe's rat babies—all seven of them. The lame party is over by nine thirty, but while it may seem as though everyone has left, there is actually a guest left behind—one of Phoebe's rat babies is in the bedroom, where he's found by a terrified Monica. (THE ONE WITH PHOEBE'S RATS)

- Joey hosts a party on the roof for his soap opera colleagues, and this year his friends are invited, too, but only because Rachel found out about it. She has a crush on Joey and wants to tell him during the party but spends much of her time gathering phone numbers from soap opera actors. When she does decide to go after Joey, she's too late—he's busy kissing Charlie in the corner. (THE ONE WITH THE SOAP OPERA PARTY)

- When Ross walks in on Joey and Rachel kissing, he insists that everything is fine. To prove his point, Ross invites them and Charlie to a dinner party, where he makes fajitas and carries them out with his bare hands. The evening is full of drama—Ross is manic; he drinks all of the margaritas and keeps telling everyone that he's fine; he wants them all to take a trip; he makes an awkward

toast to Rachel, Joey, and love; and he cries over the pressure of entertaining. After Rachel and Charlie leave, Ross finishes the evening by dancing/stripping to the *Chicago* soundtrack. (THE ONE WHERE ROSS IS FINE)

- It's Emma's first birthday party, but the guest of honor is asleep for most of it. Meanwhile, Monica and Chandler can't wait for the party to end so they can go away for the weekend. Joey finds out that he should be at an audition, Phoebe sings a terrible song, and the bunny birthday cake is actually shaped like a penis. (THE ONE WITH THE CAKE)

- Rachel and Monica host a tea party for Phoebe's bachelorette celebrations. It's all very classy, but Phoebe thinks it sucks because she wanted some dirty stuff, too. The girls hire a last-minute stripper, but when he arrives, they're shocked. Instead of a young, muscular guy, they're faced with Officer Goodbody, an old stripper who can't dance. When he demands $300 for his "performance," Phoebe refuses and makes him cry. The stripper realizes his career is over, so the girls persuade him to become a striptease teacher but not before one last dance . . . (THE ONE WHERE THE STRIPPER CRIES)

- There is a small get-together at Monica's to wish Rachel farewell before she leaves for Paris. Monica makes some questionable buffet food, Phoebe gives Rachel a swab with her DNA on it, and there are many tears as Rachel says goodbye to everyone except Ross. He asks what's going on and then they sleep together. (THE ONE WITH RACHEL'S GOING AWAY PARTY)

MENTIONED

- Joey tells Monica that Ross is planning her birthday party in an effort to stop her from going onto the balcony, where Ross is actually trying to ask Rachel out. (THE ONE WITH THE BLACKOUT)

- Mention is made of Phoebe's birthday party, where Chandler kept speaking to her breasts. (THE ONE WHERE NANA DIES TWICE)

- Chandler says that he's just been to a party where a woman literally passed through him. (THE ONE WHERE ROSS FINDS OUT)

- Chandler wants Ross to accompany him to a bachelor party for his weird lobotomist cousin, Albert. Ross thinks that lobotomists are geeks, while Chandler thinks the only reason Albert is getting married is so that he can see a stripper. The stripper in question is Crystal Chandelier, and Ross gets on so well with her that he goes on a playdate with her, her son, and Ben. Chandler, meanwhile, is happy that he got a free gift—a pen with a naked woman on it. (THE ONE WITH ALL THE JEALOUSY)

- Phoebe says that Mike's sister invited her to a party, and now she has to buy a new dress so that she can impress Mike. On the night of the party, she's all dressed up but doesn't really want to go. In the end it doesn't matter, because as she leaves Central Perk, she bumps into David and goes out with him instead. (THE ONE WITH THE DONOR)

COSTUMES

Rachel once dressed up as Little Bo-Peep for Halloween, and Ross has a naughty Princess Leia fantasy. Here are a few of the oftentimes outrageous costumes featured on the series.

- Rachel once dressed up as Little Bo-Peep for Halloween. Chandler and Joey borrowed the blow-up sheep as pillows when they went camping. *(THE ONE WHERE NO ONE'S READY)*

- While trying to teach Ben about Hanukkah, Ross dresses up as the Holiday Armadillo— and then along comes Chandler as Santa and Joey as Superman. *(THE ONE WITH THE HOLIDAY ARMADILLO)*

- During a Halloween party, Monica comes as Catwoman, Phoebe is Supergirl, Chandler is a big, pink bunny, Joey is Chandler, Ross is dressed as a potato that looks like poop, and Rachel comes as herself because she soon won't be able to fit into her dresses. *(THE ONE WITH THE HALLOWEEN PARTY)*

- Ross dresses as a sailor to whisk Rachel off her feet, but she causes so many delays that he ends up plopping her on the Central Perk sofa instead. *(THE ONE WITH THE CHICKEN POX)*

- To fulfil Ross's fantasy, Rachel dresses as Princess Leia in a gold bikini, but thanks to something Chandler said, all Ross can see is his mother dressed as Leia. *(THE ONE WITH THE PRINCESS LEIA FANTASY)*

GAMES

Joey and Chandler add a Foosball table to their kitchen, Phoebe gifts Monica and Chandler a giant Ms. Pac-Man, and Joey hopes to be the new host of a game show called *Bamboozled*. Here are all the games featured on *Friends*.

- After a depressing phone call from the bank, Rachel tearfully declares that it's time to play Twister. The girls eventually play with Joey, Chandler, and Ross when they return from a hockey game. *(THE ONE WITH GEORGE STEPHANOPOULOS)*

- During a slumber party with Monica and Rachel, Phoebe brings Operation. She's lost the tweezers, so they can't operate, "but we can prep the guy!" *(THE ONE WITH GEORGE STEPHANOPOULOS)*

- A Monopoly board is on the coffee table surrounded by candles during the blackout. *(THE ONE WITH THE BLACKOUT)* In *THE ONE WITH THE CHICKEN POX*, Phoebe and her boyfriend Ryan play the game while trying to keep their minds off the chicken pox. Phoebe rubs the dice all over her itchy spots.

- Chandler and Joey buy a Foosball table when their kitchen table breaks. *(THE ONE WITH THE DOZEN LASAGNAS)* It is seen (and played on) frequently, including when they're arguing over who should keep it when Joey moves out. Finally, Joey's new chick gets stuck inside the table, and the table is smashed to pieces. *(THE LAST ONE, PARTS 1 AND 2)*

- Chandler and Ross's Scrabble game ends in disaster when Marcel eats some tiles. *(THE ONE WITH TWO PARTS, PART 2)*

- The boys play poker with the girls, but the girls are terrible. Monica asks her aunt to teach them how to play properly, and things get competitive between Rachel and Ross. *(THE ONE WITH ALL THE POKER)* In *THE ONE WHERE HECKLES DIES*, the friends are playing poker when Chandler comes home from his date with Joan.

- The gang plays Pictionary, but Monica freaks out when nobody guesses her drawing. *(THE ONE WITH ALL THE POKER)*

- The board from Trouble is laid out on Monica's table when Chandler is obsessing about the girl who doesn't call him back, and Rachel admits to sleeping with Barry. *(THE ONE WITH THE EVIL ORTHODONTIST)*

- Chandler buys Travel Scrabble for Rachel's birthday, but she hands it straight back. *(THE ONE WHERE RACHEL FINDS OUT)*

- Malcolm keeps Mad Libs in his stalker bag just for fun. *(THE ONE WITH THE JAM)* In *THE*

ONE WITH THE KIPS, the friends play Mad Libs, but Monica ruins it with her strict rules.

- Joey demonstrates his magic skills to his friends by guessing which card Monica picked. He gets it right but only because he stared at the card before guessing. (*THE ONE WHERE CHANDLER CAN'T REMEMBER WHICH SISTER*) In *THE ONE WHERE RACHEL SMOKES*, Joey tries another card trick and fails immediately.

- While in the beach house, Joey wants to play strip poker, but instead they play strip *Happy Days*, and he loses. (*THE ONE AT THE BEACH*)

- Monica and Chandler play gin while contemplating why they could never be a couple—primarily because Chandler will always be the guy who peed on her. (*THE ONE WITH THE JELLYFISH*)

- Monica, Chandler, and Rachel are playing cards when Joey tells them about his new job at the museum. (*THE ONE WITH PHOEBE'S UTERUS*) In *THE ONE WHERE ROSS MOVES IN*, Rachel and Phoebe are playing cards when Danny comes over to borrow a ladle. In *THE ONE WITH THE GIRL WHO HITS JOEY*, the friends are playing cards when Chandler apologizes to Monica by proposing.

- When the guys and girls think they know everything about each other, Ross comes up with a quiz that will prove it one way or another. What nobody could guess, however, is that it would become so competitive that by the end of the game, Monica and Rachel would lose their apartment to Chandler and Joey. (*THE ONE WITH THE EMBRYOS*)

- While trying to trick Joshua into kissing her, Rachel organizes a game of spin the bottle.

Unfortunately for her, when the bottle points in Joshua's direction, Phoebe's baby kicks and everyone loses concentration. (*THE ONE WITH THE FAKE PARTY*)

- When Monica and Rachel want their apartment back, Phoebe devises a game that pits the girls against the boys, and it includes ludicrous questions. When that doesn't work out, Phoebe comes up with a card game, which is just as unsuccessful. In the end, the girls take the apartment back when the boys are at a Knicks game. Monica and Rachel tell them that if they let them keep their apartment, they'll kiss for one minute. (*THE ONE WITH ALL THE HASTE*)

- When Ross can't decide what to do about Emily's demands to stop hanging out with Rachel, he asks the Magic 8 Ball. It tells him to ask again later. When Monica asks if Chandler will have sex that night, the ball says not to count on it. (*THE ONE WHERE PHOEBE HATES PBS*)

- When Ross moves in with Joey and Chandler, Joey organizes his boxes to create a fort, and then all the guys play in it, complete with hats. *(THE ONE WHERE ROSS MOVES IN)*

- When Ross is bored after going on sabbatical, Joey teaches him a game that he's played for the past six months—calling Chandler and pretending he's a crazy woman with a crush on him. *(THE ONE WITH THE INAPPROPRIATE SISTER)*

- Chandler and Joey invent a crazy game called Fireball involving a tennis ball, lighter fluid, and a fire extinguisher, while Joey is supposed to be writing a script. Ross calls it a crazy lawsuit game, but that's nothing compared to Joey's next idea—Ultimate Fireball, with a bowling ball and blowtorch. *(THE ONE WITH THE INAPPROPRIATE SISTER)*

- Joey and Phoebe compete against each other to see if the chick or the duck will be the first to find the Nutter Butter. *(THE ONE WITH CHANDLER'S WORK LAUGH)*

- When Ross and Joey throw a ball back and forth, they realize that they've been playing the game for about an hour. They're happy to see how long they can throw the ball, but then Monica takes over and becomes so competitive that she calls in sick at work and tries to stop "dropper" Chandler taking part. An exhausted "Team Monica" plays throughout the night until Phoebe comes in, catches the ball, and places it on the table. *(THE ONE WITH THE BALL)*

- When the friends head to Vegas, they spend plenty of time in the casino. Monica finds a chip on the floor and wins at the craps table, Joey discovers his hand twin at a cards table, and Phoebe plays (and lurks) at the slot machine. Ross and Rachel, meanwhile, play blackjack in their bedroom, where a drunk

Rachel makes up her own rules. *(THE ONE IN VEGAS, PARTS 1 AND 2 / THE ONE AFTER VEGAS)*

- In order to give Joey money without him knowing, so he can pay his rent, Chandler invents a crazy card game called Cups. Joey wins $1,500 but then plays the game with Ross and loses all of the money. Chandler steps in to win it back and makes up some new, lucrative rules. *(THE ONE ON THE LAST NIGHT)*

- Ross and Chandler are playing chess in Central Perk when Joey arrives to tell them that the audition for *Mac and C.H.E.E.S.E.* went well. *(THE ONE WITH MAC AND C.H.E.E.S.E.)* In *THE ONE WITH RACHEL'S BIG KISS*, Phoebe and Joey play chess in the apartment but with their own rules.

- During Thanksgiving, the friends see if they can name all the states in six minutes. Ross thinks it's insanely easy but only manages to name forty-six. He vows to name them all before he has dinner, which happens in the middle of the night, even though he has Nevada written down twice. *(THE ONE WHERE CHANDLER DOESN'T LIKE DOGS)*

- Phoebe buys a giant Ms. Pac-Man as a late wedding present for Monica and Chandler. It's fun at first, until Phoebe knocks Monica's name off the winners' board, and then Chandler gets addicted and his hand turns into a claw shape. When it's discovered that the high score names are all made up of dirty words, Monica tries to erase them before Ben comes to visit. She fails, so Phoebe takes over, only to launch into a swearing rant just as Ben walks into the apartment. *(THE ONE WHERE JOEY DATES RACHEL)*

- When Phoebe wants her boyfriend Parker to be quiet, she suggests a game of who can

stay silent the longest. He deliberately loses because he wants to play Jenga. *(THE ONE IN MASSAPEQUA)*

- Joey hopes for a big break on a new game show called *Bamboozled*. He practices with Chandler and Ross, but the rules are almost too incredible to be believed (or understood!). *(THE ONE WITH THE BABY SHOWER)*

- When Rachel is late having her baby, Monica and Phoebe get into a battle betting on when the baby will arrive. When Ross and Rachel find out, they want in on it, too. *(THE ONE WHERE RACHEL IS LATE)*

- Joey plays Ping-Pong by himself while wishing he was back living with Chandler. *(THE ONE WHERE EDDIE MOVES IN)* Monica and Mike play a game of Ping-Pong in Barbados. What Mike doesn't say is that he's awesome at the game, knows all the rules, and

is fiercely competitive. When Monica hurts her hand, Chandler steps in to play for her. He's surprisingly good and wins the match. *(THE ONE IN BARBADOS, PARTS 1 AND 2)*

- When the friends argue over who can leave Emma's birthday party, Monica comes up with the idea of a race between all of the windup toys. The person who bets on the correct toy to win can leave. Unfortunately for her, her dog doesn't even finish, and Joey and Phoebe leave. *(THE ONE WITH THE CAKE)*

- Joey is invited to be on the soap opera edition of the Donny Osmond game show *Pyramid*. Paired with database specialist Gene Lester, Joey is absolutely hopeless and keeps giving the answers away and getting stuff wrong. When he's partnered with him again for the final round, he accidentally gets some right until it all goes wrong again. *(THE ONE WHERE THE STRIPPER CRIES)*

MOVIES, TV SHOWS, AND ADS

From movies and home videos to shows and advertisements, the friends watch a lot of TV on their downtime, none more perhaps than Joey and Chandler, whose favorite show is *Baywatch*.

- The friends watch an unnamed foreign soap opera, which they try to interpret. (THE ONE WHERE MONICA GETS A ROOMMATE)

- Rachel watches *Happy Days* on her first night at Monica's and laments that Joanie really did love Chachi. (THE ONE WHERE MONICA GETS A ROOMMATE) The friends also watch *Happy Days* in THE ONE WITH THE RACE CAR BED, and Ross says that when he was young, he used to pretend to be Richie.

- Chandler figures this episode of *Three's Company* is the one where there's some kind of misunderstanding. (THE ONE WITH THE SONOGRAM AT THE END)

- The friends watch *Lamb Chop's Play-Along!* while Chandler is in a terrible mood after giving up smoking. (THE ONE WITH THE THUMB)

- Chandler wants to watch *Weekend at Bernie's* instead of seeing his mother being interviewed on a chat show. (THE ONE WITH MRS. BING)

- Chandler's mother, Nora Tyler Bing, promotes her raunchy new book on the *Jay Leno Show*. (THE ONE WITH MRS. BING)

- Marcel changes the language on the television, which affects *Laverne and Shirley*, *The Waltons*, and *Bugs Bunny*. (THE ONE WITH TWO PARTS, PART 1)

- While watching TV, Ross quips that, ironically, sumo wrestlers were the kids who got picked last in gym. (THE ONE WITH ROSS'S NEW GIRLFRIEND)

- The friends watch Joey's porno during an evening at Ross's apartment. (THE ONE WITH PHOEBE'S HUSBAND)

- Joey is watching a rabbi play guitar because he can't find the remote. (THE ONE WHERE ROSS FINDS OUT)

- The friends gather at Monica's to watch Joey as neurosurgeon Dr. Drake Ramoray on *Days of Our Lives*. Joey tells them that his costar taught him a technique called "smell the fart acting." (THE ONE WITH THE LESBIAN WEDDING)

- To try and convince Joey's stalker, Erika, that he is not really Dr. Ramoray, Rachel switches on *Days of Our Lives*. Unfortunately, Erika cannot tell the difference between television and real life. (THE ONE AFTER THE SUPERBOWL, PART 1)

- The friends watch *Days of Our Lives* when Joey reveals that his next story line has him win a medical award for separating Siamese twins, and then he and his half-sister, Amber, go to Venezuela to meet their other half-sibling, Ramón. While there, Drake finds the world's biggest emerald—but it's cursed. Later, after Joey claims to write many of his own lines for the show, the writers take revenge—they decide to kill off his character by making Drake fall down an elevator shaft. *(THE ONE WHERE DR. RAMORAY DIES)*

- After Drake has been saved, thanks to a brain transplant, Rachel visits Joey on set. She watches in the monitor as Drake is told that his body is rejecting his new brain and the only hope is to extract tissue from Jessica's (his donor's) body and introduce it into Drake's brain. Unfortunately, when they try to exhume Jessica's body, it isn't there. *(THE ONE WITH RACHEL'S DATE)*

- Rachel watches Drake kiss his costar on the studio monitor and then later has a dream that she and Joey are rehearsing a romantic scene together. *(THE ONE WITH RACHEL'S DREAM)*

- *Days of Our Lives* is seen on the hospital television when Phoebe is talking to her latest crush, Cliff. Unfortunately, Joey had just been imitating Dr. Ramoray shortly before the episode is on television. *(THE ONE WHERE RACHEL HAS A BABY, PART 2)*

- Judy and Jack Geller watch Steffi Graf play tennis and a house paint commercial that they like while they're at Monica's apartment. *(THE ONE WITH THE PROM VIDEO)*

- The friends discover a home video. It shows Rachel (with her old nose), Monica (with her old weight), and Ross (with his curly hair and playing the keyboard). The girls are getting ready to go to the prom, but Rachel's date, Chip, doesn't show. Ross's mother asks him to volunteer as a date, but by the time he's ready, Chip has arrived, and the girls are headed out of the door. *(THE ONE WITH THE PROM VIDEO)*

- *The Dick Van Dyke Show* is one of the first shows the friends watch, after Joey buys a huge TV and Barcaloungers. They also watch basketball, *Xanadu*, and *Beavis and Butt-Head*. *(THE ONE WHERE ROSS AND RACHEL . . . YOU KNOW)*

- *Baywatch* is Joey and Chandler's favorite show. They watch it and then talk about it on the phone after Joey moves out, but when Chandler tries to get new roommate Eddie into it, he fails. *(THE ONE WHERE EDDIE MOVES IN)* The guys also watch *Baywatch* in *THE ONE WITH THE FLASHBACK*, and Chandler and the chick watch it together in *THE ONE WITH A CHICK AND A DUCK*. In *THE*

ONE WHERE CHANDLER CROSSES THE LINE, Chandler watches the show while sitting in the canoe, and in *THE ONE WHERE ROSS MOVES IN*, Ross accidentally tapes over Joey's copy of *Baywatch* with a show about bugs.

- Monica and Ross argue over what they'll watch on television—*Entertainment Tonight* or a documentary about the Serengeti. (*THE ONE WHERE EDDIE MOVES IN*)

- Monica, Richard, Rachel, and Ross watch *Old Yeller*. They're all crying, but Phoebe is confused. She has always thought it's a happy tale because her mother turned it off before the end to save her from the pain of what happens. When she finds out the truth, Phoebe rents other films, including *Love Story*, *Brian's Song*, and *Terms of Endearment*

to see how they end, too. (*THE ONE WHERE OLD YELLER DIES*)

- Phoebe and Ben watch *Sesame Street* at Monica's apartment. (*THE ONE WHERE OLD YELLER DIES*)

- Joey watches *Wheel of Fortune* in his apartment. When he shouts out the wrong answer, Chandler tells Joey he should go on the show. (*THE ONE WITH THE PRINCESS LEIA FANTASY*)

- Monica picks up a box of Civil War videos that she'd ordered for Richard. Heartbroken that they've split up, she watches them while sniffing a cigar. (*THE ONE WITH THE PRINCESS LEIA FANTASY*)

- The friends watch Joey's *Amazing Discoveries* infomercial, demonstrating the Milk Master 2000. Later, Rachel uses the same device to open her own milk. (THE ONE WITH THE METAPHORICAL TUNNEL)

- The Mattress King—Janice's ex-husband—is on TV, mourning the loss of his wife. He's so depressed, he's going to slash his prices. (THE ONE WITH THE RACE CAR BED)

- While Ross is trying to spy Rachel coming home from her date with Mark, Chandler entertains himself by watching basketball. (THE ONE WITH THE TINY T-SHIRT)

- Joey watches a news report pleading with people not to buy poultry as pets, so he goes out and buys a chick. Later, Chandler attempts to leave the chick at the shelter, but instead he comes home with a duck. (THE ONE WITH A CHICK AND A DUCK)

- Joey is watching *Wonder Woman* just as Chandler comes in and admits his love for Kathy. (THE ONE WHERE CHANDLER CROSSES THE LINE)

- Ross watches rugby on ESPN as research for his upcoming match. Joey tries to explain the rules and then advises Ross that the players are going to kill him. (THE ONE WITH ALL THE RUGBY)

- The guys discover free porn on their television. Scared that they might lose access to it, they refuse to turn it off and become obsessed with the erotic films. (THE ONE WITH THE FREE PORN)

- *Die Hard* is the guys' favorite film, and they first mention it while sitting in Central Perk. (THE ONE WITH THE INVITATION) In THE ONE WITH THE NAP PARTNERS, they watch it again, twice.

- While Joey is in his London hotel room, he watches *Cheers* and gets homesick for the States. (THE ONE WITH ROSS'S WEDDING, PART 1)

- When Joey tries to get into his London hotel room, Chandler and Monica pretend they are watching *My Giant*. In reality, they were planning on sleeping together. Joey and Felicity watch the movie, which makes Joey question why he can never be a giant. (THE ONE AFTER ROSS SAYS RACHEL)

- When Phoebe gives birth, she's irritated that not only is her doctor a huge Fonzie fan, but he also insists on watching *Happy Days* as she gives birth. When Rachel mentions that she always liked Mork, the doctor is offended because Mork once froze Fonzie. (THE ONE HUNDREDTH)

- After her mother's suicide, Phoebe wrote to *Sesame Street*, care of PBS. She later received a key ring, but by that time she was living in a box with no keys. Phoebe has hated PBS ever since. (THE ONE WHERE PHOEBE HATES PBS)

- Rachel and Ross are supposed to see *How Stella Got Her Groove Back*, but Ross is too busy contemplating whether or not he can bow to Emily's demands not to see Rachel anymore. (THE ONE WHERE PHOEBE HATES PBS)

- While Monica insists that she and Chandler change hotel rooms, Chandler tries to watch a high-speed police chase on TV. (THE ONE WITH THE KIPS)

- Phoebe, Joey, and Ross are supposed to be going to see *You've Got Mail* at the cinema, but Ross is too depressed after hearing that Emily is getting remarried. (THE ONE WITH CHANDLER'S WORK LAUGH)

- When Rachel says that Phoebe looks like a cross between the Six Million Dollar Man and Kermit the Frog when she's running, Ross says that Monica once had a crush on him. Rachel assumes that Monica had a crush on the Six Million Dollar Man, but it was actually Kermit. (THE ONE WHERE PHOEBE RUNS)

- Monica, Chandler, Phoebe, and Joey watch *E.T.* and then they talk about how sad *Bambi* is, especially when his mother died. Chandler doesn't agree, and it's revealed that he's just not a man who cries—or, as Joey and Monica describe it, he's dead inside. Monica then spends the next few days trying to entice some tears, until finally Chandler starts crying and can't stop. (THE ONE WHERE CHANDLER CAN'T CRY)

- Ursula makes the following porn movies under Phoebe's name: *Sex Toy Story 2*, *Lawrence of a Labia*, *Inspect Her Gadget*, and *Buffay the Vampire Layer*. (THE ONE WHERE CHANDLER CAN'T CRY)

- Ross and Joey are watching a basketball game on TV when Chandler tells them he's going to propose to Monica. (THE ONE WITH THE RING)

- While teaching a class, Ross presents a theory of how he came up with the idea for *Jurassic Park* first. (THE ONE WITH RACHEL'S BOOK)

- According to Chandler, Joey cries every time anyone talks about *Titanic*. (THE ONE WITH ALL THE CANDY)

- When Ross and Rachel argue over who came on to whom on the night that she got pregnant, Ross presents a videotape, which shows the truth. Rachel was the one who seduced him, using a romantic backpacking story that Joey made up to seduce women. (THE ONE WITH THE VIDEOTAPE)

- While Monica is cooking Thanksgiving dinner, Chandler pretends to watch the game so that he doesn't have to help. Phoebe finds out, and she wants in on it, too. (THE ONE WITH THE RUMOR)

- When Joey returns from a date, Rachel is watching *Cujo* by herself, so he offers to watch with her. The only trouble is, Joey thinks he's falling in love with her, so when she cuddles into him, he gets really scared. (THE ONE WHERE JOEY DATES RACHEL)

- Chandler is watching *Road Rules* when Monica tries to talk him into taking a relaxing bath. (THE ONE WHERE CHANDLER TAKES A BATH)

- When Chandler discovers that Monica's closet is full of junk, he reckons he's been living with Fred Sanford from the TV show *Sanford and Son*. (THE ONE WITH THE SECRET CLOSET)

- Phoebe loans Rachel a birthing video to prepare her for having her baby, but when Chandler finds it, he reads the title—*Candy and Cookie*—and thinks it must be a porn film. He pops it into the VCR and is so traumatized that he refuses to watch a real porno that Monica has rented for him. Monica and Rachel are freaked out, too, but then Rachel decides to watch it from beginning to end—only she accidentally watches the porn film. (THE ONE WITH THE BIRTHING VIDEO)

a woman wearing cowboy boots. Chandler is appalled, and then Monica is insulted when she realizes that the woman isn't her—Richard must have taped over her sex tape. *(THE ONE WITH ROSS'S INAPPROPRIATE SONG)*

- When Charlie asks Rachel where she would find jackets with shoulder pads, Rachel tells her she'd find one on Melanie Griffith in *Working Girl*. *(THE ONE WITH THE DONOR)*

- *Miss Congeniality* is one of Chandler's favorite movies. He recognizes it through the wall while in Barbados, and then on their return to New York, he begs Monica to watch it with him even though she can't understand why he loves it so much. *(THE ONE AFTER JOEY AND RACHEL KISS)*

- While trying to make everyone cry during a speech for her parents' anniversary, Monica brings up the part in *Terms of Endearment* when Debra Winger has to say goodbye to her children. *(THE ONE IN MASSAPEQUA)*

- Monica goes to visit Chandler in Tulsa but walks in on him watching a porn film. As he jumps up, he changes the channel to a shark documentary, which leads Monica to think that he gets turned on by angry sharks. She finally finds out the truth when she rents a shark documentary for Chandler, and he is thoroughly confused. *(THE ONE WITH THE SHARKS)*

- When Richard sells his apartment, Chandler and Joey take a tour and find a video with Monica's name on it. They watch the tape later, and it shows Richard making love to

- After seeing Chandler get into a strange woman's car, Phoebe calls to ask if he'd like to go to the movies with her and Rachel. They pretend that they're going to see *Liar Liar*; *Betrayal*; *An Affair to Remember*; or *Dude, Where's My Car?* *(THE ONE WHERE CHANDLER GETS CAUGHT)*

- While visiting Dr. Green in the hospital, Ross watches a dinosaur movie on TV. *(THE ONE WHERE JOEY SPEAKS FRENCH)*

SINGERS, GROUPS, AND SONGS

There are several musical influences and mentions of singers and bands on *Friends*, including Joey's (but not Rachel's) favorite original "Morning's Here."

- When Rachel is feeling down, Phoebe sings her "My Favorite Things" from *The Sound of Music*. (THE ONE WHERE MONICA GETS A ROOMMATE)

- Monica, Phoebe, and Joey sing "Top of the World" by the Carpenters, unaware that Ross is being attacked by a cat on the balcony. (THE ONE WITH THE BLACKOUT)

- Ross sings "Hey Hey We're the Monkees" to Carol's bump. (THE ONE WHERE UNDERDOG GETS AWAY)

- The friends hum the theme from the *Odd Couple* while sitting in Central Perk. (THE ONE WITH THE DOZEN LASAGNAS)

- As Marcel wakes up after his Scrabble tile emergency, "New York Minute" by Don Henley is playing. (THE ONE WITH TWO PARTS, PART 2)

- The friends whistle the "Colonel Bogey March" while stuffing envelopes. (THE ONE WITH ALL THE POKER)

- As Rachel waits for Ross to come into the arrivals lounge, "Take a Bow" by Madonna plays in the background. (THE ONE WHERE RACHEL FINDS OUT)

- The whole group is supposed to go to a Hootie and the Blowfish concert, but Joey, Phoebe, and Rachel can't afford it. Monica, Ross, and Chandler buy the others concert tickets, but the others see it as charity and turn it down. Monica, Ross, and Chandler go anyway and attend an after-show party, where Monica receives a hickey from a Blowfish. (THE ONE WITH FIVE STEAKS AND AN EGGPLANT)

- While Monica and Chandler are working out, "Macho Man" by the Village People plays in the background. (THE ONE WHERE ROSS FINDS OUT)

- Ross asks a radio show to play "With or Without You" by U2 to show how sorry he is for making Rachel a pros and cons list. She calls the station and tells them what happened, and the presenter pulls the song off the air. (THE ONE WITH THE LIST) This song is also played in THE ONE WHERE ROSS AND RACHEL TAKE A BREAK while Ross dances with Chloe and Rachel sits alone in the apartment.

- While Ross and Marcel walk around New York, "Looks Like We Made It" by Barry Manilow plays in the background. (THE ONE AFTER THE SUPERBOWL, PART 2)

- Monica and her Moondance Diner colleagues dance on the counter to "YMCA" by the Village People. *(THE ONE WITH THE BULLIES)*

- Rachel sings "Copacabana" by Barry Manilow during Barry and Mindy's wedding. *(THE ONE WITH BARRY AND MINDY'S WEDDING)*

- Chandler and Phoebe sing "Endless Love" by Lionel Richie and Diana Ross when Chandler is heartbroken over Janice leaving him. *(THE ONE WITH THE GIANT POKING DEVICE)*

- Joey sings "You've Got to Pick a Pocket or Two" from *Oliver!* during an audition for a Broadway musical. *(THE ONE WITH ALL THE JEALOUSY)*

Emotional Knapsack

- When Ross is paranoid about Rachel's work relationship with Mark, he hires a barbershop quartet to sing a song about her new job and "ever-loving boyfriend, Ross." Later, Monica hires them to sing a song for creepy Julio, calling him a butt munch, who is bad in bed. *(THE ONE WITH ALL THE JEALOUSY)*

- Phoebe and her date Sergei sing a version of "American Pie" by Don McLean while sitting in Central Perk. *(THE ONE WHERE ROSS AND RACHEL TAKE A BREAK)*

- When Monica and Phoebe cater a funeral, the widow is too busy singing "You're a Grand Old Flag" and "Jeepers Creepers" to pay her bill. *(THE ONE WITH THE DIRTY GIRL)*

- The guy across the way from Joey's apartment sings "Morning's Here" every day. Joey loves him, but Rachel hates him, especially when he sings the song on a Saturday. *(THE ONE WITH ALL THE HASTE)*

- When Ross gets his ear pierced, he compares himself to David Bowie. Chandler wonders if he knows that Wham! broke up and then asks him to wake them up before he go-gos. *(THE ONE WITH ALL THE HASTE)*

- When Ross moves in with Joey and Chandler, he changes their answering machine message to his own "special" version of "We Will Rock You" by Queen. *(THE ONE WHERE ROSS MOVES IN)*

- When Ross and Chandler had their own student band, they penned songs such as "Emotional Knapsack" and "Betrayal in the Common Room." *(THE ONE WITH ALL THE THANKSGIVINGS / THE ONE WHERE THE STRIPPER CRIES)*

Betrayal in the Common Room

- Chandler once rushed the stage at a Wham! concert, and George Michael slapped him. *(THE ONE WITH ALL THE THANKSGIVINGS)*

- When Joey says he's going to take proper guitar lessons, ex-teacher Phoebe says that he better not go crying to her when everyone is sick of him playing "Bad, Bad Leroy Brown" by Jim Croce. *(THE ONE WITH ALL THE RESOLUTIONS)*

- Chandler videotaped himself singing "Space Oddity" by David Bowie (complete with an ornament as a microphone), and later it's accidentally shown to the friends after Joey's faked *Law & Order* scene. (THE ONE WHERE ROSS CAN'T FLIRT)

- While alone in the apartment, Rachel dances naked to "Love to Love You Baby" by Donna Summer. (THE ONE IN VEGAS, PART 1)

- "Viva Las Vegas" by Elvis Presley is playing as Ross and Rachel dash out of the Las Vegas wedding chapel. (THE ONE IN VEGAS, PART 2)

- On the way home from Las Vegas, Joey sings "Rock and Roll All Nite" by KISS and "Space Oddity" by David Bowie. Phoebe thinks that Joey has a beautiful voice. (THE ONE AFTER VEGAS)

- When Rachel mistakenly thinks that she, Monica, and Chandler are going to be roommates, she sings the first line of "Come and Knock on Our Door," the theme song from *Three's Company*. An embarrassed Monica sings the next line. (THE ONE WHERE ROSS HUGS RACHEL)

- Monica and Ross perform their routine to "Trouble with Boys" by Loreta. (THE ONE WITH THE ROUTINE)

- While listening to a mixtape version of "The Way You Look Tonight" by Tony Bennett, Monica is shocked to hear Janice's voice calling Chandler her little Bing-a-Ling. Also on the mixtape is "My Funny Valentine," sung by Janice herself. (THE ONE WITH UNAGI)

- While Paul is trying to give himself confidence for dating Rachel, he sings "Love Machine" by the Miracles in front of the mirror. Ross overhears him while he's hiding under the bed. *(THE ONE WHERE PAUL'S THE MAN)*

- After their engagement, Monica and Chandler dance to "Wonderful Tonight" by Eric Clapton. *(THE ONE WITH THE PROPOSAL, PART 2)*

- When Janice invites herself to Monica and Chandler's wedding, Chandler worries that she'll want to sing "Part-Time Lover" by Stevie Wonder. However, Janice suggests she sing either "Careless Whisper" by George Michael or "The Lady in Red" by Chris de Burgh. *(THE ONE WITH ROSS'S LIBRARY BOOK)*

- Ross tries to play "Celebration" by Kool & the Gang on his bagpipes. *(THE ONE WITH JOEY'S NEW BRAIN)*

- Chandler wants the Swing Kings to play at his wedding after hearing their music in a Gap commercial. *(THE ONE WITH THE CHEAP WEDDING DRESS)*

- When Monica and Chandler go to Vegas, "Believe" by Cher is playing in the nightclub where Charles Bing is about to perform. *(THE ONE WITH CHANDLER'S DAD)*

- In his Las Vegas review, Charles Bing as Helena Handbasket sings "I Feel Pretty" from *West Side Story* and "It's Raining Men" by the Weather Girls. *(THE ONE WITH CHANDLER'S DAD)*

- When Joey's sister Dina announces her pregnancy, Bobby (the father) tells Joey that he's in a band called Numbnuts with his pal Rooster. *(THE ONE WITH MONICA'S BOOTS)*

- Phoebe is excited to hear that Ben goes to the same school as Sting's son, because she wants a ticket to Sting's sold-out concert. She takes it upon herself to visit the family apartment but ends up getting a restraining order against her. Thankfully, when Ross is able to get tickets, Phoebe can still go because the seats are more than fifty yards away from Sting, his wife, or a member of his family. *(THE ONE WITH MONICA'S BOOTS)*

- Chandler listens to Enya while enjoying his relaxing bubble bath. *(THE ONE WHERE CHANDLER TAKES A BATH)*

- When Monica tries to fix the mess Chandler has made of the CD collection, she comes across his *Miami Vice* album. Chandler assures her that they were giving them away at the store . . . in exchange for money. He also has two copies of the *Annie* soundtrack and knows all the words from the song "Tomorrow." *(THE ONE WITH THE TEA LEAVES)*

- While Rachel thinks that Joey is proposing and Ross exits the elevator on his way to see her, "Sign on the Window" by Bob Dylan plays in the background. *(THE ONE WHERE RACHEL HAS A BABY, PART 2)*

- When Rachel hires Sandy as the male nanny, Ross doesn't approve of his "too sensitive" ways. One of his talents is to play "Greensleeves," "Hot Cross Buns," and "Three Blind Mice" on his recorder. That's when he's not making beautiful madeleines, performing puppet shows, or giving counseling. *(THE ONE WITH THE MALE NANNY)*

- Ross sings "Baby Got Back" by Sir Mix-A-Lot and it makes Emma laugh. Rachel thinks the song is offensive, but then she ends up singing it as well just to get the same reaction from Emma. *(THE ONE WITH ROSS'S INAPPROPRIATE SONG)*

- When Mike runs a karaoke evening at the piano bar, Phoebe sings "We Are the Champions" by Queen while a random pervert sings a literal version of "I Touch Myself" by the Divinyls. When Monica takes to the stage, her song is "Delta Dawn" by Tanya Tucker. The crowd loves her, but is it because of her beautiful voice or the way her shirt goes transparent in the light? She doesn't care, and even after finding out about her see-through blouse, she belts out "I'm So Excited" by the Pointer Sisters, before Chandler sings his rendition of "Joy to the World" by Three Dog Night. *(THE ONE WHERE MONICA SINGS)*

- While trying to seduce Chandler with her cornrows, Monica thinks she's humming "Bolero" from *10*. Chandler informs her that it's "Ride of the Valkyries" from *Apocalypse Now*. *(THE ONE AFTER JOEY AND RACHEL KISS)*

- When Ross and Monica were young, they always wanted to be Donny and Marie Osmond and used to perform for their family and friends. She's a little bit country, and he's a little bit rock 'n' roll. *(THE ONE WHERE THE STRIPPER CRIES)*

- When Officer Goodbody attempts a striptease at Phoebe's bachelorette party, he does so to "Tainted Love" by Soft Cell. He then does one last dance to "You Make Me Feel (Mighty Real)" by Sylvester. *(THE ONE WHERE THE STRIPPER CRIES)*

- On the day of Phoebe's wedding, her friend Marjorie plays the steel drums. One of the tunes is "Can't Help Falling in Love" by Elvis Presley. *(THE ONE WITH PHOEBE'S WEDDING)*

BOOKS

Rachel loves her erotic novels, Joey gives a dramatic reading of *Love You Forever*, and Monica might have a big problem when she reads *Like a Hole in the Head*. Here are all the books and magazines mentioned in the series.

- Susan reads *Yertle the Turtle and Other Stories* to Carol's bump. (THE ONE WHERE UNDERDOG GETS AWAY)

- Chandler's mom promotes her book, *Euphoria Unbound*, while on the *Jay Leno Show*. (THE ONE WITH MRS. BING)

- Rachel tries to write an erotic novel called *A Woman Undone* after being inspired by Chandler's mother. The first chapter is full of unfortunate—but hilarious—spelling mistakes. (THE ONE WITH MRS. BING)

- Joey buys *Oh, the Places You'll Go!* for Rachel's birthday. Apparently, the book got him through some tough times. (THE ONE WHERE RACHEL FINDS OUT)

- Joey gives an interview for *Soap Opera Digest*, where he states that he writes many of his lines on *Days of Our Lives*. The real writers respond by killing his character off. (THE ONE WHERE DR. RAMORAY DIES)

- Monica, Phoebe, and Rachel read *Be Your Own Windkeeper*. The self-help book introduces readers to the concept of women having an empowering wind that is frequently stolen by men. At first the girls are obsessed with the book's philosophies, until they get into

an argument while doing a quiz. (THE ONE WHERE EDDIE WON'T GO)

- Chandler reads a book about trout in Central Perk. (THE ONE WITH THE PRINCESS LEIA FANTASY)

- Joey loves *The Shining*, but when it scares him, he pops it into the freezer. When Rachel questions what's so good about it, Joey lets her borrow it but then accidentally gives away some major plot points, including the ending. (THE ONE WHERE MONICA AND RICHARD ARE FRIENDS)

- Rachel loans *Little Women* to Joey to broaden his almost nonexistent literary tastes. He doesn't understand much of the book and mixes up the genders of the main characters. When it looks as though one of the characters will die, he pops the book into the freezer. (THE ONE WHERE MONICA AND RICHARD ARE FRIENDS)

- Rachel is reading *The Last Thing He Wanted* when she encourages Bonnie to shave her head. (THE ONE AT THE BEACH)

- When an encyclopedia salesman turns up at Joey's door, he assures the guy that he has no money to buy a complete set. However, after finding $50 in his pants pocket (they must be Chandler's), Joey buys *Encyclopedia,* volume V, in the hope of impressing his friends. (THE ONE WITH THE CUFFS)

- Rachel is reading *Anthem: An American Road Story* in Central Perk when Ross tries to make her jealous with another woman's phone number. (THE ONE WITH JOEY'S NEW GIRLFRIEND)

- Still in love with Joey's girlfriend Kathy, Chandler buys an early edition of her favorite book, *The Velveteen Rabbit*. In order to find it, he had to visit a couple of bookstores, talk to dealers, and call the author's grandchildren. When Joey buys her a pen with a built-in clock, Chandler is forced to swap so that his gift is not better than Joey's. Kathy knows the book came from Chandler, however, because when Joey gave it to her, he said it was because he knew she liked rabbits and cheese. (THE ONE WITH THE DIRTY GIRL)

- Monica is reading *Like a Hole in the Head* when Rachel discovers all the holes in the wall caused by Monica's obsession with the light switch. (THE ONE WITH ALL THE RUGBY) She is seen reading it again in THE ONE WITH THE FREE PORN when the guys come over to watch regular TV instead of porn. In THE ONE WHERE ROSS HUGS RACHEL, Rachel reads this book (with a different cover) when Monica explains that Chandler is moving in.

- Phoebe says that she has read the entire baby names book and hasn't been able to come up with a suitable name for Frank and Alice's baby. (THE ONE WITH RACHEL'S NEW DRESS)

- Chandler reads *Access London* in Central Perk while planning his trip to London. (THE ONE WITH THE INVITATION)

- When Phoebe thinks she has gone into labor but isn't sure, Monica tells Rachel to pass "the book." She means the pregnancy book, but Rachel hands her the Bible. (THE ONE WITH THE WORST BEST MAN EVER)

- When Phoebe asks Chandler to fetch her book from his apartment, he brings *What to Expect When You're Expecting*. (THE ONE WITH ROSS'S WEDDING, PART 1) In THE ONE WITH THE RUMOR, Joey reads this book when Rachel is pregnant.

- Monica is reading *Practical Intuition* in Central Perk when she and Rachel discuss how Ross is coping after breaking up with Emily. (THE ONE WHERE ROSS MOVES IN) She reads it again in THE ONE WITH ROSS'S SANDWICH, when Phoebe and Rachel come back from night class.

- Phoebe reads *Wuthering Heights* and *Jane Eyre* during her literature class at the New School. (THE ONE WITH ROSS'S SANDWICH)

- Phoebe is reading *Love* in Central Perk when Ross tells her that he didn't go through with his and Rachel's annulment. (THE ONE AFTER VEGAS)

- Rachel reads *The Art of Happiness* during a conversation with her sister and then another with Ross. (THE ONE WITH RACHEL'S SISTER)

- When Joey and Monica say that Chandler is dead inside, he reads *Chicken Soup for the Soul* to try and force out some tears. (THE ONE WHERE CHANDLER CAN'T CRY)

- According to Phoebe, she has written fourteen books. Her next one is about the traps of relationships and includes a couple called Marcia and Chester, who happen to share quite a few similarities to Monica and Chandler. *(THE ONE WHERE ROSS MEETS ELIZABETH'S DAD)*

• When Joey takes a nap in Rachel's bed, he comes across an erotic book about Zelda and the chimney sweep. He enjoys teasing her about it, until she pretends that he's turning her on, and he runs away. *(THE ONE WITH RACHEL'S BOOK)*

• Ross discovers a copy of his doctoral dissertation in the university library, but it's in a quiet section where couples go to make out. *(THE ONE WITH ROSS'S LIBRARY BOOK)*

• Phoebe and Rachel are reading *Cowboy Love Poetry* when Ross and Joey arrive to talk about Chandler and Monica's vows. *(THE ONE WITH THE VOWS)*

• Ross reads *Dutch for Beginners* in Central Perk to learn to speak Dutch, but he can't understand anything that Gunther says to him. *(THE ONE WITH THE STAIN)*

• Rachel is reading *The Girlfriends' Guide to Pregnancy* when Joey tries to persuade her not to move out. *(THE ONE WITH THE STAIN)*

• When Dina and Rachel are talking about pregnancy, Dina is reading *Pregnancy for Dummies* while Rachel reads *The Girlfriends' Guide to Pregnancy*. *(THE ONE WITH MONICA'S BOOTS)*

• Rachel is reading *The Pink and Blue Baby Pages* in Ross's apartment just as he's getting ready to see Mona. *(THE ONE WITH THE BIRTHING VIDEO)*

• When Phoebe tells fortunes for her friends, she uses a book about reading tea leaves as her guide. *(THE ONE WITH THE TEA LEAVES)*

• Ross is reading *Blue Dog Love* in Central Perk while Monica tells him that she wants to give the speech at her parents' anniversary party. *(THE ONE IN MASSAPEQUA)*

• Monica looks for advice from *365 Things Every New Mom Should Know* when baby Emma won't stop crying. Phoebe, meanwhile, reads *The New Mom's Manual*. *(THE ONE WHERE EMMA CRIES)*

• While waiting at the doctor's office, Ross helps a little girl find Waldo. Spoiler: The character is hiding behind an elephant at the circus. *(THE ONE WITH THE PEDIATRICIAN)*

• When Joey says he'll do a dramatic reading of one of Emma's books, he accidentally picks up *Riding the Storm Out: Coping with Postpartum Depression*, which belongs to Rachel. *(THE ONE WITH THE CAKE)*

• Joey gives a dramatic reading of *Love You Forever* for Emma's first birthday. Phoebe suspects it will be a disaster, but everyone loves it. *(THE ONE WITH THE CAKE)*

• After Joey's dramatic reading, Phoebe wants to do one, too, but her choice of book is controversial—*Sex and the Single Mother*. *(THE ONE WITH THE CAKE)*

INSPIRATION AND QUESTIONS FROM THE BOOK

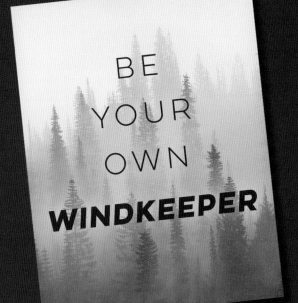

BE
YOUR
OWN
WINDKEEPER

When Phoebe, Monica, and Rachel discover a new self-help book, they're intrigued, inspired, and ultimately irritated. Here are a few gems from *Be Your Own Windkeeper*.

- Have you ever allowed a lightning bearer to take your wind?

- Have you ever betrayed another goddess for a lightning bearer?

- Don't let men (lightning bearers) steal your wind.

- Women need to become more empowered.

- The wind can make you a goddess, but lightning bearers can take the wind.

- As Rachel says, "How can you expect me to grow if you won't let me blow?"

- Lightning bearers always drink from your pool of inner power, but God forbid you should take a sip.

- You don't have to apologize.

- Don't let men wash their feet in the pool of your inner power.

- Don't let a guy into the forest of your righteous truth on the first date.

- Don't be a leaf blower.

- Don't suck wind from another goddess.

(THE ONE WHERE EDDIE WON'T GO)

RESTAURANTS

It's always a nice treat when the friends are able to go out to eat, although they don't always know what's going to be in store.

- The friends go to a Mexican restaurant with Chandler's mother, but Ross's evening is ruined when Rachel and Paolo show up late. While checking messages on a public phone, Nora talks to Ross about his love life and then kisses him—just as Joey walks past. *(THE ONE WITH MRS. BING)*

- To celebrate Monica's promotion, the friends all go to an expensive restaurant. Joey, Rachel, and Phoebe don't have as much money as the others, and the expense of the meal and other recent celebrations causes Phoebe to explode. *(THE ONE WITH FIVE STEAKS AND AN EGGPLANT)*

- Rachel goes to the Saloon with Michael. The date's a disaster when Rachel gets drunk,

laments her love for Ross, borrows a man's cell phone to call Ross, and then chucks the handset in an ice bucket. *(THE ONE WHERE ROSS FINDS OUT)*

- When Ross finds out that Rachel is in love with him, he shows up at Central Perk to talk about their relationship. They bicker about the circumstances they find themselves in, and Ross storms out. Rachel locks the doors, but then he returns and they kiss for the first time. *(THE ONE WHERE ROSS FINDS OUT)*

- During the rehearsal dinner for Ross and Emily's London wedding, their parents bicker, Joey is homesick, and Chandler makes an embarrassing speech about Ross and a blow-up doll. After Chandler's jokes fall flat, Joey takes his turn, which involves a speech about how homesick he is for New York. *(THE ONE WITH ROSS'S WEDDING, PART 2)*

- When Chandler and Monica go out for dinner with Gary and Phoebe, Monica is jealous that Phoebe seems to have a more exciting sex life than she does. She sneaks into the men's room and tries to seduce Chandler, and he realizes that she's now the one freaking out about their relationship, not him. *(THE ONE WITH RACHEL'S INADVERTENT KISS)*

- On the morning after Ross and Rachel get married, everyone meets in the restaurant of the Las Vegas hotel for breakfast. The happy couple doesn't seem to remember anything about what they did the night before until everyone else reminds them. *(THE ONE AFTER VEGAS)*

- Rachel, Ross, Paul, and Elizabeth go out to dinner, with Rachel's intention being to talk Ross up to Paul. Unfortunately, everything she says seems to backfire, especially when she accidentally tells him that Ross has been married and divorced three times. *(THE ONE WHERE ROSS MEETS ELIZABETH'S DAD)*

- When a pregnant Rachel is mourning her lack of dates, Joey offers to take her out for the evening. Before the date, he presents her with lilies and a paper bag that once housed a brownie, before Joey ate it. They go to an expensive restaurant, where they eat lobster and share their dating moves. When they get home, Joey declares it to be the best date he's ever had. *(THE ONE WHERE JOEY DATES RACHEL)*

- Joey takes Rachel to a restaurant so that he can declare his love for her. At first, she thinks he's joking, but then she realizes he's telling the truth. Rachel assures Joey that she loves him as a friend, and they both end up in tears. The waiter decides that one of them must be dying and he kind of hopes it's Rachel because he thinks Joey is really cute. *(THE ONE WHERE JOEY TELLS RACHEL)*

- When Phoebe and Joey agree to choose dates for each other, Phoebe introduces Joey to her

friend Mary-Ellen. Joey, however, forgot about the date, so he chooses the first person called Mike that he can find in Central Perk. What follows is an awkward dinner together, during which Mike lets it slip that he only knows Joey from *Days of Our Lives* when he was supposed to pretend that he knew him since high school. *(THE ONE WITH THE PEDIATRICIAN)*

- It's Phoebe's birthday, and she and Joey wait for their friends in a restaurant. The friends are so late that the waiter takes their table, and by the time everyone shows up, they're crammed into a tiny space. Monica and Chandler bicker about his smoking and her tricking him into bed, Ross and Rachel are distracted by Judy and Emma at the bar, Joey just wants his dinner, and Phoebe lectures everyone about being late on her birthday—before she receives a call from Mike and leaves. *(THE ONE WITH PHOEBE'S BIRTHDAY DINNER)*

- It's Phoebe and Mike's rehearsal dinner, but Monica the wedding planner is so bossy that she ends up being screamed at by Phoebe and then fired. Meanwhile, Rachel is tasked with deciding who will be a groomsman, Ross or Chandler. *(THE ONE WITH PHOEBE'S WEDDING)*

FOOD

We all know that Joey doesn't share food and Ross becomes an honorary Brown Bird, but we wish we could forget about Phoebe and Joey trying breast milk.

- Monica makes lasagna for her parents, but Rachel loses her engagement ring in it. (THE ONE WITH THE SONOGRAM AT THE END)

- The girls order a fat-free crust with extra cheese pizza, but they get mushroom, green pepper, and onion instead. The pizza belongs to White House adviser George Stephanopoulos, who lives across the street. They then spy on him from the window. (THE ONE WITH GEORGE STEPHANOPOULOS)

- Monica makes a dozen lasagnas for her aunt, but her aunt rejects them because they're not vegetarian. Monica offloads the pasta dish on her friends, including one to Carol and vegetarian Susan, and even Rachel's ex-boyfriend Paolo goes home with one. (THE ONE WITH THE DOZEN LASAGNAS)

- Ross, Chandler, and Rachel are freaked out when Phoebe and Joey taste bottled breast milk. However, when Susan says she's tasted it, too, Ross decides to eventually give it a go. (THE ONE WITH THE BREAST MILK)

- Mockolate is a synthetic form of chocolate that Monica has to make into various recipes for a perspective employer. Mockolate crumbles and bubbles and has a terrible aftertaste. It is so awful that Monica only adds just a tiny bit of it to her recipes after Phoebe labels it as what evil must taste like. (THE ONE WITH THE LIST)

- Monica and Rachel make cookies instead of giving Christmas tips. Mr. Treeger enjoys them, but the mailman and newspaper delivery guy do not. (THE ONE WITH PHOEBE'S DAD)

- Monica makes Rachel a birthday flan instead of a cake. The others hate the idea of the Mexican custard dessert and are pleased when it's eventually destroyed by a volleyball. (THE ONE WITH THE TWO PARTIES)

- Monica makes jam while recovering from her split with Richard. It's her plan to get over her man. (THE ONE WITH THE JAM)

- Ross volunteers to sell cookies to send a young girl to Space Camp. Monica buys some boxes even though her own experience of selling Brown Bird cookies was a disaster—her father had to buy all of her boxes because she ate them. (THE ONE WHERE RACHEL QUITS)

- On their anniversary, Ross brings a picnic to Rachel's office because she has to work late. He grinds pepper when Rachel is on the phone and accidentally sets fire to some flowers after lighting candles. This leads to a giant argument, and Rachel demands he leave. As Ross gathers up his basket, he accidentally packs up the office's three-hole punch. (THE ONE WHERE ROSS AND RACHEL TAKE A BREAK)

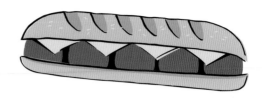

- After eating pizza with her friends, Rachel attempts to throw away the box only to be shouted at by Mr. Treeger for clogging up the trash chute. Joey then goes down to confront him, and Treeger tells him that he's going to evict the girls because Monica has been illegally subletting her apartment. (THE ONE WITH THE BALLROOM DANCING)

- After his marriage to Emily breaks up and he loses his apartment, Ross's sandwich is the only good thing going on in his life. It's a special Thanksgiving turkey leftover sandwich, with Monica's special "moistmaker" in the middle. Ross keeps it in the refrigerator at the museum, along with a little note asking others not to eat it, but it still disappears. In response, Phoebe composes a threatening message, which earns Ross the nickname Mental Geller. When it's revealed that it was his boss who ate the sandwich and threw most of it away, Ross freaks out, screams at him, and is put on sabbatical. (THE ONE WITH ROSS'S SANDWICH)

- When Ross discovers that Emily is getting remarried, he smashes up a scone in Central Perk. (THE ONE WITH CHANDLER'S WORK LAUGH)

- When Joey, Ross, and Chandler go on a ride-along with Phoebe's cop boyfriend, Gary, Joey stops off to buy a meatball sandwich. When there's a suspected gunshot, Joey

throws himself in front of Ross. Despite it being a car backfiring instead of a gun, Chandler gets jealous that Joey chose to save Ross and not him. In reality, Joey was saving his sandwich, which just happened to be next to his friend. (THE ONE WITH THE RIDE-ALONG)

- To get out of helping Rachel pack, Ross says he's looking after Ben. Knowing that Monica can see him from across the road, he creates a fake Ben with a giant pumpkin as a head. (THE ONE ON THE LAST NIGHT)

- Rachel makes a trifle for Thanksgiving dinner. The recipe consists of a layer of lady fingers, a layer of jam, custard, raspberries, more lady fingers, beef sautéed with peas and onions, custard, bananas, and whipped cream. It turns out—because the pages in the cookbook are stuck together—that she's made half an English trifle and half a shepherd's pie, so the friends find reasons why they can't eat it. Joey, however, thinks that it's delicious and eats everyone else's. (THE ONE WHERE ROSS GOT HIGH)

- When Joey's fridge breaks, he has to eat all of the food, including cold cuts, ice cream, limes, and an unidentified substance in a brown jar. (THE ONE WITH JOEY'S FRIDGE)

- Phoebe offers her grandmother's cookie recipe as an engagement present to Monica and Chandler. The fire has destroyed it, however, so she gives Monica the last cookie to dissect. After Monica makes dozens of batches, it's revealed that the cookie recipe is actually a packet mix made by Nestlé Toll House. *(THE ONE WITH PHOEBE'S COOKIES)*

- Monica makes candy for the neighbors and leaves it in a basket at the door. Her intention is to get to know them better (and for them to like her), but when "customers" start arriving in the middle of the night and almost rioting outside the front door, the free treats stop. *(THE ONE WITH ALL THE CANDY)*

- When Chandler finds a cheesecake outside his door, he and Rachel eat it even though it's addressed to a lady downstairs. A couple of days later, another one arrives. They deliver it to the right address, but when it isn't collected, Chandler and Rachel eat that one, too—with forks on the floor after it fell to the ground. *(THE ONE WITH ALL THE CHEESECAKES)*

- Monica isn't going to make a turkey for Thanksgiving, but Joey assures her that if she does, he'll finish almost the entire thing. After he spends all day eating the whole turkey, he finds enough room for Monica's home-made pie, too. *(THE ONE WITH THE RUMOR)*

- Mona gifts Ross some saltwater taffy, and he gives a piece to Phoebe. She's never had it before and can't decide if it's food or gum. Although she seems to hate it, she then wants to try a pink one. *(THE ONE WITH THE BIRTHING VIDEO)*

- At Thanksgiving, Monica prepares her annual delicious dinner. She's using her fancy wedding china, so she insists that everyone be careful. Unfortunately, Rachel and her sister Amy are fighting, and Amy takes her anger out on the plates. This prompts Monica to give a demonstration on how to cut a turkey leg without even touching the precious china. Despite all the safety, however, by the end of the day, the crockery has all been broken. *(THE ONE WITH RACHEL'S OTHER SISTER)*

- While Rachel and Phoebe go out for the evening, Ross invites Mike over for dinner and a drink. Ross is hopeful of a good night of conversation, but the guys have nothing to say to each other and end up counting the minutes until the pizza is due to arrive. In an effort to break the silence, they have an awkward discussion about the difference between beer and lager. *(THE ONE WITH RACHEL'S PHONE NUMBER)*

- When Amy comes to visit for the second time, she thinks that Ross owns a falafel cart and that she bought one from him yesterday. *(THE ONE WHERE RACHEL'S SISTER BABYSITS)*

- Monica makes Thanksgiving Day dinner, and Chandler contributes homemade cranberry sauce. When the rest of the friends are late, Monica and Chandler lock them out, and then Joey gets his head stuck in the chained door. When he eventually gets free, he ends up sliding into the middle of the food cart. All is forgiven, though, when the adoption agency calls—Monica and Chandler are getting a baby. *(THE ONE WITH THE LATE THANKSGIVING)*

FASHION

Some of the friends' fashions are memorable in a good way, and some are just plain memorable.

- When she can't get a job, Rachel uses her father's credit card to buy some "I don't need a job, I don't need my parents, I got great boots, boots." This leads to her cutting up the credit cards and taking a job at Central Perk. *(THE ONE WHERE MONICA GETS A ROOMMATE)*

- When Ross accompanies Rachel to the laundromat, she accidentally dyes her clothes pink after a disaster with a red sock. *(THE ONE WITH THE EAST GERMAN LAUNDRY DETERGENT)*

- As Barry and Mindy's bridesmaid, Rachel has to wear a huge, bright pink dress with puffy sleeves, silky bows, and a sparkly motif in the middle of her chest. According to her, it looks like something you drink when you're nauseous. The outfit is topped off with a huge hat, and to make things worse, Rachel tucks the skirt into her red panties. *(THE ONE WITH BARRY AND MINDY'S WEDDING)*

- While arguing over chair cushions, Joey dresses up in every piece of clothing that Chandler owns. *(THE ONE WHERE NO ONE'S READY)*

- After Monica accidentally hits Ben's head on the wooden post in her apartment, she and Rachel disguise the bump by dressing Ben in a Rainy Day Bear's outfit, consisting of a yellow raincoat and hat. *(THE ONE WITH THE GIANT POKING DEVICE)*

- To fill time after being fired, Phoebe creates her own shoes, complete with buttons, tassels, and pom-poms. *(THE ONE WITH JOEY'S NEW GIRLFRIEND)*

- While visiting Joshua's parents' house, Rachel strips down to her nightie in order to seduce Joshua. Unknown to her, his parents return home early, see her in her underclothes, and presume that she's a hooker. Rachel then pretends that her skimpy outfit is a new dress design and goes to a restaurant, where her boob pops out. *(THE ONE WITH RACHEL'S NEW DRESS)*

- Phoebe buys some "maternity" pants from a used clothes store, but they're really part of a Father Christmas outfit. When Chandler and Joey tell her, Phoebe denies it and says that the pants even came with a list of baby names, good and bad. *(THE ONE WITH ALL THE HASTE)*

- When Monica is tasked with picking up Emily's wedding dress, she can't resist trying it on. Before long, she's obsessed with wearing the outfit, and then Phoebe rents her own from a store called It's Not Too Late. Later, Rachel joins them with the gown she wore to her failed wedding with Barry and then freaks out Joshua when she opens the door and shouts, "I do!" *(THE ONE WITH ALL THE WEDDING DRESSES)*

- Monica chooses her perfect wedding dress but wants to buy it from a discount place in Brooklyn. Unfortunately, she tells another bride about the cheap shop, and they end up fighting over the same dress. *(THE ONE WITH THE CHEAP WEDDING DRESS)*

- Rachel sets the men up with suits for Chandler and Monica's wedding. Chandler chooses Pierce Brosnan's tux and Ross wears Val Kilmer's, thinking that it was worn in a *Batman* film. They argue over who will be cooler, but in the end, Chandler's Brosnan suit doesn't fit, and Ross discovers that his suit wasn't worn in *Batman* after all. Meanwhile, Joey says he doesn't need a tux because he intends on wearing multicolored robes and a hat. *(THE ONE WITH RACHEL'S BIG KISS)*

- When it's revealed that the father of Rachel's baby owns a red sweater, Phoebe thinks it's Tag, but the real father is Ross. *(THE ONE WITH THE RED SWEATER)*

- When Chandler hires a cleaning lady, Monica becomes obsessed that Brenda has

stolen her jeans (with an ink stain at the crotch) and her pink flowered bra (with a noticeable rip). Brenda walks out just as Monica discovers that she's wearing the bra herself and Rachel has borrowed her jeans. *(THE ONE WITH THE STAIN)*

- Monica buys some expensive boots but assures Chandler she'll get lots of wear out of them. However, they hurt so much that Chandler has to give her a piggyback, and she accidentally leaves her boots on the street. *(THE ONE WITH MONICA'S BOOTS)*

- Ross realizes he left his favorite salmon (pink) shirt at Mona's apartment and decides to get it back. She's not there, so he lets himself in anyway and then has to hide behind the sofa when Mona comes back with a guy. Her date ends up wearing the shirt after spilling wine down his own, and Ross reads a magazine on the floor while waiting for the guy to take off the shirt. When he does, Ross gets caught trying to retrieve it and then refuses to let Mona keep it as a souvenir. *(THE ONE WITH THE TEA LEAVES)*

- Rachel, Phoebe, and Charlie go shopping and end up in the changing room of a clothes store. Before Phoebe tries on a dress, she and Rachel have a conversation about Joey and Charlie, and Phoebe guesses that Rachel has a crush on Joey. When they leave the changing room, they discover that Charlie has been in the next changing room. She later says she overheard everything but thinks

that Phoebe is the one who likes Joey. *(THE ONE WITH THE DONOR)*

- Rachel and Phoebe offer to take Ross shopping so that he can get something to wear on his date. He hates the silver shirts, the hairy shirts, and the padlocked shirts and refuses to pay the exorbitant price for a sweater. He does like a leather jacket, however, until he sees the sparkly Boys Will Be Boys logo on the back. Rachel says that she'll pick out some great clothes for him, but then the bags get mixed up, and Ross ends up going on a date wearing a woman's shirt. *(THE ONE WITH THE BIRTH MOTHER)*

HOLIDAY EPISODES

Holidays are an important part of the friends' lives, especially Thanksgiving, and provided some of the most memorable scenes in the series.

- It's Thanksgiving, and Monica is cooking dinner because her parents are going out of town. She cooks various types of potatoes to suit her friends' requirements, but everything is ruined when they get locked out of the apartment. In the end, everyone eats grilled cheese sandwiches instead, and Chandler declares it a great Thanksgiving because it didn't involve divorce or projectile vomiting. (THE ONE WHERE UNDERDOG GETS AWAY)

- Phoebe writes and performs two depressing Christmas songs, and Joey is rejected as a store Santa but hired as an elf. There's a New Year's Eve party at Monica's, which is taken over by strange guests, arguments, breakups, and Marcel the monkey. (THE ONE WITH THE MONKEY)

- A holiday party at Monica and Rachel's turns tropical when the radiator breaks. Meanwhile, Chandler and Joey steal/buy their Christmas presents from a gas station because it's too late to shop. (THE ONE WITH PHOEBE'S DAD)

- The friends organize a football game, which gets competitive when Monica and Ross fight over the Geller Cup. While they continue to argue at the park, their friends eat Thanksgiving dinner at the apartment. (THE ONE WITH THE FOOTBALL)

- Ross becomes an honorary Brown Bird and sells holiday cookies to himself and his friends. Joey gets a job at a Christmas tree lot, but Phoebe hates the idea of innocent trees being cut down in their prime and dressed in twinkly lights. To make her feel happier, the friends decorate Monica's apartment with old trees destined for the chipper. (THE ONE WHERE RACHEL QUITS)

- Phoebe organizes a Secret Santa gift drive, which leads to an argument when Ross is told that Rachel exchanges every gift she's given. Monica hosts Thanksgiving dinner and invites Richard's son as her guest, and Chandler gets into a box to contemplate how bad he feels for kissing Joey's girlfriend Kathy. (THE ONE WITH CHANDLER IN A BOX)

On the ornament (top left): Happy Christmas Eve Eve

On the ornament (top right): I'm the holiday armadillo

- Phoebe writes a holiday song for her friends but has trouble finding a version that everyone approves of. Monica hires Joey in the restaurant so that she can fire him in front of her hateful staff, but the great holiday tips mean that Joey is reluctant to leave. *(THE ONE WITH THE GIRL FROM POUGHKEEPSIE)*

- The friends share their Thanksgiving stories: Chandler tells the story of his parents' divorce, and Phoebe thinks back to her former lives, and then remembers when Joey got his head stuck in the Thanksgiving turkey. When it's Monica's turn, it's revealed that, as a teenager, she overheard Chandler call her fat. This led to her losing weight for the next Thanksgiving, when she pretended to seduce Chandler and accidentally cut the tip of his toe off with a knife. *(THE ONE WITH ALL THE THANKSGIVINGS)*

- Phoebe takes on a charity job collecting donations outside Macy's department store, but the shoppers enrage her by donating trash and cigarettes before the bucket eventually catches on fire. Phoebe's reaction to the events results in her being removed from her corner. *(THE ONE WITH THE INAPPROPRIATE SISTER)*

- A series of events including embarrassing secrets, arguments, a telling-off from Ross and Monica's parents, and Rachel's accidental meat trifle makes this Thanksgiving dinner one to remember. *(THE ONE WHERE ROSS GOT HIGH)*

- Janine invites Joey, Monica, and Ross to the taping of *Dick Clark's New Year's Rockin' Eve*. This gives Joey a chance to impress Janine, while Ross and Monica showcase their childhood dance routine. *(THE ONE WITH THE ROUTINE)*

- During Thanksgiving dinner, the friends play a game of naming all the US states in six minutes. Ross thinks it is insanely easy but gets so frustrated that he doesn't eat his

dinner until the middle of the night. *(THE ONE WHERE CHANDLER DOESN'T LIKE DOGS)*

- In an effort to get to know her neighbors, Monica makes holiday candy and leaves it in a basket at the front door. Her good deed goes awry when she receives candy-demanding visits in the middle of the night, and then the neighbors revolt when Monica is late filling the basket. *(THE ONE WITH ALL THE CANDY)*

- In an effort to teach Ben about Hanukkah, Ross dresses up as the Holiday Armadillo. He is joined by Santa (Chandler) and Superman (Joey). *(THE ONE WITH THE HOLIDAY ARMADILLO)*

- Monica invites old school friend Will to her Thanksgiving dinner, where it's revealed that he and Ross were the cofounders of the school's I Hate Rachel Club and created a rather scandalous rumor about Rachel. *(THE ONE WITH THE RUMOR)*

- Ross is freaked out when girlfriend Mona suggests that they send out a holiday card together. *(THE ONE WITH ROSS'S STEP FORWARD)*

- Rachel brings her spoiled sister Amy to Monica's Thanksgiving dinner. An argument breaks out between the siblings, Chandler wonders if he'll be a good parent, and Monica's precious wedding china gets smashed. *(THE ONE WITH RACHEL'S OTHER SISTER)*

- When Chandler is forced to spend Christmas in Tulsa, the unwanted attentions from a female colleague prompt him to resign from his job, so he heads back to New York. *(THE ONE WITH CHRISTMAS IN TULSA)*

- Despite begging Monica to host Thanksgiving dinner again, everybody is late. Monica and Chandler are furious, until they receive a phone call to say that they're getting a baby. *(THE ONE WITH THE LATE THANKSGIVING)*